THE
MASTER
JEWELERS

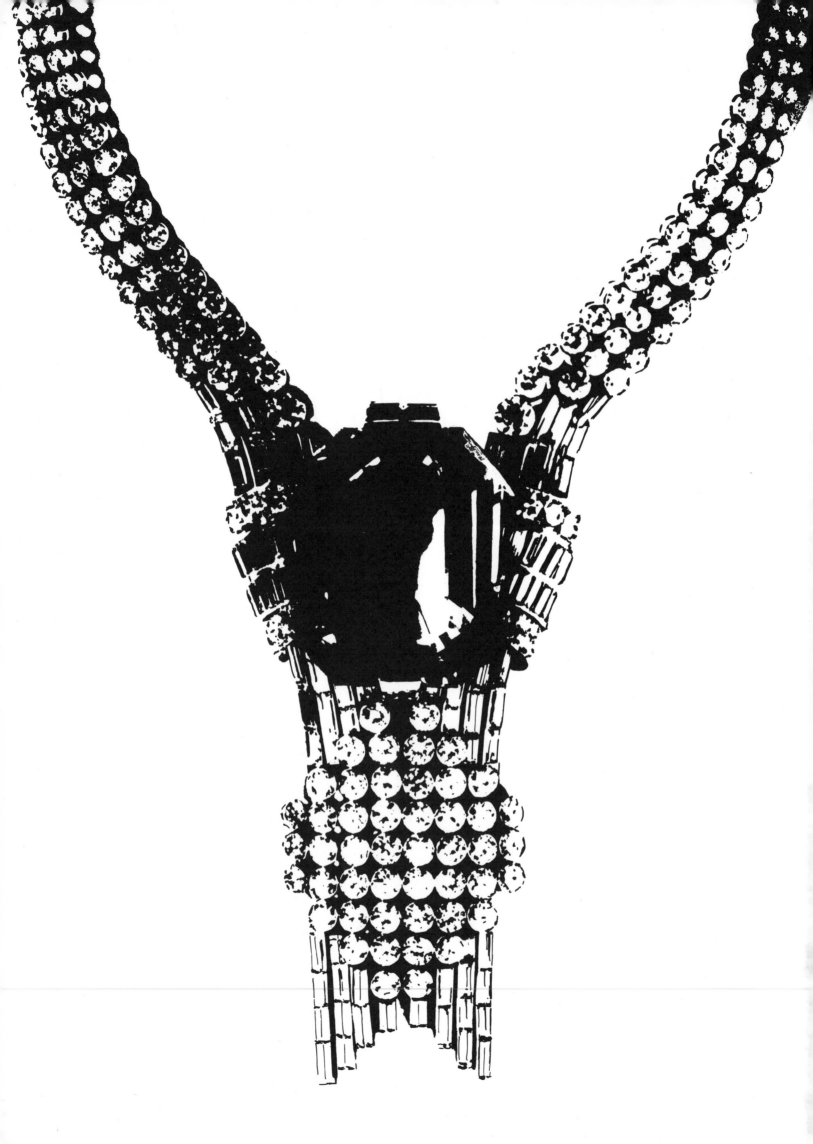

THE MASTER JEWELERS

EDITED BY
A. KENNETH SNOWMAN

HARRY N. ABRAMS, INC., PUBLISHERS, NEW YORK

Frontispiece: Tiffany necklace with
429 diamonds and a 217-carat aquamarine,
which was exhibited at
the 1939 New York World's Fair.

"Boucheron," "Vever," and "Fouquet"
translated from the French
by Augusta Audubert.
"Fontenay" translated from the French
by Francisca Garvie

Library of Congress Cataloging-in-Publication Data

The master jewelers / edited by A. Kenneth Snowman.
p.   cm.
Includes bibliographical references.
ISBN 0-8109-3606-2
1. Jewelry—History—19th century.   2. Jewelry—History—20th
century.   I. Snowman. A. Kenneth (Abraham Kenneth). 1919–
NK7309.8.M38   1990
739.27′092′2—dc20   90–32716

© 1990 Thames and Hudson Ltd, London

Published in 1990 by Harry N. Abrams, Incorporated, New York
A Times Mirror Company

Printed and bound in Japan by Dai Nippon

CONTENTS

Although many words have been devoted individually to each of the distinguished jewelers who are assembled to form this anthology, it will be seen that, more often than not, quite another picture emerges as they appear cheek by jowl. When a wide range of artifacts becomes available for close scrutiny, as in this context, it means that we are able to assess the activities of the various designers and craftsmen with that much more confidence; it allows us to exercise a comparative judgment as to the artistic merit of the objects themselves. By a judicious mixing of worthwhile ingredients, the resulting cocktail acquires a fresh piquancy – sufficient justification, it would seem, for this present endeavour.

The majority of the artist-craftsmen brought together in this study evoke a distinct period flavour which continues to please our palates today. The aim of these business houses was to furnish for their fashionable clientele the graceful accoutrements of high living, and as the pages which follow are turned, one can appreciate to the full the extent of their success.

The decorative or applied arts, as opposed to the purely fine arts, are always demanding since they are dependent upon the approval of and acceptance by the customer. The decorative artist has a more exacting task than that of so many contemporary "fine artists" who are too often happy merely to produce yards of canvas covered with dribbles or blobs of paint for the aspiring new-rich to buy and brag about among themselves; the decorative artist is obliged to sell his work to a discriminating and highly critical society comparatively free to make up its own mind about what it wants and not subject to extraneous pressures and art-critical advice.

Many of the individual artists and firms whose development is faithfully recorded here borrowed liberally from the flood of new ideas and forms which became available once the decorative arts had been released from an unyielding traditionalism. Revivalism became a highly successful movement, firmly based as it was on a theory of decorative sentimentality; throughout history, feelings of nostalgia have been eagerly welcomed by those fascinated by the arts.

The discoveries in Etruria, Egypt, and the Crimea, to take three of the most striking instances, inspired the inventive designers of Rome, Paris and St Petersburg to produce some of their most brilliant work in the 19th and early 20th centuries – not merely slavish copies of the artifacts which had been excavated in those exotic lands, but wonderfully chic shorthand transcriptions of the original material, which continue to please those fortunate enough to possess examples.

The revolution brought about in the arts when Japan was finally forced in the 1850s to open her shores to the outside world affected not only the painters, musicians and theatre people, it left the jewelers and decorative artists entirely *bouleversé* at their benches. In Russia the influence of the *netsuké* on the lapidaries who carved the animals, birds and fish for Carl Fabergé proved fundamental and many of them speak to us today with a distinct Japanese accent.

The Art Nouveau movement of the 1890s quickened the pulse of a whole generation of designers in Europe, and its compulsive drive is still potent and popular. During the first twenty years of our century, individual artists designed some of the most astonishing and original jewels ever made. They were not necessarily composed of costly materials. In fact the monetary value of many of the loveliest compositions of René Lalique or Fouquet, for example, could be reckoned intrinsically in just a few pounds or dollars. Enamel, after all, is simply a form of glass, and diamonds, if they are too large, cannot describe curves and turn corners.

As for originality in the arts, however, it must be said that to set out deliberately to attain this quality is generally and, perhaps deservedly, attended by peril. Originality pursued for its own sake is always suspect – it is, after all, an elusive ideal which, like style in a painter's work, will only emerge unsought. Novelty, a very different thing, is too often the enemy of the arts. The terror of not being up-to-date is most prevalent among the aesthetically undeveloped and the technically disadvantaged.

The extraordinary jewelers who make up the content of this book were never prepared to compromise their artistic integrity for the sake of vainglorious stunts or commercial tricks. As for ourselves, with the proliferation of unsightly plastic materials and the horrors attendant upon the hectoring voice of the media, the light appears to have dimmed somewhat; but it must surely never be forgotten that no age is automatically entitled to a great culture.

It seems all the more appropriate therefore for us to salute a group of truly dedicated originals who have bequeathed to us works of a very high order indeed, carried out in beautiful materials, which continue to give enduring pleasure to those with eyes to see.

A. KENNETH SNOWMAN

A large silver and silver gilt bangle which once belonged to Edith Holman Hunt. Made by Carlo Giuliano in the archaeological style, it is decorated with filigree and granulation and set with cabochon garnets. Although Giuliano drew heavily on classical sources in this bracelet, a certain barbaric element is reminiscent of near Eastern jewelry.
Mrs Elizabeth Tompkin

CASTELLANI
AND GIULIANO

Like William Morris we live in an age where King Shoddy reigns. A century ago craftsmanship and quality had declined in the wake of increased mechanization, and exactly the same is true today. Even our individualism is threatened by the sterility of the chainstore and hypermarket. It is easy to recognize as our own the aesthetic dilemma of the 19th century, but unlike our forebears we lack even the inspiration to react against it. Patronage of the arts is in the doldrums and it is therefore not surprising that we turn to the past with unprecedented enthusiasm. Almost without exception, the artists and craftsmen of the 19th century thought there was no other option open to them but to look back, and today a new spirit of revivalism thrives. In 1863 William Burges said, "There is an old proverb which says 'when things are at their worst they begin to mend'; and certainly nothing could be worse than the design of our jewellery some six years ago, for it is only since our workmen have taken to imitating the beautiful articles found in the tombs of Etruria and Magna Graecia that an artist can pass a jeweller's shop without shutting his eyes." This return to the antique in jewelry design can be attributed in the main to the Castellani family of Rome.

Fortunato Pio Castellani (1794–1865) had, by the age of 20, embarked on a career as a manufacturing goldsmith, and the business which he founded on the ground floor of the Palazzo Raggi in the Via del Corso was devoted for the most part to the manufacture of ornaments in precious metal but also dealt in works of art. It was later to become the venue of a rich English "milord" who, whenever he heard that Castellani had acquired a picture, came round to the premises "cheque-book in hand" and refused to leave without purchasing it. This procedure was, we are told, irritating to Castellani who would have preferred a little more time to commune with his latest discovery.

The jewelry manufactured by Castellani in the first few years was in the contemporary French, English and Swiss taste and was greatly influenced by a Russian craftsman called Zwerner who worked in Rome in the 1830s. Russian jewelry of the period is characterized by a sumptuous display of precious stones in tight and neatly executed openwork settings. Rome had never been considered a centre for this sort of jewelry and it seems unlikely that the traditional pieces produced by Fortunato Pio Castellani could successfully compete with similar ornaments available in St Petersburg, Geneva, Paris and London. Regrettably, none of this early jewelry has been traced, possibly because of its derivative nature but more probably because it did not bear any one of the distinctive monograms of crossed C's found on later Castellani works.

In the mid-1820s Fortunato was lucky enough to win the friendship of the famous archaeologist Michelangelo Caetani, who later became the Duke of Sermoneta (1804–82). He was a man of great erudition, a patron of considerable private fortune and one whose wide-ranging and important connections throughout Europe and America must have been invaluable to Castellani's growing business. Among his cultivated circle of friends were Rossini, Chateaubriand, Stendhal, Liszt, Balzac and Witte. The relationship with Caetani was to prove one of the strongest influences on the Castellani firm. It was he who in 1851 encouraged Fortunato Pio and his two sons Alessandro (1823–83) and Augusto (1829–1914) to abandon jewelry of foreign inspiration and concentrate on antique themes; but more importantly he remained a consistent and generous mentor for the rest of his life. Alessandro Castellani was

Top, *a selection of gold-mounted mosaic jewels by Castellani showing various influences –* Byzantine, Roman, early Christian, medieval. Christie's, Geneva

Bottom, *two similar Castellani bracelets, decorated with white and gold mosaics and spelling out the Latin* NON RELINQUES *("You will not give up").* Private collection and The Cooper Hewitt Museum of Decorative Art and Design, New York

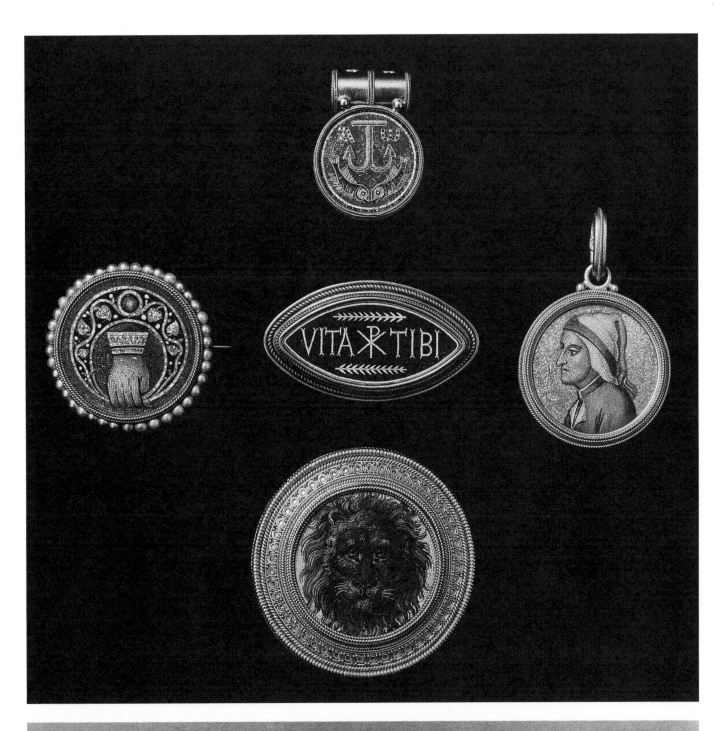

Top, *a circular gold brooch by Castellani with the popular motif of a snake in the grass.* Museo Nazionale Etrusco di Villa Giulia, Rome

Above, *a gold ring in the Byzantine style by Castellani. The bezel is set with red micromosaic in the form of* Chi-Rho, *the holy monogram of Christ.* Private collection

later to acknowledge the Duke as a man "whom we consider as our master, and as a most certain and learned guide in the whole art of design". It was under Caetani's close influence that the revival of Italian and Greek jewelry was given the name Italian Archaeological Jewelry.

Alessandro Castellani was unable to participate in the day-to-day running of the firm in the same way as his brother Augusto since he had lost an arm in a hunting accident when quite young. This misfortune meant that he was precluded from any practical involvement with the workshop which went beyond the designing of jewelry. His main role was to continue the tradition of the firm by dealing in the finest antiques and works of art, and the trade was to provide him with a livelihood and a consuming interest for the rest of his days. Unfortunately, Alessandro's mental health was somewhat finely balanced and was ultimately pitched into disorder as a result of being imprisoned by the Papal Government. The political stance of the Castellani family was essentially liberal and Alessandro's life was to be moulded by his strict adherence to these ideals. His membership of the commission set up for the selection of Government employees during the Roman Republic of 1849 led to his arrest and that of his brother when the Papal Government was restored in the same year. They were released as a result of the father's reputation and his generosity in paying the fines. Alessandro, however, was not easily deterred and continued to cultivate the friendship of the exiled Republican Giuseppe Mazzini. In August 1853 a revolutionary plot was uncovered and numerous arrests were made. Alessandro was imprisoned in the Castel Sant'Angelo, and the combination of interrogation and fevers he contracted there drove him temporarily insane. In 1856 he was released. Three years later, however, the Papal Government presented him with an ultimatum: to accept banishment or return to prison and judicial interrogation. Not surprisingly, he fled to Paris in June 1860 and took an apartment in the Rue Taitbout. The premises he was subsequently to open at 85 Champs-Elysées were to form the core of the Archaeological School of Jewelry in France. Circumstances had decreed that Alessandro was to become foreign ambassador of the firm as well as of the aesthetic

disciplines in which it so fervently believed.

While in Paris, Alessandro gave a lecture called "Mémoire sur la Joaillerie chez les Anciens" to the Académie des Inscriptions et Belles Lettres. The English version, entitled "Antique Jewellery and its Revival", was published to complement the Castellani display at the 1862 International Exhibition in London. It took the form of a brief history of the firm, its aims, inspirations and relentless pursuit of those classical goldsmiths' techniques, which were such an enigma to the 19th-century jeweler. Among them was the method used by the Greeks and Etruscans to decorate the surface of gold with tiny globes or granules so fine that they appear to the naked eye like the finest dusting or frosting. Furthermore, the delicacy of the filigree which is so often applied to Classical jewelry seemed to the Castellani to be virtually impossible to achieve. This extraordinary facility with materials coupled with an ability to achieve a bold and tasteful effect made the Greeks and Etruscans peerless in the Castellani family's estimation.

They had assembled their own collection of ancient jewelry, which was freely exhibited at the premises to customers and scholars, and they had also been intimately involved in Cavaliere Campana's collection of some 929 ornaments in gold and silver. Thus the Castellani were not short of prototypes on which to base the pastiches they made under the direction of Caetani. They offered these for sale to the enormous number of tourists who visited Rome every year. Although the Castellani believed that Etruscan and Greek jewelry was aesthetically and technically supreme, their pastiches were not limited to these two groups alone. Recognizing the dramatic qualities of Roman jewelry, the firm used Roman sources from time to time despite the reservations they were so quick to voice.

The Etruscans and inhabitants of Magna Graecia attained the highest perfection in the early years of Rome; but with the rise of the imperial power the art of jewellery lost its beauty, as has happened in all times to those arts which flourish in the free life of nations, but languish and die when liberty grows weak and disappears. The excavations of Pompeii have brought to light works of the Greco-Roman period inferior to those found in Etruria and Magna

Graecia. And although in the Pompeian ornaments we find sometimes the elegant forms of more remote antiquity, showing the well-known persistence of archaic types, still the workmanship is in every way inferior. From this we deduce that the decay had already begun; and that the gold ornaments of imperial Rome, both in design and execution, fell short of those remote periods.

Similar scorn was poured on the jewelry of the early Christians of the Eternal City, who,

being chiefly poor men and taught to despise all external magnificence and show, had neither means nor desire to possess personal ornaments or costly vessels for sacred use. Their altars were adorned with terracotta and bronze; the bread of the Eucharist ceremony, and the relics of the dead, were enclosed in copper lockets; and the few jewels found in the catacombs of Rome, similar in form to those of the Dark Ages, are so deficient in art that they can

only be compared with the roughest works of the primitive eras. Of this kind are the medallions, rings and fibulae, used by them to distinguish each other in days of persecution and danger, and on which the various Christian symbols are generally represented in a very inartistic manner.

Despite these reservations, the Castellani family were aware that the majority of visitors to Rome were deeply devout Christians making something of a pilgrimage. Nothing would give them greater pleasure than to bring back a jewel decorated with an early Christian symbol or a Byzantine-style mosaic. Unlike the other jewelers working in Rome in the second half of the 19th century, the Castellani exploited rather than suppressed the severity of these religious jewels; as a result they have a monumentality simply not found in the work of other goldsmiths.

Alessandro Castellani had only harsh words for the jewelry of the 16th and particularly the 17th century:

Castellani's shop in the Piazza Fontana di Trevi, in which antique vases were displayed along with modern jewelry. Original Castellani photo: Signora Saraceni, Rome

It is not certain whether the Italian masters of the art of jewellery of the 15th century had lost, or disregarded, all the traditions of the ancient schools, or whether, guided by their native genius, they laboured to create new methods of working in this art, harmonizing it with the forms under which the sister arts were reviving. . . . These masters at all events studied and used at their discretion methods totally different from the ancient. They availed themselves of the punch, burin and chisel; of enamels, nielli, cast ornaments and figures, and precious stones. And their best works are those in which these precious materials are combined according to the free and original fancy of the artist, without showing the slightest similarity either to ancient processes or designs.

But in the decline of painting, sculpture and architecture in the days of Michelangelo, jewellery underwent the same fate. In the seventeenth century it was already in an advanced stage of decay and lost every merit, and every reminiscence of good taste, under the fatal domination of the Spaniards and Austrians over Italy.

Such criticism of the high and late Renaissance goldsmith and jeweler notwithstanding, the Castellani family appreciated the brightly coloured three-dimensional qualities of this jewelry and did not flinch from adding them to their already highly successful repertoire. Such pastiches are some of the most colourful and impressive made by the firm.

Despite his career as an antique dealer, Alessandro had opened premises in Paris, London, and Naples and had lectured on behalf of the firm in many parts of the world. When he died in June 1883, *The Times* recorded his passing thus: "A man who will be mourned by many a personal friend and political admirer and whose death will be regarded as an irreparable loss by every European and every American who cares for Classical Archaeology."

There is no doubt that Alessandro's death coincided with the beginning of the decline of the Archaeological School of Jewelry throughout Europe. His brother Augusto was to survive him by thirty years and to see the business, which had once been the focus of European royal, aristocratic and artistic circles, slowly peter out, because of its uncompromising attitude towards art. Augusto's place was taken on his death in 1914 by his son Alfredo, whose sad task it was to close down the once world-famous business. At the same time that the Parisian jewelers were making incomparably chic jewels from frosted rock-crystal, black onyx, coral and diamonds, Alfredo was selling archaeological fringe necklaces of granulated gold and scarabs to the tourists. The position of the shop in the Piazza Fontana di Trevi and the considerable reputation of his forebears allowed this to go on until his death in 1930.

The Castellani family understood the importance of the Great Exhibitions and showed jewelry in Florence in 1861, London in 1862 and 1872, Paris in 1867 and 1878, Vienna in 1873, Philadelphia in 1876 and Turin in 1884. Through their own writings and foreign travel, their influence on European and American jewelers is quite inestimable. The intentions of the entire family are summed up in Alessandro's words, "We do not reserve everything for ourselves, being fully satisfied that others will follow us, and, progressing in the mood we have chosen, will help to recall the attention and admiration of the modern world towards worthy objects."

Alessandro Castellani (1823–83)

Giuliano

It was in England, more than anywhere else, that the aesthetic ideals of the Castellani family were enthusiastically accepted. By the early 1860s the spirit of revivalism had already taken a firm grip on the arts. By 1856 C.F. Hancock had created the sumptuously eclectic Devonshire parure incorporating Classical, medieval, and Renaissance themes into one of the most magnificent suites of jewelry ever made in the 19th century. It is small wonder that Alessandro Castellani felt the moment was ripe to come to London; in 1861 he presented in English to the Archaeological Institute the lecture he had previously given in Paris, and this was circulated the following year as a privately printed booklet entitled "Antique Jewellery and its Revival".

It is now generally agreed that Carlo Giuliano accompanied Alessandro Castellani to London in about 1860 with the intention of managing a branch of the old firm at 13 Frith Street, Soho, much like the premises recently vacated at 85 Champs-Elysées. Why there is scant evidence of Castellani's part in the foundation of Giuliano's business in London remains a mystery; it may be that Carlo wished to disassociate himself from his master and deliberately suppressed the facts. It is significant, however, that the catalogue of the 1862 exhibition describes Castellani as a firm of Rome and London. Apart from this we have to rely on a small number of hazy clues to elucidate this important connection.

Carlo Giuliano's will begins thus: "I, Carlo Giuliano, late of Naples but now a naturalized British subject . . ." Given that Alessandro Castellani had a base in Naples, it has been suggested that he brought one of his principal craftsmen from there to London. However, if it is not possible to place the opening of the Naples workshop any earlier than in 1863, Carlo Giuliano must have come from the Castellani workshops in Rome. Certainly all the evidence of his early goldsmithing techniques suggests that he was trained by Castellani. Another, more substantial hint of the connection between the two organizations comes from the already mentioned obituary of Alessandro Castellani in *The Times* which, referring to the Archaeological

Carlo Giuliano (1831–95)
Courtesy W.F. Little Esq.

School of Jewelers, reads as follows: "The Art has been carried to still greater perfection by another Italian, settled in London – Signor Giuliano, whom we believe, had his first hint from Alessandro Castellani."

In the early years in London, Carlo Giuliano made a number of Revivalist jewels, some elaborately worked in the Archaeological taste more often associated with Castellani. Several of these pieces bear a gold label so close to Castellani's own that it was, until relatively recently, taken for the same. It is, in fact, a monogram of C and G rather than C and C as had previously been supposed. Perhaps Carlo Giuliano chose to use a signature different from that of his master but close enough not to incur his displeasure. By 17 February 1863, Carlo Giuliano entered a much smaller mark with the Worshipful Company of Goldsmiths and from time to time jewels bearing both the more conspicuous monogram and the later trade label come to light. This use of a clearly separate mark suggests that the relationship with Alessandro Castellani may already have been over by this time. The premises at Frith Street run by Giuliano were not a retail jewelers' establishment but, as later described, a "laboratory". The ornaments created there were offered for sale through notable jewelers' shops in the West End of London. This is a common trade practice which continues to this day. Regrettably outworkers' names were often concealed by leading retail houses, who preferred their customers to

The shop of Carlo and Arthur Giuliano at 115 Piccadilly, London, in 1904.

believe that everything in their showcases was of their own manufacture. These outworkers, although heavily subjected to the company name of their hosts, were sometimes referred to as "designers"! It is difficult to believe that some reference to Giuliano's Italian origins would not have been made during the course of a transaction, since the jewels were often obtrusively signed and his name must have carried some cachet. In one instance we know this to be true. Mrs Henry Adams, visiting from the United States, wrote in 1879, "The daily temptations of London are enormous. . . . [for instance] Giuliano, Phillips."

Robert Phillips (1810–81), whose business later became Phillips Brothers and Son of Cockspur Street, has been credited by trade tradition with Giuliano's establishment in London, but this is probably an exaggeration. Phillips was arguably one of the most prominent jewelers working in the Revivalist taste and he was clearly influenced by Castellani. The fact that Giuliano supplied him is now no longer in dispute and even some of those jewels which bear Phillips' trade label (back-to-back Ps and the Prince of Wales's feathers) can be firmly attributed to Giuliano.

Carlo Giuliano also supplied several other retail houses, among them C.F. Hancock, Hunt and Roskell, and Harry Emanuel. By 1874 his business was sufficiently established to encourage him to open retail premises at 115 Piccadilly. This tiny shop was to become the resort of the aristocratic, intellectual and artistic communities for many years to come. Shunning the image of the simple tradesman, Carlo Giuliano preferred to be seen as something of an historian and scholar of precious metalwork.

As a result he was able to attract the attention of the famous archaeologist Heinrich Schliemann. In "Ilios: the City and Country of the Trojans", Schliemann records how he took King Priam's treasure to Giuliano's shop to have it weighed and assayed and to ask the famous jeweler's opinion on how it was made. Giuliano said, "How the primitive goldsmith could do all this fine work, and in particular, how he could accomplish the minute granular work on the earrings, where grains of gold infinitely minute were to be soldered into the microscopic grooves – how he could do all this without the aid of a lens – is an enigma. But it was done, and with a powerful lens we can easily distinguish the soldering, even on the smallest rings."

These remarks are particularly valuable to us today, since the treasure under discussion was lost almost entirely during the Second World War. Furthermore, Schliemann's own integrity is now in question and so, therefore, must the treasure be.

The near hysterical interest of the British public in archaeology and their willingness to assimilate a style of jewelry, based on ancient prototypes, which had originated in Italy was not to last. Although Archaeological Jewelry was to be made well into the 20th century, Carlo Giuliano soon decided to focus on the Renaissance as his primary source of inspiration. It conveniently provided him with a more colourful palette and a softer effect, which the English ladies found more amenable. Little by little, openwork necklaces of candy-twist enamel were to replace the severity of plain gold diadems and fringe necklaces. Enameling was invariably used to evoke French and Italian jewelry of the 16th and 17th centuries, and sometimes even the necklaces and bracelets of Moghul India. Giuliano and his contemporaries never flinched from mixing entirely disparate sources of inspiration in a single jewel in order to achieve an effect.

CASTELLANI: above, *a parure in the Italian medieval taste, consisting of a coronet, necklace, brooch and earrings, set with cabochon rubies, sapphires and pearls and decorated with filigree. The crosses can be detached from the coronet to form separate brooches. The ensemble was created for the wedding of Princess Margareta of Prussia (1892).* Ares Antiques, New York
Below, *an enameled gold diadem, set with brown agates and white glass beads, which draws its inspiration from a classical jewel in the Campana collection which dates from the third century* B C.
Private collection (formerly Pierpont Morgan collection)

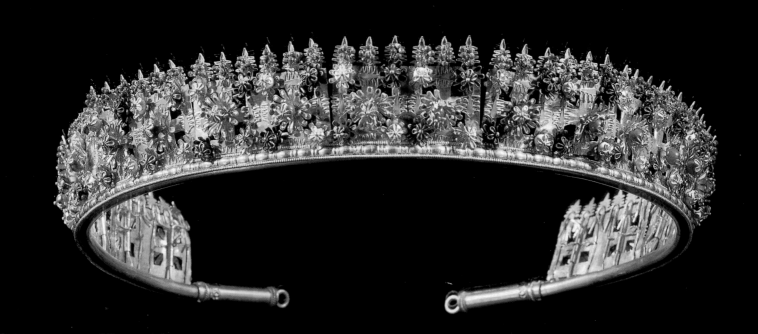

CASTELLANI: top, *a gold pendant, based on a Campana jewel. This version, which is one of several, is in the form of the head of Bacchus, adorned by a garland of vines. A small souvenir can be kept in the compartment at the rear. Private collection.*

Below, *a gold box in the Roman taste. A 19th-century green jasper cameo depicting Daphne and Apollo is set into the lid, while the base (not shown) is set with a panel of translucent, rust-coloured agate. In gold letters on an enameled white background runs the following Latin inscription:* BENE.REM.GERAS.ET.VALEAS.DORMIAS.SINE.CURA. *("May you succeed and may you fare well; may you sleep without care.")* S.J. Phillips, London

CASTELLANI: opposite, *a parure adorned with pearls, rubies, drop-shaped emeralds and late 16th-century onyx cameos (although the gem in the pendant to the necklace may be modern), mounted in enameled gold. Private collection*

18

A granulated gold necklace by ALFREDO CASTELLANI, *set with ancient and modern cornelian scarabs. Private collection*
Within the necklace, a circular micromosaic of a parrot, mounted in gold by Castellani as a brooch, the border of which is decorated with cloisonné enamel. Private collection

A gold fringe necklace by CARLO *and* ARTHUR GIULIANO, *decorated with black and white enamel
and set with Indian diamonds taken at the battle of Seringapatam in 1799. Private collection
Within, a gold pendant by* CARLO GIULIANO *decorated with enamel and set with pearls and
rubies. The central oval aperture contains a repoussé gold portrait of Queen Victoria, who gave the
jewel to her goddaughter, Alexandra Elizabeth Grey. Engraved on the reverse: "To V.A.E.D on
her marriage June 6th 1877 from the Queen." Private collection*

CARLO GIULIANO: right, *an exuberant gold brooch in the Egyptian style, adorned with polychrome enamels, pearls, diamonds and a ruby, which depicts a crowned Nubian and his plumed horses.* Wartski, London

Below, *a parure of openwork gold jewelry in the Indian taste, set with chrysoprase, rubies and pearls.* Private collection

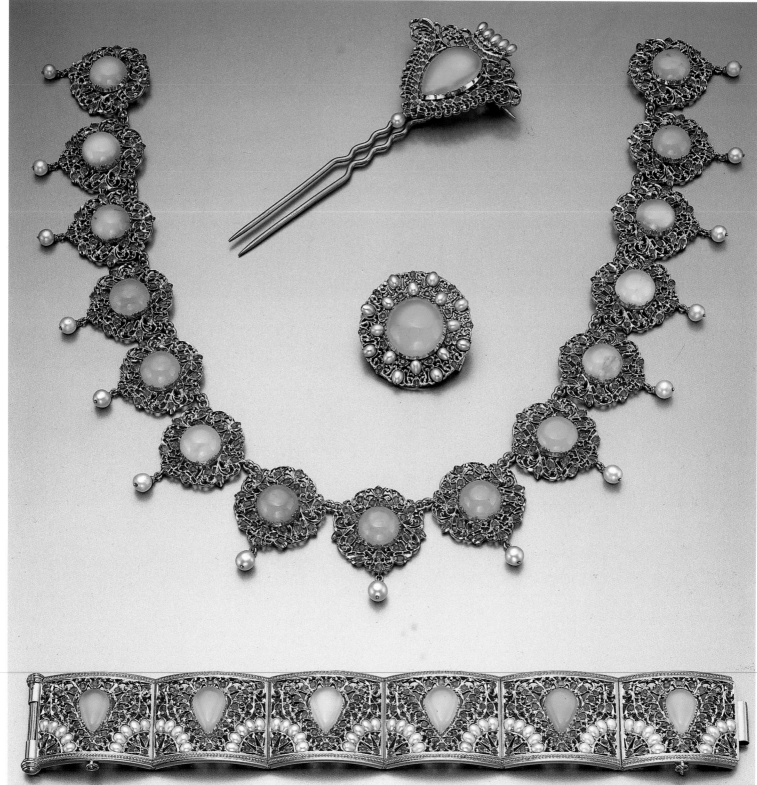

Two pendants by CARLO and ARTHUR GIULIANO: left, a gold Renaissance-style locket of Pegasus drinking at the fountain of Hippocrene (1901). The enameled locket, set with pearls, garnets and rubies, was made for Katherine Bradley to contain a miniature of Edith Cooper. The Fitzwilliam Museum, Cambridge

Right, "The Descent of Psyche into Hell", an enameled gold pendant set with emeralds, sapphires, chrysolites, carbuncles and a pink topaz, which was designed by Charles Ricketts for the wedding of Mrs Sturge-Moore in 1904. The Fitzwilliam Museum, Cambridge

Below, an openwork gold brooch pendant in the form of a bird perched on an olive branch, designed by Sir Edward Burne-Jones and made by CARLO GIULIANO. The brooch is decorated with translucent red and green enamel, and set with a ruby, pearls, and cabochon coral and turquoises. It is possible that Burne-Jones may have been influenced by late medieval mosaics of olive trees in Venice, which he saw when he visited the city in 1862. Private collection

Bottom, a pair of hair ornaments and a brooch by GIULIANO from the collection of Mrs William Holman Hunt in the form of marguerites – the petals carved from coral and the centres of enamel set with a coral bead. The signed brooch cannot be later than 1895 but the box dates from 1912–14. It has been suggested by Mrs Elizabeth Tompkin, adopted daughter of Gladys Holman Hunt and current owner of the jewels, that the date of the box might be explained if the combs, which are unsigned, were made between 1912 and 1914 to match the existing brooch.

The Pre-Raphaelites and their circle recognized in the eclecticism of Carlo Giuliano's work an echo of their own ideals. Sir Lawrence Alma-Tadema (1836–1912) went to Giuliano to borrow a gold jewel for his painting "The Conversion of Paula". Sir Edward Poynter asked Giuliano to make the jewelry for his model in "Helen of Troy", but perhaps the most famous commission from an artist was the bird brooch which Sir Edward Burne-Jones asked Giuliano to make up. In her biography of her husband, called *Memorials*, Lady Burne-Jones says, "Much later in his life his thoughts turned to jewel work, but I only remember one thing he carefully and completely designed and saw executed, a brooch, representing a dove, made of pink coral and turquoise mounted in olive branches of green enamel." The version which belonged to Burne-Jones's daughter Margaret was shown at the New Gallery in 1892–93, and appears to have influenced the jewelry designs of several of his contemporaries. Among them were John Paul Cooper, Charles Voysey and Charles Ricketts. Furthermore, the designs for jewels left with Giuliano by Sir Edward Burne-Jones seem to have influenced the commercial repertoire of the firm and from time to time pieces in the form of enameled hearts and laurels are found which owe their origins to Burne-Jones's restless imagination.

No doubt Charles Ricketts (1856–1931) sought out Giuliano not only because of the Burne-Jones connection but also for the firm's skill in interpreting Renaissance themes. The British Museum has a small album, prepared by Ricketts at Richmond in about 1899, which contains numerous jewelry designs represented in rich and beautiful colours, often heightened with gold. Among them are ideas for jewels to be given to a small group of friends. Ricketts published some of the work of the poets Katherine Bradley (1846–1914) and her niece Edith Cooper (1862–1913), who collaborated under the pseudonym of Michael Field. Katherine was known to him as

Michael and Edith Cooper assumed the name Henry. They spoke of Ricketts as "Fairy Man" or "Fay" in reference to the wizardry of his various talents. On 8 December 1899 Ricketts gave Katherine Bradley a pendant he had designed in the form of a large oval turquoise held in an enameled gold mount that was further decorated with pearls and hung with an amethyst, and Giuliano had been asked to make it up. Also in the series of jewels designed by Ricketts and made by Giuliano was the pendant called "Pegasus Drinking at the Fountain of Hippocrene" now in the Fitzwilliam Museum in Cambridge; it was made to contain a miniature of Edith Cooper by Ricketts and given to Katherine Bradley by him in May 1901. The poets were consulted during the designing of the jewel and Henry wondered whether Giuliano would make it "daintily absurd enough". Eventually the jewel was complete and Ricketts confessed that, at first, he could not have been more pleased but then, like "God on Sunday", he began to reflect and found two places where the work was not up to standard.

Between 1899 and 1904 a number of other pieces were made, but as Edith Cooper had predicted these experiments were relatively short-lived. She found that the "jeweller's work coarsens the design, the setting often robbing the stone of its size, and then the objects get lost, and, with the future in mind it's not worth doing." The cost of using Giuliano to execute the designs must have worried Ricketts' generous nature. "Michael Field" were so apprehensive concerning the forthcoming bill for the "Pegasus" jewel that they considered selling their clothes to an intimidating old gipsy woman. Giuliano and his substantial bills were so much part of Ricketts' life at the time that he introduced the theme into the plot of a play he and "Michael Field" were to write together, based on the story of Madame de Chateaubriand and her jewels at the court of François I. It was to be called "Giuliano or Never Never Let Us Part"

The artist/illustrator Charles Ricketts, who designed jewelry for many of his friends. Sotheby's

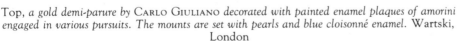

Top, *a gold demi-parure by* Carlo Giuliano *decorated with painted enamel plaques of amorini engaged in various pursuits. The mounts are set with pearls and blue cloisonné enamel.* Wartski, London

Above, *a gold fringe* Giuliano *necklace, decorated with enamel and set with cabochon rubies and moonstones.* H.R.H. The Princess Margaret, Countess of Snowdon

Within it, a Vesta case (1863–95) by Carlo Giuliano, *made up of two panels of rock-crystal, which are mounted in gold decorated with black and blue champlevé enamel of exceptionally fine quality. The enamel is apparently the work of Kempson and Mauger, outworkers for Giuliano.*

Top, left, *a watercolour portrait of Princess Louise by Blanche Lindsay, in which the princess is wearing a silver articulated necklace (as shown below) by Guiliano, or a version of it. Queen Victoria seems to have commissioned a series of this necklace, one of which she gave to Jenny Lind, the Swedish soprano (top, right)*

Right, *Clara Bell, sister of the painter Sir Edward Poynter, was a customer of Giuliano's. Private collection*

Top, *two daughters of Constantine Ionides, an important client of the firm: they are wearing enameled gold brooches by Giuliano (c. 1880). Private collection*

Left, *a portrait of Fanny Holman Hunt, wearing a pendant necklace by Castellani and Giuliano. Toledo Museum of Art*

Above, *the woman in this painting by Alma-Tadema is wearing a gold jewel by Giuliano in the form of the river god Achelous.*

Before his death in 1895, Carlo Giuliano had taken care to see that the business would continue under the ownership of his two sons Arthur Alphonse (1864–1914) and Carlo, and he clearly acknowledged to whom his success in business was due. His will directed that all his devoted retail customers should receive a small jewel from his stock up to the value of £50 and, furthermore, seventeen *grenaille* works of art made by him were to be left to the English Government on his death, together with enamel work from his stock to the value of £200 to be selected by the director of the South Kensington Museum, now the Victoria and Albert Museum. Ultimately the bequest of Giuliano's jewels was housed there in a glass case by the tea rooms.

In 1899 the case was broken into and the jewels stolen. Today only a few fragments remain to give us some idea of the superlative quality of this collection. Carlo and Arthur Giuliano were obviously distressed by the theft; in 1900 they gave the Museum seven more items made by their father and the Museum purchased a necklace by Carlo for £250.

Arthur Giuliano continued in the way his father had taught him and artistic, intellectual and aristocratic circles continued to patronize the business, as well as Queen Victoria, Queen Alexandra, King Edward VII and Queen Victoria's daughter the Empress Frederick of Prussia. The pattern was broken in 1910, however, with the accession of King George V and his consort Queen Mary, who is believed to have held certain prejudices against the "foreign" origins of the establishment. Despite continual Royal patronage there is no record of any member of the Giuliano family being granted warrants, invariably an outward sign of such a relationship.

Arthur Giuliano is universally remembered as having enormous charm. Charles Ricketts was sufficiently captivated by him to write, "When I last saw the glorious Giuliano he received me in emeralds . . ." His happy and winning personality, coupled with wide-ranging artistic gifts, concealed a complicated private life. He was married to Eleanor Gertrude Gray on 27 September 1893 and separated from her after twenty years of marriage to take up residence with Amelia Sarah Barker. Amelia was the beneficiary of his will and the mother of several children. It may be that the outbreak of the First World War, the difficulties of maintaining the business in a new location (48 Knightsbridge from 1912) and his own colourful domestic circumstances led Arthur Giuliano to take his life with a revolver on the last day of August 1914. His tragic suicide caused the closure of a firm that had occupied a leading position in London as art jewelers for some fifty-five years.

A necklace by Carlo Giuliano in gold, cave-pearls and green and blue enamel (probably c. 1863). Hancock & Co., London

FONTENAY

"**A**man of rare intelligence, much spirit and a very sure taste. A genuine artist, a distinguished writer . . ., with an open and pleasant nature, wonderfully talented in all things, he was passionately interested in everything connected with his profession." Fontenay could not have hoped for a greater tribute than these words written by his young colleague Henri Vever, in his remarkable work on French 19th-century jewelry. And Vever added: "Fontenay was one of the greatest figures in jewelry; like Castellani he created a style which will also bear his name and which no one has managed to repeat since."

More than a century after his death – Eugène Fontenay died on 6 March 1887 – it is only right to give him his due place within that generation of skilled and distinguished artists who marked the second half of the 19th century. A keen defender of *bijouterie* (metal jewelry) – at a time when *joaillerie* (stone-setting) reigned supreme – he managed to combine perfect mastery of his craft with inventiveness and great erudition; he learned in depth from the example of antiquity and restored gold jewelry to its former high rank.

What remains today of the incredible quantity and variety of jewels created in his ateliers during a career spanning thirty-five years? The few pieces that have been identified, the valuable albums of published photographs and engravings, the testimony of his contemporaries and his own historical writings on jewelry may help us to gain some idea of his works; but the sad fact remains that the major part of his production has disappeared and all his drawings and papers are lost.

Fontenay was born in the heart of Paris on 19 May 1824. The grandson and son of jewelers – his father Prosper, who lived at 32 Rue du Caire, had specialized in costume jewelry chains – he soon made it clear that he wanted to continue the family tradition and was lucky enough to be apprenticed to two excellent Parisian jewelry-makers: Edouard Marchand, inventor of new forms of jewelry, especially elastic or spring-based bracelets, and Dutreih who had rediscovered the brilliant effect of enamels on pure gold, in the manner of the 16th-century craftsmen.

When he was 24, Fontenay set up his own modest atelier at 2 Rue Favart. Presumably remembering his own difficult beginnings, he later reminded his colleagues in the jewelers' guild of "the very democratic basis of the jeweler's profession: most jewelry-makers . . . began by being workers."

We know little about his first ten years of activity, from 1848 to 1858. Vever mentions only two prestige works: a piece of jewelry with historiated decoration inspired by the Renaissance, the fan commissioned in 1852 for the Queen of Portugal and executed in collaboration with the enameler Lefournier whom Fontenay knew from his years with Dutreih; and the masterpiece of stone-setting made for the 1855 Exposition Universelle, a diadem formed of two branches of bramble. In the case of the latter, Fontenay produced an original interpretation of a headdress already in favour under Louis-Philippe, showing a particularly lively naturalism, accentuated by the very light setting and carried out partly in platinum.

An entirely different spirit imbued the elegant diadem he executed in March 1858 for the Empress Eugénie. Aware that a diadem must be effective from a distance – as a result of "the lines, the wide and easily intelligible divisions", presenting "little more than silhouettes" – he composed a headdress whose arrangement offered two different aspects, which could be altered at will: the nine large fleurons – enhanced with emeralds or sapphires – could be replaced with seventeen "large pendant pearls

Top left, *the two different forms of the diadem made in March 1858 for the Empress Eugénie, after an etching made and published by Fontenay in 1867. One view (above) shows the diadem decorated with emeralds and diamonds, while the other shows it transformed by the substitution of large pendant pearls.*

Top right and above, *a plate, cutlery and fruit bowls of chased gold, blue enamel and diamonds from the dinner service made between 1858 and 1867 for Said Pasha, the Viceroy of Egypt, after etchings made and published by Fontenay in 1867.*

pointing downwards, which produced a lovely effect", or seventeen "large pendant diamonds which formed part of the imperial rivière and which could be detached for that purpose". With his usual sense of precision, Fontenay made it clear that these crowns – Princess Mathilde had a similar one with pearls – "were not strictly heraldic; in many ways they were works of fantasy but they complemented the toilet admirably."

The next decade marked a decisive stage in the artist's career and culminated in his brilliant success at the 1867 Exposition Universelle. By joining forces with a major dealer in precious stones, Joseph Halphen, Fontenay secured for himself a flood of commissions from an extremely wealthy Eastern clientele and began to diversify his production to satisfy these export demands.

On Fontenay's death, his colleague Massin paid him warm tribute, describing this success: "Thanks to his astonishing variety of talents, together with the resources of a thoroughly skilled technique and ability, he was better placed than any of his colleagues to further the reputation of our Parisian arts and taste abroad. A goldsmith when he created dinner services . . ., he became an armourer when asked to make sabres. The weapon that emerged from his hands was constructed in accordance with all the rules of the art . . . and as suited to display as to war."

The royal caprices, these betel-nut boxes, pipes, sword-belts, mirrors, parasols, fly-whisks, parade weapons – even a complete harness with bit, saddle, bridle, stirrups, riding-whip, etc. – made for the King of Siam, the Shah of Persia or the Indian princes, were designed mainly to set off a profusion of stupendous precious stones. The Viceroy of Egypt's dinner service, begun in September 1858 and completed in February 1867, was quite beyond imagination and unbelievably lavish.

Conscious of the reputation he acquired from these extravagant commissions – although aware too that they were only a pale reflection of his real artistic aims –

Fontenay took a certain pride in them: "We feel we cannot conclude this summary of the history of our industry . . . without mentioning the dinner service executed in gold, diamonds and precious stones . . . and made for Said Pasha. This service, consisting of 42 table settings in gold and enamel covered in diamonds, each of which was worth 60,000 francs, was completed by a large fruit dish which made up the centrepiece of an ensemble that included 2 six-branched candelabra . . . worth 1,800,000 francs by themselves, and 6 fruit bowls representing large natural leaves."

Thanks to his profits from these exports and the confidence shown in him by his faithful customers, he managed in the 1860s to free himself from reliance on the dealers for whom he had set many stones, which had been exhibited to advantage in industrial shows since 1855. He had to wait until 1863 to stamp his own hallmark, and it was only in 1865 that he first exhibited works under his own name, in Porto. Henceforth he was to be a full exhibiting member at these world fairs and to help open their doors to the other jewelers.

Now that he felt ready to show his works to the public, he realized that the 1867 Exposition Universelle offered him an ideal opportunity to make his works known, benefiting skilfully from the widespread infatuation with the *néo-grec* style.

He proudly affirmed that none of the works he exhibited had been made for the occasion: "My showcase is the exact and sincere expression . . . of what I make . . . and represents the objects I am currently selling." Apart from three jeweled humming-birds, executed by one of his colleagues, Hommassel, his showcase was indeed devoted entirely to gold pieces.

Presumably he was already aware that his name would remain linked more closely with the series of jewels he had designed and executed in the space of a few years, with the more intimate and personal demi-parures, than with the masterpieces of stone-setting executed purely on commission, of which he had supplied so many to the East.

Top, *a miniature painted by Pierre-Paul de Pommayrac in 1861 which shows the Empress Eugénie wearing the diadem made by Fontenay in 1858. The fleurons could be embellished by sapphires or emeralds, or replaced by pearls and diamonds.* Private collection
Left, *a pair of gold earrings (c. 1864–67), each of which bears a lapis-lazuli bust of a small boy.* Musée des Arts Décoratifs, Paris
Below, *a bracelet in gold, black enamel and lapis-lazuli (c. 1870–80).* Musée d'Orsay, Paris

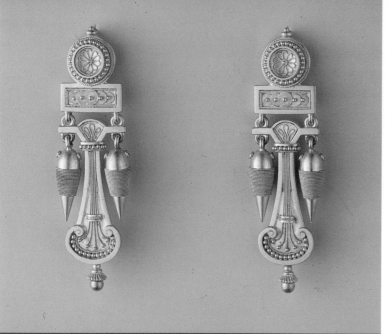

Left: top, *a pair of gold earrings (c. 1864–67).*
Musée des Arts Décoratifs, Paris
Centre, *a pair of earrings composed of gold and jade.*
Fontenay began to use jade from 1860; this pair of
earrings in the form of amphorae, designed a few years
later (c. 1864–67), is among his best creations.
Musée des Arts Décoratifs, Paris
Bottom, *gold earrings (c. 1864–67).* Musée des Arts
Décoratifs, Paris

Opposite, *a demi-parure (c. 1864) consisting of a gold*
pendant and earrings. The enamels were painted by
Eugène Richet. This set, together with some thirty
similar demi-parures, appears in an album of
photographs of Fontenay's jewels which dates from
1864. Asprey, New York

Above, *a brûle-parfum, made of gold, enamel, diamonds and lapis-lazuli. Fontenay's masterpiece, this was specially created for the 1878 Exposition Universelle. It was exhibited once more after his death at the Exposition of 1889.*
Opposite, details of the enamel allegories, by Eugène Richet, representing discord, sensual delight, work and love. Renouncing the matt painting of antiquity, Richet combined translucent enamel on a guilloché background, basse-taille enamel and enamel painted in relief. Musée d'Orsay, Paris

Gold "Chimera" brooch (c. 1864–67), with enamels painted by Eugène Richet. Private collection

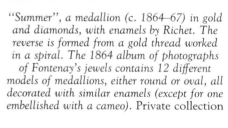

"Summer", a medallion (c. 1864–67) in gold and diamonds, with enamels by Richet. The reverse is formed from a gold thread worked in a spiral. The 1864 album of photographs of Fontenay's jewels contains 12 different models of medallions, either round or oval, all decorated with similar enamels (except for one embellished with a cameo). Private collection

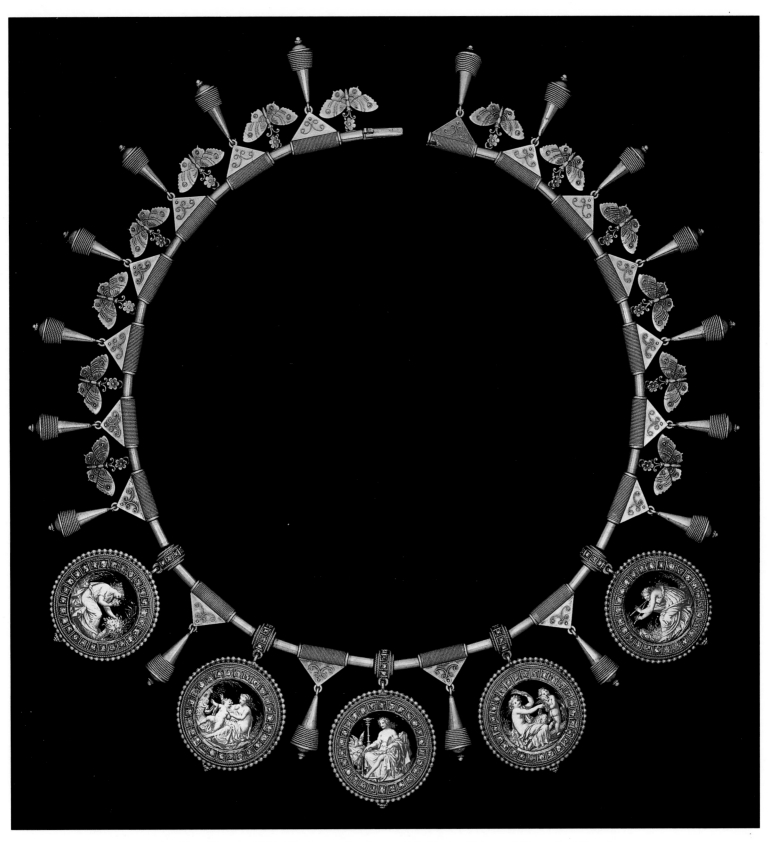

A gold necklace (c. 1864–67), decorated with enamels by Eugène Richet and diamonds. Although a matching brooch has now been lost, the necklace still has its jewel case bearing the mark of the House of Boucheron, at 152/153 Galerie de Valois in the Palais-Royal. Fontenay continued to produce jewelry for Boucheron until 1881. British Museum, London (Hull Grundy Gift)

Gold necklace, decorated with enamels by Richet and diamonds (c. 1864). The medallions represent Spring, Summer and Autumn. The necklace is a variant of a shorter version which appears in the photograph album of 1864. Kunstgewerbe Museum, Cologne

The 1867 Exposition Universelle was largely dominated by the *néo-grec* style. This vogue for classical antiquity, heralded by a few isolated earlier works, enjoyed general favour during the last decade of the Second Empire. In 1854 Prince Napoleon had set the tone by commissioning a Pompeian house from the architect Alfred Normand, which was erected at 18 Avenue Montaigne in Paris. In his turn, Emperor Napoleon III also encouraged this fashion when he decided in 1861 to acquire the collection assembled in Rome by Cavaliere Campana. The presentation of this collection – which consisted of 1,200 Greek, Etruscan and Roman jewels – first in the Palais de l'Industrie and then from 1863 in the Louvre was a sensational artistic event.

As early as the 1862 exhibition in London, several Parisian craftsmen – Marret, Baugrand, and Mellerio, among others, had transposed supposedly "Etruscan" motifs into the setting of stones. But what was merely to be for most of them a passing fashion, based on current artistic taste, was in Fontenay's case to give rise to a genuine style and to remain for many years an inexhaustible source of research, study and reflection.

He was neither the first nor the only one – in Paris, Rome, London, Vienna, or elsewhere – to draw inspiration from the jewelry of antiquity. In Italy, Castellani had of course rediscovered certain manufacturing procedures and successfully reproduced a large number of known examples. In Paris itself, other jewelers – Wiese, Rouvenat, Gueyton, and Falize, to mention only a few – had also drawn on this archaeological heritage and adapted it temporarily to their work. Vever took notice of the huge success of the "Campana type" jewels.

He especially admired Fontenay's parures, reproducing no fewer than 64 different models in his reference book on 19th-century French jewelry: "The parures of the heroes and gods of whom Homer sang, of the beauties of Mycenae, Cyprus and Tyre, came back to life under his hands to adorn the Parisian women of the Second Empire."

Fontenay managed by a tour de force to combine the heritage of antiquity in its purest form, the gold jewel, with Parisian traditions which had culminated in the 18th century in the manufacture of chased gold boxes and chains, hard stones and enamels, to propose a subtle synthesis which belongs distinctively to his era. He was only too well aware of the dangers of pastiche, given the prevailing eclecticism. "These styles, all of them, have become our heritage . . . which, like a new shirt of Nessus, is destroying our very marrow." With great foresight, however, he defended the creations of his colleagues against those who accused them of having no style: "The contemporary producers, who are reproached for lacking any real character of their own, have made far greater efforts than the ancients did when, treading a well-worn path, they calmly followed in the well-defined and undefined footsteps of their styles."

Fontenay managed to avoid the pitfall of too great a familiarity with antique and exotic styles. Although he occasionally indulged in the caprices of fashion – by designing a few Egyptian or Chinese jewels commemorating the opening of the Suez Canal and the capture of Peking – he still remained loyal to the rules of composition and ornamentation he had set himself.

Wherein lies the mark of his originality and the vigour of his style? First, in direct, unequalled knowledge – for he travelled throughout Europe to visit museums and private collections – and in his enthusiastic nostalgia for the jewelry of antiquity. He liked to speak of this enthusiasm, and spoke of it well: "I like to imagine the gold of the diadems, the necklaces, the fibulas, the pendants, standing out against black hair, running like streaks of fire over brown and warm flesh-tints, and tracing fantastic glinting arabesques on the simple folds of the lovely white tunics."

Antique Egyptian and Assyrian jewelry, Gallo-Roman and Byzantine jewelry, modern jewelry from the French provinces, from Scandinavia, China and Japan, even from Africa and the Indies – where he no doubt found some distant memories of antiquity – nothing escaped his intellectual curiosity. But above all, he was one of those artists who managed to go beyond the production of what are often poorly understood imitations of antique works; and by constantly questioning the models he studied he came to a profound understanding of the principles of ornamentation: "I like an art . . . that can subordinate knowledge to taste."

Châtelaine of chased gold, inscribed "FUGIT IRREPARABILE" (c. 1860).

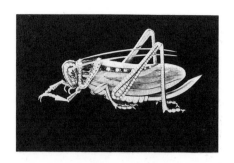

Grasshopper and scarab brooches made from jade and precious stones (1860).

His jewelry, often enhanced by a discreet polychromy – achieved sometimes by the use of enamels, sometimes by hard stones, coral, pearls, and the like – always retained their homogeneous, lofty and measured style. Even if he was occasionally carried away by his virtuosity, especially in the use of filigree, at least he was always careful to ensure that every motif, however detailed, remained clearly legible and formed an integral part of the whole. He turned to stone-cutters to cut and polish the jade and lapis-lazuli. He turned to the art of enameling to represent the mythological figures he liked so much: Artemis, Atalanta, Athena, Circe, Danaë, Leda, Omphale, Penelope, Sappho, each surrounded by her familiar emblems. Even to enameling, which was experiencing a brilliant revival at the time, he brought his own entirely original contribution, calling on a pupil of Thomas Couture, Eugène Richet, who produced for him matt enamels treated like miniature antique paintings.

The few pieces of jewelry rediscovered today allow us to appreciate the extraordinary perfection that was the hallmark of his production. None of the procedures of jewelry-making – embossing, chasing, repercé work, filigree work, and so forth – held any secrets for him.

Vever tells an anecdote which clearly reveals his exacting approach to his trade. Finding one day in his workshop that a piece he was to deliver the following day was defective, Fontenay did not hesitate to remake it entirely himself, working until nightfall: "Next day, the workman found on the workbench . . . side by side, the failed piece and the remade piece . . ., ready for delivery to the client."

With his knowledge of antique jewelry and his professional perfectionism, he was an intransigent champion of jewelry made entirely of gold. Although he hit on the idea of making cheap jewelry, he left it to others to carry out the work. Whole-hearted and demanding as he was, he could not persuade himself to embark on what seemed to him an impoverishment of his chosen profession, even though he had to face the growing competition from imitation jewelry in gold plate or copper gilt.

For this nostalgic lover of antique jewelry, 22-carat fine gold remained the ideal material, and one that could not be rivalled by any alloy: "You have to look at jewelry made of this material, worn out of doors, in the greenery, under the canopy of the skies, in full sunlight, to experience its magical effects."

When it became impossible to use 22-carat gold as freely as before, he proposed plating 18-carat gold with it – to combine "the charm of the one with the solidity of the other" – and reserved for himself the pleasure of using pure gold for particularly delicate ornaments: "I have executed works in 22-carat gold, which are almost sleights of hand, absolutely unfeasible with a lower alloy, such as soldering a series of microscopic granulations to a very heavy moulded piece."

He was more adept than other goldsmiths at producing the most varied effects from the tone of gold. He remembered how, as a young apprentice, he had tried to combine different colourings by mixing silver with red copper or brass. When he became a master jeweler in his turn, he preferred not to produce the facile effects of coloured golds and to retain the rich yellow tonality of native gold, "which improves with use". He also knew how to give worked gold a matt finish, "very pleasing to the eye", which avoided the excessively bright and superficial brilliance generally produced by polishing.

This respect for the noble metal, this care to preserve its intrinsic qualities – in a period when the rise of industry encouraged all kinds of factitious processes – clearly reflects the nostalgic idealism of an artist who found it difficult to accept the many upheavals produced by the industrial revolution: "Our society, so keen to enjoy itself, is content with approximations."

More perspicacious than others, he realized that following the example of antiquity did not mean confining oneself to a simple repertory of forms and ornaments but must involve careful reflection on the principles of design and the rules of composition. And he deplored the fact that "modern jewelry creations have . . . neither the character, nor the fullness of form, nor the purity of line" of jewelry of the past.

As with many of his contemporaries – Viollet-le-Duc, for example – it was of course a long way from a theory enunciated with unusual foresight to actual works, which depended too much on fashion, on the demand of the client and on the routine of the workshop. And yet, within this

Opposite: top, *necklace and earrings in gold (c. 1864), from a contemporary photograph.* Centre, *"embroidered" necklace made of chased matt gold, decorated with filigree (c. 1875).* Bottom, *"grains of oat" diadem of chased gold, decorated with filigree (c. 1875–80); from a photograph in the Boucheron Archives.*

artistic circle where the spread of eclecticism encouraged all kinds of mixed styles, he remained one of the rare creators to return to a unity of material and style. In the most beautiful pieces he created, seeking to avoid an excess of superimposed decoration, he managed to attain that naivety, that elegance born of simplicity, that he appreciated so much in antique jewelry, drawing his inspiration from the life and nature around him. He was to become a keen apostle of this return to nature, which anticipated the great flowering of Art Nouveau, and in his *Confession d'un Orfèvre* (1885), he told of the different stages that led him to this awareness: "I spelled out the tiniest details of nature, one by one . . . and each of these studies, which seemed at first quite devoid of meaning, became, at a certain point and quite without my knowledge, the point of departure for a complete piece of jewelry; a grain of oat or wheat provided the motif for an entire necklace."

Over the years, then, if we look at the pieces we know, we can see those in which he displayed this love of the natural environment: from the headdress of brambles (1855) to the jade brooches (he was the first European jewelry-maker to use jadeite) in the form of scarabs, grasshoppers or dragonflies (1860) and the familiar demiparures with grains of oat or wheat (1867). This inspiration from nature, less evident at first sight, also imbues a number of compositions dating from 1870–80, especially the pieces he made for Boucheron. A piece of jewelry like the châtelaine inscribed "FUGIT IRREPARABILE" surprises by the suppleness of the furled foliage, which is very close in spirit to Art Nouveau.

With his complex and often baffling character, Fontenay leaves us with the impression of an artist difficult to define, as capable of designing the plainest and boldest forms as of producing enormous, almost unwearable pieces. There are necklaces as voluminous as antique pectorals, headdresses such as those that appear in the Boucheron archives, which are more reminiscent of theatre jewelry and anticipate the analogous jewels Alphonse Mucha was later to design for Georges Fouquet.

However, even in the parures in a heavy orientalist taste, Fontenay had a vigorous sense of composition; the amplitude and dynamism of some of his spiral motifs are reminiscent of the articulated breast-plates

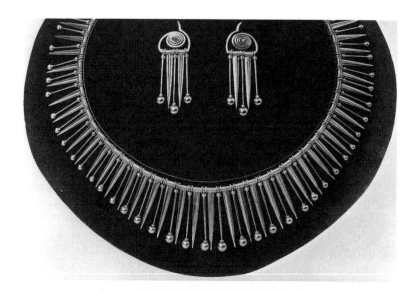

and Roman or Gallo-Roman bracelets whose design he had noted during his travels.

The more measured style of his matt gold, supple bracelets and necklaces, also referred to in Boucheron's archives, harks back to earlier successful models – once again the Campana jewels with grains of wheat and oat – but also gave rise to new creations, new successes: the "embroidered" necklaces, with their filigree design running all the way round, on a series of small tongues decreasing in length, display a remarkable originality.

He created one of his masterpieces for the 1878 Exposition Universelle – for which he was appointed a member of the jury awarding the prizes, which meant that he could not compete. This was a small *brûle-parfum* formed of an egg covered in filigree and enamel, supported by dolphins and sirens, resting on a lapis-lazuli stand. This unique jewel, which used all the resources of the jeweler's art, can stand as the testament of an accomplished artist who had completely assimilated the heritage of antiquity: composed like a small-scale monument, this tour de force of a jeweler at the height of his career represents a perfect synthesis of the styles he most admired, those of classical antiquity and the Renaissance.

The allegorical theme he chose – the stages of life, shown on four medallions: the life-giving force of love, work, sensual delight, the destructive force of discord – the composition and the rich polychromy (here Richet returned to translucent and iridescent enamels) – all seem to pay tribute to the goldsmith-jewelers of the Renaissance. The work of a sculptor, a painter, a founder, a chiseler, an enameler, a stone-cutter, the *brûle-parfum* of 1878 prefigures the famous Fabergé eggs.

Fontenay was 59 years old when he decided, in 1882, to hand over his business to his main colleague, Henri Smets. The honoured and respected jeweler gave way to the historian of jewelry, working sometimes as a lecturer, sometimes as a writer. During the last five years of his life, he travelled the length and breadth of Europe to study, compare and draw all the known specimens of the art of jewelry. The articles he published in the *Revue des Arts Décoratifs* (from 1881), in his books *Diamants et Pierres Précieuses: Bijoux, Joyaux, Orfèvreries* (1881) and *Les Bijoux Anciens et Modernes*, which appeared soon after his death in 1887, showed him to be one of the first to attempt to retrace the history of jewelry since antiquity, and to do so with enormous passion and enthusiasm.

A learned artist and an admirable craftsman, Fontenay was entirely a man of the 19th century, when erudition was the accompaniment of all artistic creation. With his meditative spirit and eye for life, he was one of the first to free himself from the prevailing eclecticism and to preach the principle of learning from nature, well before the flowering of Art Nouveau. In a period which loved an at times meretricious richness and a great profusion of forms, his purest creations – simple jewels, entirely in gold, free of any allegorical reference – look strikingly bold and honest and surprisingly "modern".

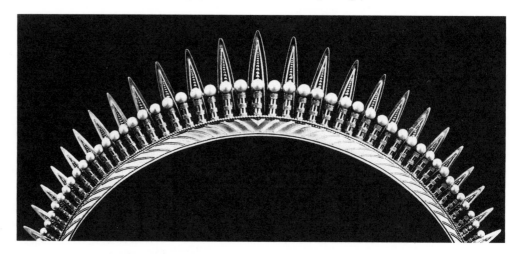

A diadem in the néo-grec style made of chased gold (c. 1864), from a contemporary photograph.

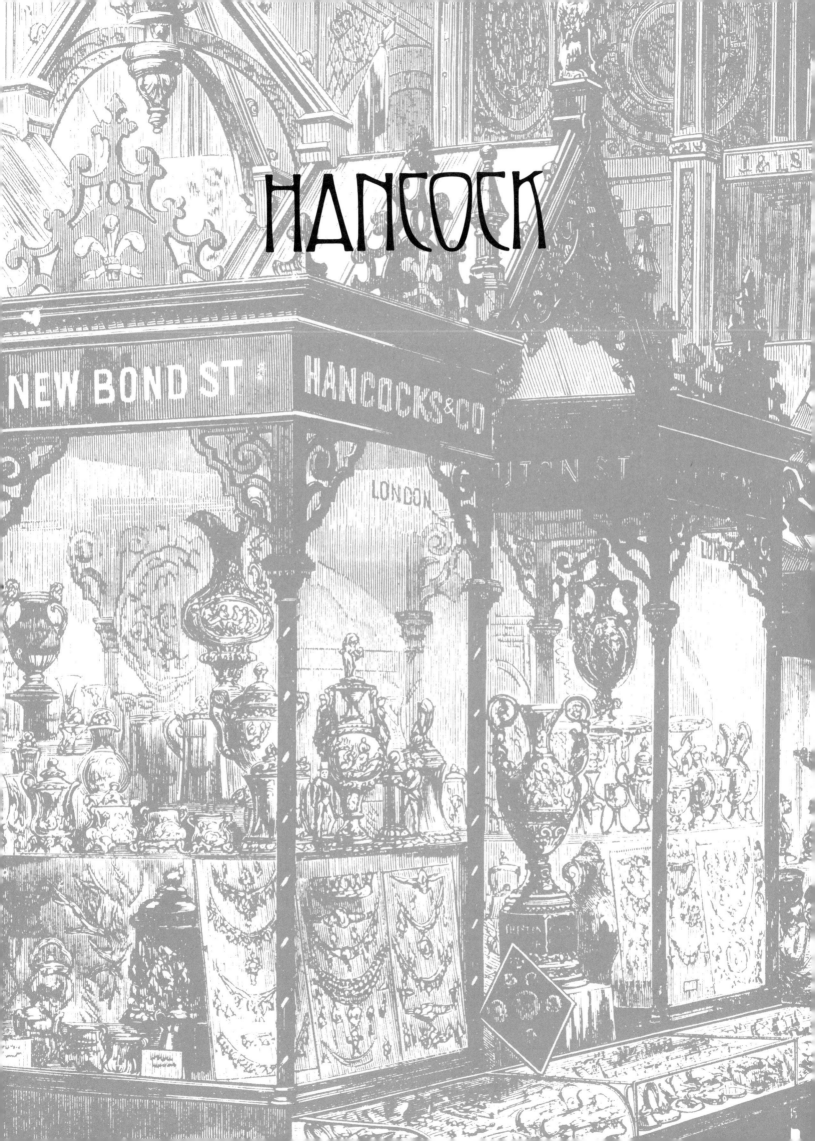

Among the state, splendour, and brilliant displays of wealth and taste at the coronation of the Emperor of Russia, at Moscow, will doubtless be remembered the celebrated suite of jewels worn by the Countess Granville, and known as 'the Devonshire Gems'. The collection is the property of the Duke of Devonshire, who intrusted the gems to Mr. C.F. Hancock, of Bruton Street, to be set en suite as ornaments to be worn upon the above memorable occasion by his Grace's noble relative. Mr. Hancock has accomplished his tasteful work with great success. The difficulty in arranging the gems in such a manner as to bring out their peculiar beauties and render them the principal objects in the ornamental suite, and at the same time to avoid the heaviness which might be produced from the darkness and opacity of many of them has been surmounted; and the result has been their disposal in seven ornaments – viz. a Diadem, a Coronet, a Stomacher, a jewelled Bandeau, a Necklace, a Comb and a Bracelet – each of which is in itself matchless; while united they display a concentration of elegance the superiority of which will be apparent to everybody in any degree acquainted with the fine arts, and with the progess of the manufacture of the precious metals in the hands of the best artists. (*Illustrated London News*, 9 May 1857, p. 441)

In the summer of 1856 Earl Granville, nephew of the sixth Duke of Devonshire, set out with his wife Marie on the long journey to Moscow, where they arrived in mid-August. Lord Granville had been appointed to represent the Queen at the coronation of Alexander II, Tsar of Russia. They installed themselves in the Graziano Palace and prepared to join in the month-long celebrations surrounding this event of Byzantine splendour. In their baggage, along with valuable pieces of plate also lent by the Duke of Devonshire, was the fabulous parure described above. Of enameled gold set with large diamonds and incorporating 88 engraved gems from the historic Devonshire collection, this suite of ornaments furnished Lady Granville with jewelry of almost royal grandeur to wear in her role as consort to the British Ambassador.

The Duke himself had attended the coronation of the previous Tsar, Nicholas I, in 1825, in a similar capacity, and was thus well able to advise his nephew on the necessary preparations for his embassy. The Russian love of jewelry and precious stones was famous and in order to match the almost barbaric opulence of Russian aristocratic taste this parure in the "Holbeinesque" style was devised. If the collection of antique engraved gems had not been used, the problem of providing the Countess with jewelry would have been formidable. C.F. Hancock was to claim that the idea was his own; the Duke, too, was credited with it. Sir Joseph Paxton, it is said, was instructed to act as intermediary in placing this important commission and it was he who selected Hancock's to carry out the work. The design for the settings of the gems seems to have been based on the surviving Tudor frame in enameled gold of one of the portrait cameos of Elizabeth I. The authenticity of Hancock's chosen pattern of four-lobed formalized flower-heads outlined in white is confirmed by comparison with a contemporary piece which survives from the Tudor period, the "Gresley" jewel, similarly set with a portrait cameo and enclosing in the reverse two portrait miniatures by Nicholas Hilliard, as did the Devonshire cameo. The "Gresley" jewel is depicted in a portrait of Catherine Walsingham, once attributed to Holbein (now in Birmingham City Art Gallery). These motifs of three- and four-lobed flower-heads outlined in white derived from the courtly jewels of France and Austria, examples of which, dating from the 1560s, are in the collections of the Bibliothèque Nationale in Paris and in the Kunsthistorisches Museum in Vienna.

Of the Devonshire parure the correspondent of the *Illustrated London News* wrote:

The ball given in Moscow during the coronation festivities in 1856 by the British Ambassador
Extraordinary, Earl Granville, and his wife. The host and hostess are shown standing at the right
in the tented ballroom devised for the occasion by Sir Joseph Paxton. Photo courtesy Sotheby's London

Below, The stand of Hancock & Co. at the Vienna Exhibition of 1873.

The settings are after the manner of Holbein, they are remarkable for their tracery and the minute delicacy of the component parts, both in design and execution. The successful performance of this most difficult commission has not only established the fact that in this country the arts have of late years attained a state of perfection unsurpassed at any period since the renaissance, but that the workmen employed in connection with them are second to none in any country in the world.

This praise for the workmanship must have gratified Hancock, but in fact the name of the workshop responsible for it is not recorded. Although jewelry accounted for an important part of Hancock's trade, it is unlikely that their own workshop was equipped to carry out this skilled enamel work as well as the very different silversmithing work for which the firm was principally celebrated. It has been suggested that the clue to this mystery may lie with C.F. Hancock's marriage, for his wife was a member of the Edington family whose firm, Edington and Staudinger, were manufacturing goldsmiths and jewelers. Possibly some of the great number of "Holbeinesque" pieces that were made to satisfy the demand created by the remarkable parure can be ascribed to this same firm – at least, those supplied to Hancock's themselves.

Ironically the parure itself seems rarely to have been worn. Of the Russian occasions little is recorded. It is said that Lady Granville wore the stomacher for the ball given at the Graziano Palace. The great wonder of the evening, a temporary ballroom improvised by Paxton in a great marquee supplied by Benjamin Edington and shipped out from England, was described by the reporter from the *Illustrated London News*, but Lady Granville's dress was not mentioned and the jewelry is not recognizable in either the illustration to this report or that in the Russian souvenir album presented to each of the guests.

The parure – or rather selected pieces from it, since it is not feasible to wear all seven ornaments together – was worn at the inauguration of the New State Supper Room at Buckingham Palace in 1857.

Again we are indebted to the indefatigable correspondent of the *Illustrated London News*: "At the ball the Countess Granville wore the magnificent parure of the Devonshire gems which the Duke of Devonshire had arranged by Mr. Hancock expressly for the Countess to wear at the coronation of the Emperor of Russia at Moscow." On its own, however, this would not be enough to explain the rapid spread of the enthusiasm for the "Holbeinesque" style. We learn from a report in the *Morning Chronicle* (30 April 1857) that the Duke had allowed the suite of jewels to be exhibited (at the Mechanics Institution in Manchester, February to March 1857), thus giving the public an opportunity to see it and Hancock's competitors the means to imitate the enameled settings.

It was to be exhibited thrice more, in 1861 at the Archaeological Institute in London and again in London at the 1862 and 1871 International Exhibitions.

Hancock himself is credited with the decision to lighten the richly coloured gems and their toning settings with the large diamonds that were placed at intervals on all the seven pieces. He feared that the effect would otherwise be too sombre. It is significant that only he among the many exhibitors to display "Holbeinesque" pieces at the 1862 International Exhibition should have shied away from re-creating directly the pattern of enamel work used for the Devonshire parure. The bracelet in the "Holbeinesque" style re-creates fairly closely the interlaced work of the parure, but that too is set with gems predominantly, the enamel work being of less importance. He did not resist for long the pressure of fashionable demand and his surviving "Holbeinesque" pieces echo, like those of other firms such as Howell and James, John Brogden and Hunt and Roskell, the enamel work of the parure.

It is possible that Edington was the supplier of "Holbeinesque" pieces to some of these other firms. Brogden was a manufacturing jeweler, not a retailer, and the survival of his design book, with its many versions of "Holbein" pieces, suggests that he was also an important source for these jewels.

A group of designs for jewels in the "Holbeinesque" style, from John Brogden's album of jewelry drawings, dating from the 1850s and '60s (now in the Victoria and Albert Museum, London).
Photos courtesy Sotheby's London

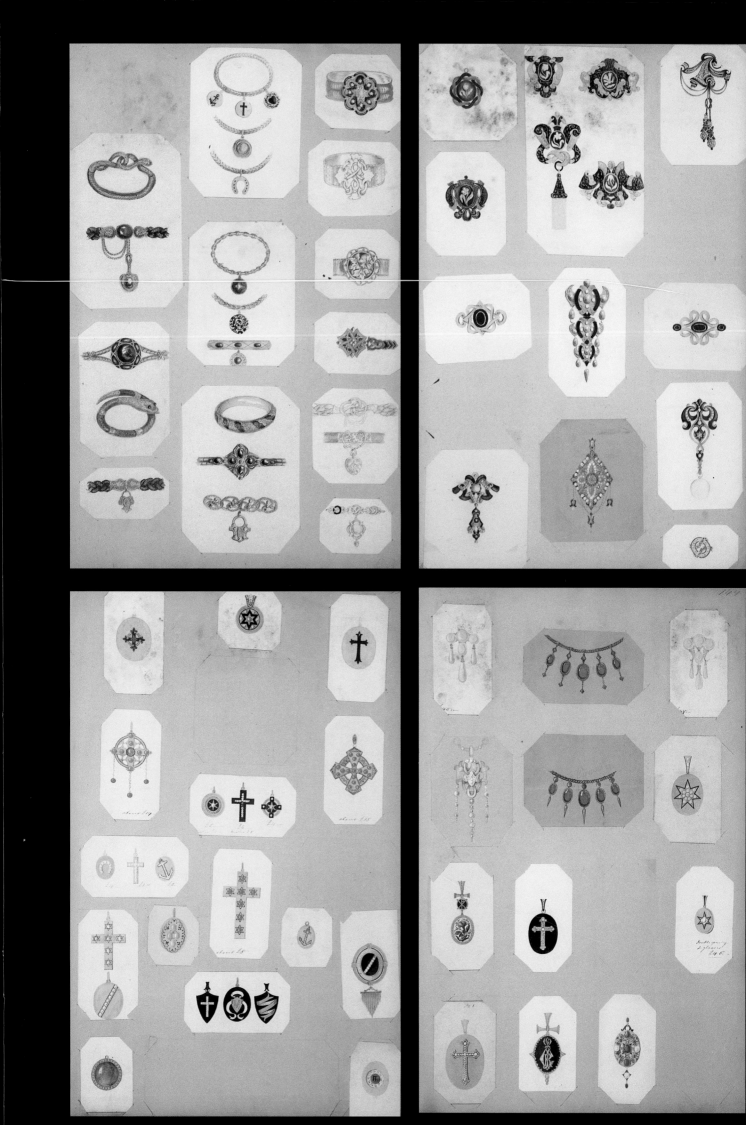

Scenes of events in Moscow during the coronation festivities in 1856, for which occasion Hancock's designed the Devonshire parure. Photos courtesy Sotheby's London

Below, the Devonshire parure by C.F. Hancock. This illustration (plate 203 in J.B. Waring's Masterpieces of Industrial Arts and Sculpture at the International Exhibition of 1862) is a marvel of organization in which the problem of depicting all seven pieces of the set has been brilliantly solved. This could not have been achieved with photography. Photo courtesy Hancock & Co.

Opposite, the stomacher from the Devonshire parure: enameled gold set with engraved gems from the collection of the Dukes of Devonshire and glass pastes in place of the original diamonds. Trustees of the Chatsworth Settlement

Opposite, *a group of "Holbeinesque" jewels in enameled gold. Three pendants, a necklace, and a pendant* en suite, *plus a pair of earrings, all in the typical taste of the 1870s. The central pendant in the top row is similar to surviving examples cased for Hancock's. Courtesy S.J. Phillips Ltd, London*

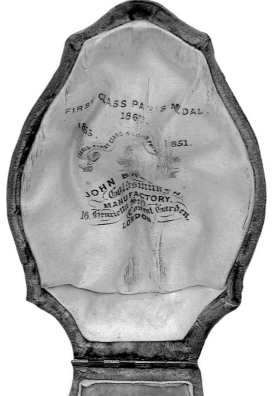

Left and left below, *a "Holbeinesque" pendant of enameled gold set with diamonds, in the original Hancock's case. It was probably made prior to the 1862 Exhibition, since the satin label in the lid includes the medal Hancock's put in after the 1851 Exhibition, but none of the later awards. The reverse of the pendant shows the delicate engraving of many of these pieces. Photo courtesy Hancock & Co.*

Left, *a "Holbeinesque" pendant in its original case, supplied by John Brogden, manufacturing jeweler of Henrietta St., Covent Garden, in the 1860s. Courtesy Philip Antrobus, London*

Above, *Tudor-style pendant (front and reverse) by Carlo Giuliano in enameled gold. The high quality of Giuliano's enamel work is particularly evident in this piece.*

53

Opposite, *the "Tennyson" Vase, a celebrated example of Hancock's sculptural silverwork. Designed and modeled by H.H. Armstead, it represents motifs from Tennyson's* Morte d'Arthur *and was exhibited in Paris in 1867. Photo courtesy Hancock & Co.*

Above, *three jewels in Hancock's cases showing something of the range of fashionable pieces supplied by the firm.* Photo courtesy Hancock & Co.

Left, *the "County Cavan" or "Queen's" brooch, made by West of Dublin and cased by Hancock's soon after the firm was established in 1849.* Photo courtesy Hancock & Co.

55

A matching bracelet, brooch and earrings of coral set in gold and decorated with filigree enamel. The set was cased for Hancock's and probably dates from the 1870s.

It is remarkable that the highly important Devonshire commission should have gone to Hancock's. The firm had been established only six years earlier, and at neither of the two great exhibitions (1851 and 1855) was Hancock's jewelry particularly noticed. The Royal jewelers at this date were Garrards (they still hold this appointment); Robert Phillips had been established for nearly ten years and was beginning to make a considerable reputation; other possible contenders for this valuable commission included Hunt and Roskell, or John Brogden, whose impressive display with his one-time partner Watherston at the 1851 Exhibition in London had attracted favourable attention. Another impressive display in 1851, that of Rowlands and Son of London, even included a bracelet in the "Holbein" style.

Charles Frederick Hancock (1807–91) opened his own shop at 39 Bruton Street in 1849. Until that year he had been a partner in the firm of Hunt and Roskell of 156 New Bond Street, successors to the celebrated Regency firm of Storr and Mortimer. Hunt and Roskell were important rivals to Hancock, particularly in the field of sculptural silverwork, and it is significant that Hancock styled himself a successor to Storr and Mortimer also, presumably a shrewd exercise in commercial credibility. Possibly the naming of Queen Adelaide as his patron was related to his claims on these august origins, since the Queen died in the very year Hancock set up his business and she cannot by that time have had much interest in commissioning jewelry or plate.

A surviving piece from this early date, cased for Hancock, is an example of the "County Cavan" brooch, an archaeological revival jewel by West of Dublin patented in 1849 and a popular exhibit at the 1851 Exhibition.

These devices that Hancock employed to set up the business in the early days may not have been necessary. A man with great entrepreneurial flair, he was clearly destined to succeed in spite of the strengths of his well-established rivals. Between 1849 and his retirement in 1869 he managed to entice Royal clients from all over Europe to his shop. The firm's jewel-cases proudly list Queen Victoria and the Prince and Princess of Wales on the labels, but the letter- and bill-headings go much further, listing the crowned heads of nearly all the Western European countries as well as "Their Imperial Majesties" of Russia.

Many of the English aristocratic families patronized Hancock's; Mrs Disraeli, too, was a frequenter of the shop. But Disraeli was not entirely defenceless against the extravagances that he might have suspected Hancock of luring her into. C.F. Hancock is portrayed – or rather caricatured – as the egregious Mr Ruby in the novel *Lothair* (1871), rubbing his hands with glee as he bamboozles the hero into a far greater expenditure than he had intended.

Hancock's own display at the Great Exhibition was concentrated on the firm's speciality, the elaborate silver groups, sculpted by Rafaelle Monti and Henry Hugh Armstead – for example, the "Goodwood Cup", a group in silver mounted on an ebony pedestal based on the legend of Robin Hood, and another representing "Guy of Warwick contending with a dragon". Another ambitious production was "The entry of Queen Elizabeth on horseback into Kenilworth Castle". The Queen is accompanied by the Earl of Leicester and a page, with two greyhounds in the foreground. This was modeled by an even more famous sculptor, Baron Marochetti. In Paris in 1855 Hancock staged a repeat performance with models of Napoleon I crossing the Alps and Napoleon III on horseback; these were modeled by Eugène Lami, a French artist much favoured by the French Imperial couple. The former of these models was commissioned by the Emperor, and the latter subsequently did duty as the "Doncaster Cup".

Above, *a "Holbeinesque" pendant, designed by a rival firm, London and Ryder, and shown at the 1862 International Exhibition, recreates Hancock's Devonshire parure settings with careful accuracy. (From the* Art-Journal Illustrated Catalogue, *1862)*

Below, *two of Hancock's jewels that appeared in the* Art-Journal Illustrated Catalogue *of the 1871 Exhibition.*

One of the "rich and rare" Hancock's jewels, based on antique ideas, illustrated in the Art-Journal Catalogue of 1871.

It was at this point that C.F. Hancock first conceived the idea of mounting the engraved gems from the Devonshire collection as a suite of jewelry. He is said to have approached the Duke with this suggestion and to have been permitted to make a selection from the collection which was shown at the Paris exhibition. This important display went unremarked by the reporter from the *Illustrated London News*, but Hancock's initiative does explain why he was chosen to execute one of the most important jewelry commissions of the 19th century. For Hancock, 1856 was a sort of *annus mirabilis*: not only did he supply the Devonshire parure, but he was also chosen by Lord Panmure to be responsible for supplying the Victoria Cross for the newly instituted order for gallantry that had initially been ordained by Queen Victoria to reward conspicuous bravery in the Crimean War. The crosses were made of metal from guns captured during the Crimean campaign. The awards in this new order were first presented in June 1857, and the Cross is still supplied by the firm to this day.

In spite of this enormously auspicious beginning, Hancock's, while mounting suitably impressive displays at successive international exhibitions, failed to maintain the momentum of the Devonshire commission. Their trade in jewelry remains something of an enigma, with apparently no surviving marked pieces to give a nucleus of documentary evidence; and the history of their activities in the remaining years of the 19th century has to be put together from contemporary publications.

Catalogues of the international exhibitions reveal that Hancock's continued with the elaborate sculptural silverwork: in 1862 a series of vases dedicated to Shakespeare, Milton and Byron was shown in London to considerable acclaim. In Paris in 1867 the "Tennyson" vase won a gold medal for the firm; a vase modeled by Raffaele Monti and Owen Jones was bought by Napoleon III. The Emperor also purchased jewelry valued at £1,765.

By this date C.F. Hancock had virtually retired. In 1866 his son Mortimer had joined the business, and when his other son, Charles Frederick, entered the firm in 1869 C.F. Hancock retired completely. It is perhaps to the sons that the emphasis on jewelry in these years is owed.

Hancock's most impressive jewelry display was mounted in 1871, with a glittering show of brilliants, rubies and both black and white pearls contrasting with historical and archaeological revival pieces in the manner of Castellani. Writing of the jewelry in the 1871 Exhibition, the correspondent of *The Queen* remarked: "We have already spoken of Messrs. Hunt and Roskell's very meritorious jewellery. The only two other English celebrities are Messrs. Brogden and HANCOCK. The latter firm shows a fine display of precious stones, one pendant containing an emerald of remarkable size. Their Byzantine and Etruscan tablet bracelets are good examples of the respective styles, and unexceptional in workmanship."

Included in this display was also a necklace in cloisonné enamel, probably in the Japanese taste, by Falize of Paris. In 1867 C.F. Hancock had spent six months in Paris, remaining for the whole duration of the Exhibition. He would have had many opportunities to make valuable contacts, and this collaboration with Falize may have been the result.

A surviving cased parure of enameled gold set with corals is probably of this date as it fits in well with the style of not very authentic "archaeological" goldsmiths' work favoured by the British public. Other cased examples of this type of filigree enamel-work suggest Hunt and Roskell as the source, possibly as importers, since the work is typical of Roman jewelry of this date. Jewels in the Assyrian style shown by Hancock's in 1871 are also difficult to pinpoint to a particular maker. Both Brogden and Edwin Streeter were certainly suppliers of similar pieces. Brogden could have been the supplier to Hancock's as well as to other retailers. On the other hand, Streeter had a considerable and complicated involvement with Hancock's which has yet to be fully documented, and the Assyrian pieces, which resemble examples advertised by Streeter, may well have been provided by him.

In two portrait drawings of his wife, the artist Frederick Goodall has depicted her jewelry in unusually minute detail. At her neck, in one of them, Alice Goodall is wearing an Assyrian-style brooch which is now in the British Museum (Hull Grundy Gift). The unmarked gold brooch is worked in shallow relief with a representa-

tion of King Ashurnasirpal pouring a libation over a dead lion, taken from the reliefs in the throne room of the great palace at Nimrud, which were discovered by Sir Austen Henry Layard and displayed at the British Museum from the late 1840s. The very elaborate necklace that Mrs Goodall wears in the companion drawing is in the Egyptian taste, recalling Goodall's Orientalist inclinations and his travels in search of subject matter. The form of the necklace recalls Hancock's 1871 exhibit, and it is apparent from an illustration of the firm's display at the 1873 Vienna Exhibition that they continued to favour this type of model. The large lotus bud pendants on Mrs Goodall's necklace might even be ancient Egyptian faience, obtained by the artist in the East. Also a feature of Hancock's 1873 display was a group of the crescent-and-star head ornaments like the one Mrs Goodall wears in her two portraits which, incidentally, were executed only a year later in 1874.

The star item in the 1873 showcase, however, was an emerald and diamond tiara which had been purchased on the eve

Two portrait drawings by Frederick Goodall of his wife Alice (1874). On the left she is wearing a heavy festoon necklace of Egyptian inspiration, and two wide bracelets, one in the archaeological revival style and the other a stiff bangle with a square central motif. In the other she wears a brooch with earrings en suite in the Assyrian taste.

Left centre, a gold brooch with an applied relief showing a libation scene from the Nimrud Palace reliefs. This is the same as the one worn by Alice Goodall in the portrait above. It has been suggested that the brooch was made by George Goodwin of London, whose registered designs (1873–74) in the Assyrian style conform most closely with this piece. British Museum, Hull Grundy Gift

Left bottom, a ram's head brooch in gold, ornamented with filigree and chased with anthemion motifs. The fashionable Assyrian style was a speciality of Hancock's. The brooch may have been supplied by John Brogden. Private collection

HANCOCK

of the opening of the Exhibition by the Earl of Dudley, a patron with a penchant for magnificent jewelry. The points of the tiara were finished with drop-shaped emeralds, facet-cut rather than polished *en cabochon* – a great technical feat.

As to other details of Hancock's activities that can be gleaned from contemporary sources, the firm had from the early years enjoyed Royal patronage, and their press-cutting books and diaries record some of the Royal commissions.

For the wedding of Princess Louise, daughter of the Prince and Princess of Wales, to the Duke of Fife in 1889 Hancock's supplied the wedding tiara and brooch and made up the bridesmaids' bracelets with the "LF" monogram surmounted by coronets in diamonds from designs by the princess herself. In 1893, for the wedding of Princess May of Teck to the Duke of York (later Queen Mary and King George V), more valuable presents were supplied. The exiled Empress Eugénie, perhaps remembering the jewels purchased from Hancock's by her husband in Paris in 1867, ordered an elegant peacock feather in diamonds, very much in the French taste of that date. If it survives it may well now be described as French, since it was so closely modeled on similar pieces produced by Boucheron.

In the previous year the firm had been involved in an important transaction. Hancock's sold to W.W. Astor an outstanding ruby and diamond necklace for £7,500, on 15 January 1892. This necklace had once been part of the great ruby and diamond parure from the French Crown Jewels, sold by order of the Third Republic in 1887. The complete parure consisted of twelve items, nearly all of which sold for more than the estimates. The House of Bapst had been responsible for the mounting in 1816 of the diadem, and much of the work of resetting the pieces for subsequent use, first for the Royal Princesses during the reign of Louis XVIII, and then for the Empress Eugénie, was done by the firm. Both of the necklaces from the parure were bought at the sale by Bapst, the "great necklace" (the one sold later to Astor) for FF 77,500.

After that sale an American banker, Mr Bradley Martin of New York, the partner of Pierpont Morgan, managed to buy the diadem, a pair of bracelets and a pendant in the form of a Greek cross from the parure. These he gave to his daughter, Cornelia, Countess of Craven. After her death a sale took place at Sotheby's on 30 November 1961 of her "Magnificent Casket of Jewels". At some point a ruby and diamond necklace resembling the "great necklace" from the parure had also come into her possession, and it too, with the suggestion that it was in a somewhat altered state from the original, was included in the sale. In fact the actual necklace from the parure was sold twenty-one years later in Geneva by Christie's and a colour illustration is included by Bernard Morel in his monumental work on *The French Crown Jewels* (published by Fonds Mercator, Antwerp 1988).

Hancock's history is typical of many similar firms in the second half of the 19th century. The mixture of selling, exhibiting, dealing in rare pieces, supplying Royal gifts and devising elaborate silver trophies matches the activities of many of their rivals; yet they have survived the upheavals of the present century while some once more celebrated firms have disappeared.

An example of Hancock's work in the Art-Journal Catalogue *of 1871.*

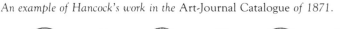

FALIZE

Design for a Moorish style châtelaine by Alexis Falize (c. 1852). Source: Eugène Fontenay, Les Bijoux Anciens et Modernes, 1887

Lucien Falize (1839–97) wrote in 1893: "Enameling is a precious art which, owing to its prominence in the works of bygone days, has occupied a privileged place in public and private collections. It is the duty of contemporary artists to create, for our own use and for our museums, works of art that lend themselves to enamel." This was a weighty challenge from a jeweler whose contribution to the enameling revival was outstanding.

Lucien's extraordinary career, however, should never be allowed to eclipse the achievements of his father Alexis (1811–98), nor should the influence of Alexis on his son be underestimated. Alexis's introduction to jewelry took place when he joined the Mellerio brothers' thriving Paris business in 1833. Initially taken on as a bookkeeper, he soon applied his prodigious talent for drawing to the designing of a wide range of precious ornaments. His brother Guillaume had started working for a jeweler named Maudoux the previous year, and was soon to be joined by another younger brother, Hyacinthe. These two had no doubt inspired Alexis and helped to determine his career. It took no time at all for Alexis Falize's elaborate Second Empire jewelry designs to become much sought-after. By 1838, he had been supplying the highly successful Restoration jeweler Janisset for three years, and was rapidly making a name for himself with other Houses. Even though he acquired his own premises in Galerie de Valois, in the fashionable Palais Royal, by buying out Aristide Joureau-Robin's firm of manufacturing jewelers, Janisset still demanded exclusive rights in Alexis's designs. By 1840, he was mentioned in the trade directory and established at 6 Rue Montesquieu, under the description "Falize aîné" – no doubt to distinguish him from his brothers, who were shortly to join in partnership. The following year, Alexis registered this stamp ◁A|F▷ at the Garantie des Métaux Précieux.

The revolution of 1848 bankrupted many businesses, including that of Janisset; like all the firm's suppliers, Alexis suffered. In the end, however, these troubled times finally opened the way for him to supply without hindrance any of the numerous manufacturing and retail jewelers of Paris who sought his designs.

Henri Vever (1854–1942), the famous jeweler and historian of his trade, wrote: "Alexis Falize is one of the very rare industrial artists of our time who created true innovations and was capable of freeing himself from the themes of decoration with which we had contented ourselves until then. . . . He applied his talent with equal success to every aesthetic discipline; he was thoroughly acquainted with a wide range of styles and took care to respect every one of them."

Alexis Falize had no interest in intrinsic value for its own sake, treasuring art above all precious stones. Like many other talented jewelers of the 19th century, he worked as a supplier; he never contributed to an Exposition Universelle under his own name. It is therefore often difficult to identify his jewelry and to assess its extraordinary range. Certainly, the vast array of watercolour designs published in *La Bijouterie Française au 19ème Siècle* testify to the breadth of material which inspired him; there one finds neo-Renaissance brooches and Moorish châtelaines as well as Egyptian and néo–Grec bracelets. However, he finally achieved much-deserved recognition when he took the decisive step of introducing enamels into his jewelry.

After exploring the possibilities of using "Limousin"-style painted enamels, Alexis turned his attention to Far Eastern sources, including Persia, India and China, and above all Japan. The opening up of Japanese ports in the late 1850s and the

Above, *a diamond-set necklace in the form of stylized flowers and a brooch in the form of a branch of wild bramble, both by Lucien Falize (1889). Source: Henri Vever, La Bijouterie française au XIXe siècle, 1908*

Below, *a gold laurel wreath in the neo-classical taste, tied at the back with a ribbon bow inscribed:* O ELLENISMOS IS TON ARISTON TON PANELLINON ELEFTHERION VENIZELON *("To the best of the Greeks from the rest of the Greeks, Eleftherion Venizelon"). Venizelon (1862–1936) became Prime Minister in 1910. Signed "Falize Orf., Paris".* Sotheby's

resumption of trade with the Western world provided Europeans with opportunities to see Oriental works of art at first hand. An important collection of Chinese and Japanese lacquer work, bronzes and earthenware, largely owned by Sir Rutherford Alcock, was shown at the 1862 International Exhibition in London. At the Exposition Universelle in Paris in 1867, the public were offered an unprecedented range of works of art made by the Japanese, all of which exemplified their unfailing sense of style and their appreciation of the natural world.

Significantly, the firm of Christofle exhibited at the same time some twenty examples of vases and other objects embellished with enamels in the "cloisonné" style, designed by Emile Reiber and made up by the talented enameler Antoine Tard. A highly successful collaboration between Falize and Tard was soon to follow, in which the matt cloisonné enameled decoration in the Japanese taste was applied to jewelry, the gold "cloisons" replacing the copper partitions which had been used in Christofle's pieces.

The successful experiments of Tard and Falize seem to have begun while the Exposition was still open, since there is documentary evidence of a necklace by Falize having been purchased in Paris in 1867; although Lucien Falize recollected that his first cloisonné enamels were made in 1868, it must be one of the earliest examples of its kind. Two pendants are also illustrated in Philippe Burty's *Les Emaux Cloisonnés Anciens et Modernes* (1868), suggesting that jewelry of this nature had been produced well before the publication date. A quantity of these highly distinctive jewels were exhibited at the Union Centrale des Arts Décoratifs in 1869 under Alexis Falize's name, alongside a display of Oriental works of art, some from Japan. Although inspired by Japanese work, Falize's intricate and brightly coloured cloisonné enamels owed their vivid palette to Chinese prototypes. The painstaking craftmanship in Falize's lockets, necklaces, châtelaines, earrings, dress studs, cufflinks, frames and scent bottles made them expensive items to purchase. As Burty recognized, however, their attractiveness overcame any reluctance to buy caused by their high price: "These jewels go beautifully with the bright colours women are wearing today. This must be the reason for their success, since they are very costly. They are unlikely to come down in price, for the problems of manufacture and the uniqueness of the design have to be taken into account."

Top left, *set of bachelor buttons of cloisonné enamel in the Japanese taste, one with a fan decorated with a figure looking out to sea, the other with a vase containing yellow waterlily flowers (c. 1869). Silver, London*
Top right, *a similar set of bachelor buttons of the same period, each decorated with a dragon and signed* ◁⫯▷. *Silver, London. (A similar set was exhibited at the Union Centrale des Arts Décoratifs in 1869.)*
Centre, *pendant of shaped triangular form framed by diamonds and centred on a cameo depicting a theatrical mask, surrounded by three panels of gold leaves against a green enameled ground; hung with a baroque pearl drop. From the collection of the chaser Louchet and engraved* "Falize 1907" *on the border. Hartley Brown, London.*
Above the pendant, *an articulated enameled bracelet (c. 1880) decorated with holly motifs applied with translucent enamels against a matt enameled ground, the centre panel decorated with a diamond-set "h", possibly for "hiver". Signed* ⫯▷. *Ulf Breede, Munich.*
Below the pendant, *a bracelet composed of 9 lavishly decorated enameled panels, one side with various mythical beasts in the medieval taste, the other with stylized lilies and exotic flowers (c. 1880). Ulf Breede, Munich.*
Bottom left, *an enameled tie-pin decorated with translucent enamels against a cream matt enameled ground (c. 1880). Wartski, London. Next to it, a circular pendant of cloisonné enamel, with beaded border (c. 1869). Decorated on one side with pink flowers, on the other with a bird on a bamboo branch. Signed* ◁⫯▷. *Silver, London.*
Bottom right, *intricately enameled circular bonbonnnière (c. 1880) decorated on the base with a crowned "F" for François I (1515–47) of France, the inside with two crossed "C"'s, also surmounted by a crown, for his consort, Claude. The lid decorated with a salamander, the king's emblem. Hancock's & Co., London*

Above, châtelaine of cloisonné enamel in the Japanese taste (1869), which formed part of the
Vever gift to the Musée des Arts Décoratifs in 1924. Signed ◁Ⅎ▷ three times.
Photo L. Sully-Jaulmes

Left, necklace and earrings of cloisonné enamel on both sides in the Japanese style. These were
purchased in Paris by H.F. Makins for his wife Kezia Elizabeth, the daughter of John Hunt of the
Court jewelers Hunt and Roskell. The provenance which accompanies the suite indicates that it
was acquired in 1867, which suggests these would be among the very first jewels of this nature to be
produced by Falize. Each earring is signed ◁Ⅎ▷. The Ashmolean Museum, Oxford
Inside the necklace, two cloisonné enameled lockets, one in the Indian taste (bought by the Museum
in 1869 for £13.4s.), the other in the Chinese taste. By courtesy of the Board of Trustees of the
Victoria and Albert Museum

Above, gold necklace and earrings by Lucien Falize, the necklace hung with three pendants centred on painted enameled portraits by Alfred Meyer, with another smaller forming the clasp. Each historical personage is related, by birth or marriage, to the de Foix family. Engraved "L. Falize 1887" on reverse of the centre pendant. Museum für Angewandte Kunst, Köln (Dauerleihgabe der Förderer des Museums)

Right, pendant in the Renaissance taste decorated with enamels and set with diamonds, framed by two fantastic creatures, centred on a pearl and hung with a pearl drop (c. 1889). The jewel is illustrated in H. Vever's history of 19th-century French jewelry (v. III, p. 501), and identified as forming part of L. Falize's display at the 1889 Exposition Universelle. Private Collection

Right, gold necklace hung with a pendant centred on a painted enamel portrait of a lady, the elaborate chainwork interrupted by three open-work gold panels framing the interlaced white enamel initials "H" and "D" for Henri II of France (1547–59) and his mistress Diane de Poitiers. The detachable pendant, hung with a pearl and decorated with diamonds, has a brooch fitting.

Within the necklace, a gold open-work bracelet similarly decorated with white enamel, centred on a painted enamel portrait of a lady; the side is engraved "L. Falize à Paris". Both pieces are dated 1880–90, and were retailed by Boin-Taburet, 3 Rue Pasquier, Paris. Badisches Landesmuseum, Karlsruhe

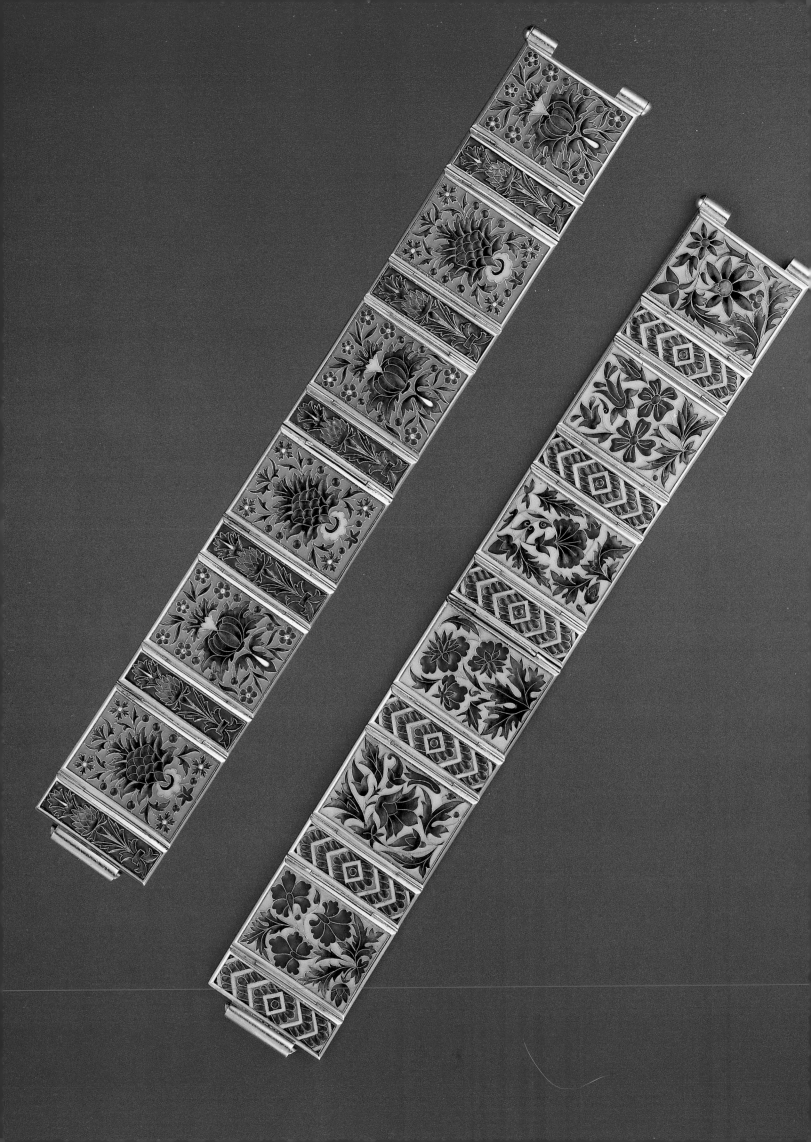

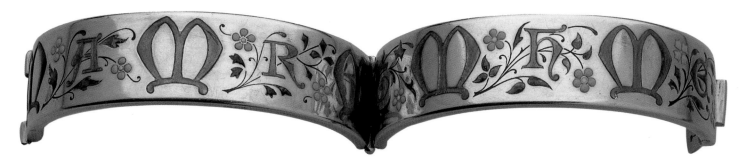

Above, gold bracelet decorated with the name "Marthe" in medieval script carried out in red enamel, the initial "M" repeated between each letter. The surface also embellished with blue enameled forget-me-nots and the inside pierced in the shapes of forget-me-nots revealing blue counter-enameling and inscribed "Jeanne et Fernand, à leur Marton" (c. 1880). Wartski, London

Left, reversible bracelet by Lucien Falize lavishly decorated with translucent enamels, one side depicting stylized flowers, the other with stylized pineapples (1880–90). Christie's, New York

Right, hinged bangle inscribed "Laisse Dire, Fais Bien", the initial of each word in gold against a cloisonné enameled ground. Signed ◁AF▷ (c. 1870–75). Schmuckmuseum, Pforzheim

Above, brooch inscribed with the word "Forever" in medieval script, the initial carried out in translucent "sur paillons" enameling, the border interspersed with diamonds (c. 1880). Wartski, London

Left centre, hinged gold bangle decorated with enameled camomile, the centre of each flower set with a diamond. Inside the bangle, an elaborate Bapst et Falize signature (c. 1889). Purchased by the Musée des Arts Décoratifs at the 1889 Exposition Universelle for FF2,000. Musée des Arts Décoratifs

Left, articulated bangle by Bapst et Falize decorated with raised gold motifs against a red enameled ground, the inside elaborately signed "BF" with their symbol of a ring suspended with a pearl drop (c. 1885). S.J. Phillips, London

71

Left, crown, orb, sceptre and clasp (for the Royal mantle) carried out in red, white and blue enamels, the colours associated with Serbia. The crown is decorated with white enameled double-headed eagles, the emblem of the medieval Serbian rulers, separated by blue enameled fleurs-de-lis. Historical Museum of Serbia, Belgrade

Left below, King Carol II of Roumania's distaff, decorated with auroch's heads and eagles in gold against a red ground, symbols of Moldavia. At one end, the Roumanian crest chased in gold, with the legend "Nihil Sine Deo", at the other a blue enameled cross centred on two crossed C's. Signed "FALIZE ANCIEN JOAILLIER DE LA COURONNE DE FRANCE" and dated 1930, the year in which the Crown Prince returned as king after five years of exile. Photo courtesy Prince Paul of Hohenzollern-Roumania

Below, a comb in Art Nouveau style composed of horn, the petals of each narcissus carved from opal and set with cabochon rubies. Museum für Kunst und Gewerbe, Hamburg. Bottom, an Art Nouveau style comb of blond tortoiseshell, the leaves decorated with green enamel and hung with pink pearl berries (c. 1900). Silver, London

Lucien Falize, who had joined his father's firm in 1856, was a great enthusiast of Japan, and was very eager to go there to recruit native craftsmen (which other firms, such as Tiffany, did later). His parents, however, were opposed to such a lengthy voyage. As small compensation, he buried himself in the albums of Hokusai prints borrowed from the connoisseur and critic Philippe Burty, the writer Théophile Gautier, the ceramist François-Eugène Rousseau, or purchased from the famous Orientalist Madame Desoye. Models were also available in E. Collinot and A. de Beaumont's *Recueil de Dessins pour l'Art et l'Industrie*, which first appeared in 1859 and was reissued in an enlarged form between 1871 and 1883, under the new title *Encyclopédie des Arts Décoratifs de l'Orient*. These French translations of Japanese images were to be used as a source of imagery for French designers, and their emphasis on natural ornament attracted Lucien; nonetheless, he was fully aware of the dangers of slavishly imitating these new-found motifs without understanding the symbolism which inspired them, and advocated a careful study of Japanese art and culture. It is when Lucien wrote about Japan that he was at his most eloquent and lyrical: "Japanese art points us towards a return to nature, a path through this infinite world which envelops us and to which we have been blind. We had to read Japanese albums and see their ceramics, lacquers and bronzes, to remind ourselves that we too have a sky, fields, woods, waters, seething with birds, flowers, grasses, insects and multicoloured fish; they have taught us the poetry of this world, its life, the charm of a fleeting moment captured by a sketch."

There are conflicting reports concerning which Falize was responsible for the first use of cloisonné enamel in jewelry; even the story of the firm, recounted by Lucien to Henri Vever, fails to clarify the matter: both father and son are named as Antoine Tard's collaborators. Under the pseudonym of Monsieur Josse (the name of the goldsmith in Molière's *L'Amour Médecin*), Lucien emphatically states that the innovation was his father's. The only certainty seems to be that it was Lucien who visited the 1862 International Exhibition in London and who therefore saw the first important display of Oriental works of art, but albums of prints had been available in Paris for some time before. In addition, both Alexis and Lucien saw Christofle's display of cloisonné enameled objects at the 1867 Exposition Universelle. However, there must be some significance in the fact that Alexis exhibited such a large number of these cloisonné pieces in 1869 under his own name. In museum collections, cloisonné enameled jewels are often, but not always, attributed to him. Significantly, the Musée des Arts Décoratifs in Paris, which was given many such examples by Vever in 1924 (and which must have been acquired directly from the Falize family), credits both father and son with them.

Further contradictions arise over the introduction to their repertoire of another technique which has come to be called cloisonné enamel *sur paillons*. The first examples of this technique emerged in the early 1870s, when Alexis and Lucien were working closely together. The translucent enamels over tiny fragments of gold introduced a shimmering quality to their jewelry and achieved a unique warmth and richness of colour. Reliefs were also achieved by using matt enamels as background, with raised *sur paillons* enameling to emphasize a particular legend, such as a proverb, pet name or message of love, illustrated vividly in Gothic manuscript style lettering. Lucien proudly declared: "[These] bracelets are intimate mementos . . . They will no longer be broken up, but will be handed down as family heirlooms, as precious as illuminated parchments."

One of the founder members of the Chambres Syndicales des Bijoutiers et Joailliers, Alexis Falize had become its first President in 1864. By the time he retired in 1876, he was considered a high-ranking member of the jewelry profession. Lucien, in partnership with his father since 1871, took over the running of the business which had since that year occupied the prestigious site of 55 Avenue de l'Opéra.

In 1878, Lucien Falize took part in the Exposition Universelle, exhibiting for the first time under his own name; he was decorated with the Légion d'Honneur and was awarded one of the Grands Prix. The other two went to Oscar Massin and Frédéric Boucheron. His display was extremely varied, and his wide range of inspiration most striking. Listed in the

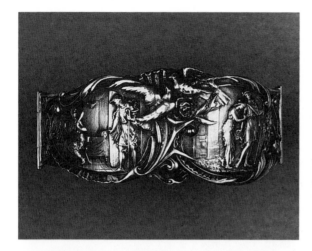

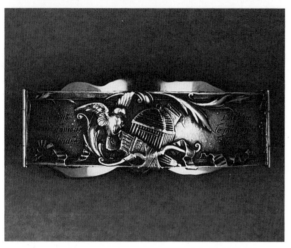

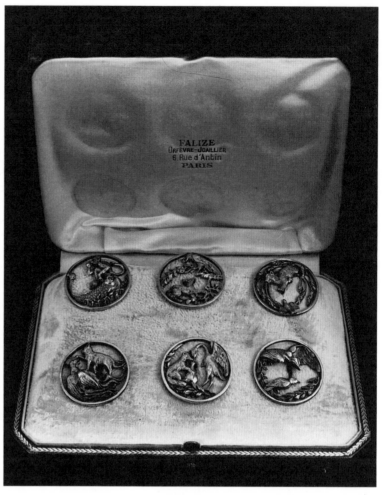

Above left, *a hinged silver bangle inspired by "Les Deux Pigeons" of La Fontaine; on one side two pigeons are being chased, on the other are inscribed two lines from the fable. Signed* ◇AXF◇ *1889. Ruth and Joseph Sataloff (photo Wartski, London)*

Above right, *a set of six silver-gilt buttons by Falize, each inspired by a La Fontaine fable, in their original case (c. 1880)*

jewelry section are such diverse items as a hunting bracelet in the 14th-century manner, a badge of St George after Albrecht Dürer, an enameled head ornament in the 16th-century taste, an Indian-style necklace, a Japanese-style cloisonné enameled *bonbonnière*, a Chinese-style hair ornament, and a *basse-taille* enamel after Van Eyck. The contributions of his highly specialized craftsmen did not go unacknowledged, and no fewer than twenty-nine were listed by name in his "Notice" for the exhibition, with Tard, Houillon and Pye particularly singled out as collaborators.

Lucien found the Renaissance a limitless source on which to draw, and the heroes of the 16th century included Henri II and Diane de Poitiers. Portraits were reproduced in *basse-taille* enamel to great effect. *Pendants-de-col*, inspired by jewels designed by Renaissance masters such as Adrien Collaert, were frequently exhibited, as well as corsage ornaments in the 17th-century taste after Gilles Legaré. Articulated bracelets were much favoured, usually decorated with vivid coloured enamels on both sides;

fantastic medieval creatures were treated as decorative motifs as readily as were flowers and fruit.

Eugène Fontenay aptly described the beauty and skill of Lucien's jewelry: "Most often, opaque enamels served as a background to the translucent enamels of the most wonderful vividness, which sometimes reproduced mottos in old French, at other times heraldic attributes and emblems which were widely used in the 16th century. The interplay of the enamels, placed with careful precision on different planes, the accuracy of the design, and the fineness of the cells which form the contours make these jewels innovative, and have turned them into little masterpieces in their own right."

In 1880, Germain Bapst, descendant of the famous Crown jewelers, approached Falize and proposed a partnership between the two firms. This was a generous gesture on Bapst's part, since, although Lucien's successes at the 1878 Exposition had certainly helped his reputation, the name "Bapst" carried enormous respect and

Lucien certainly benefited from this illustrious association.

The new firm of Bapst et Falize moved to premises at 6 Rue d'Antin that same year, and they exhibited together at the 1889 Exposition Universelle. Lucien's contribution earned him the decoration of Officier de la Légion d'Honneur. Among the numerous objects they showed were a particularly poetic bracelet decorated with camomile flowers and a silver bracelet with two pigeons and verses taken from La Fontaine's poem of the same title. As Lucien commented, "Just as with an engraving or painting, the subject for a bracelet may be borrowed from the poets: the fables of La Fontaine offer excellent themes for compositions chased in low-relief." The poet inspired many more of Falize's creations, including a set of six silver-gilt hunting buttons, each based on a different fable. The Bapst et Falize stamp ⟨BꝯF⟩, officially registered only in 1892 at the end of their association (replacing the previous mark ⟨AⱵF⟩ registered in 1875), was often used as a decoration in their jewelry.

It is in his writings that Lucien Falize reveals the extent of his research and knowledge of jewelry past and present, and he was frequently called upon to write official reports for various exhibitions; for this reason he was *hors-compétition* in 1876 and 1889. His most famous and lengthy document was the one published after the 1889 Exposition Universelle, in which the remarkable scarcity of precious stones in his *oeuvre* is explained: "The precious stone is not enhanced by sophisticated mounts and setting, it defies all forms of embellishment. Its fires interfere with every conceivable type of decoration; they scintillate with geometric shadow and light. Elegant modeling, finely chased detail and depths of ornamentation are lost as if in a gigantic firework display in which the architect's designs have vanished, leaving only dazzling light and wonderment." Nevertheless, Lucien did make concessions to contemporary taste, almost invariably choosing nature as his source of imagery. He was also a regular contributor to serious art journals, including *La Revue des Arts Décoratifs*, in which he frequently appeared under the pseudonym of Monsieur Josse; his articles appeared in many other publications, including Siegfried Bing's *Artistic Japan*.

Lucien was a widely travelled man who had an intimate knowledge of public collections at home and abroad. (He particularly favoured the "South Kensington Museum", as the Victoria and Albert Museum was then known, and was well acquainted with Sir Henry Cole and Sir Owen Cunliffe, the first and second directors of the Museum.) Frequently called upon to deliver lectures, he was certainly respected as much for his erudition and scholarship as for his reputation as a jeweler. His writings occasionally reveal glimpses of irony, particularly when he is discussing Louis Gonse's book *L'Art Japonais*: "M. Gonse is a privileged author who has undertaken the voyage [to Japan] in his bedroom." The fact that Lucien Falize and Oscar Massin frequently voiced differences of opinion regarding the use of precious stones in jewelry did not prevent them from being close friends. Indeed the warmth expressed towards Falize by his colleagues was remarkable for its unanimity.

Lucien Falize was an industrious member of the Union Centrale des Arts Décoratifs and in that capacity strove to reestablish proper respect for the art of the jeweler and goldsmith. Devoted to that organization's task of advertisement and teaching, he proposed and had adopted a project for a series of technological exhibitions. These advocated the essential value of bringing together works of art past and present, and at the same time the tools which had fashioned them were also displayed. In July 1890 Lucien submitted an idea for an exhibition devoted to the plant world, which was enthusiastically received and planned for 1892. Unfortunately it was adjourned and never came to pass. However, his predilection for plants and vegetables as ornamental devices made him one of the most significant precursors of the Art Nouveau movement. Although his spirit lay firmly in the Revivalist tradition, he recognized that a modern age was upon him and that it would survive him.

It is particularly fitting that the Union Centrale should have commissioned one of Lucien's masterpieces, the gold and enameled Hanap (Goblet) de la Vigne et des Métiers. This ambitious work, lavishly decorated with every form of enameling to be encountered in Falize's *oeuvre*, incorporates two themes: vines interpreted in eight

The Hanap de la Vigne et des Métiers, elaborately decorated with enamels that required almost forty firings, and took seven years to complete. Purchased by the Museum in 1896 for FF 20,000. The base of the goblet is engraved L'AN MDCCXCV, LUC. FALIZE ORF. ET EM. PYE GRAV. ONT FAIT CE VASE D'OR A L'EXEMPLE DES VIEUX MAITRES.
Musée des Arts Décoratifs, Paris (photo L. Sully-Jaulmes)

FALIZE

Top, *King Peter Karageorgevitch of Serbia riding through the streets of Belgrade after his coronation in 1904.* Photo courtesy the Historical Museum of Serbia, Belgrade

Below, *King Carol II holding the distaff he generally used as a sceptre (December 1938).* The Illustrated London News Picture Library

different styles, and eight of the various craftsmen's guilds. On the base is a portrait of Lucien himself as a Renaissance goldsmith, examining a cup handed to him by his favourite engraver, Pye. On the table beside him is a vase containing flowers, and on his lap a book, symbolizing the pursuit of nature and erudition, the two essential qualities of his profession. This intensely retrospective and above all introspective work was completed and displayed in 1896, a year before Lucien's untimely death. His father Alexis was to outlive him by one year.

André Falize (1872–1936), Lucien's eldest son, had joined the firm in 1894. When his father died, he formed a partnership with his two brothers, Jean (1874–1943) and Pierre (1875–1953), and they became known as Falize Frères. Together they prepared for the 1900 Exposition Universelle, for which their father had already begun to plan some objects and jewelry. Their display, which won them two of the Grands Prix, therefore contained examples of Lucien's work as well as their own; the latter was very much in the Art Nouveau style which was so fashionable then, and which the firm was to embrace for the next decade.

Much improved relations between France and Russia had provided Lucien Falize with important commissions for official gifts. Further orders were received by his sons, and the reputation of the firm was now international. Among the most prestigious commissions undertaken was that of the Crown Jewels for King Peter I of Serbia, ordered by the Serbian Ambassador to Paris in 1904. These were completed in just under three months, for the sum of 19,000 francs. Designed by architect Mihailo Valtrovic̀, the regalia was composed of bronze taken from a Turkish cannon captured by the Serbian hero and leader of the War of Independence, Karageorge. The coronation was held in Belgrade Cathedral on 8 September 1904, after which the King rode through the streets of the capital to the Palace. André and Jean Falize, as well as their collaborator, M. Bouchon, were awarded the Serbian Order of St Sava for their work.

The firm also made several presentation swords for the most prominent officers of the First World War, including the Marshals Foch and Pétain. The Belgian town of Liège (birthplace of Alexis Falize) commissioned one for the King of Belgium; and others were made for French authors elected to the Académie Française.

Further notable commissions included a laurel wreath for Eleftherion Venizelon, Prime Minister of Greece, and several pieces for the Roumanian royal family. Falize Frères made a crown for Queen Marie in 1922, as well as a distaff for King Carol II in 1930.

The partnership of the brothers existed only in name since Pierre, a precocious and talented artist, had from the beginning intended to pursue a career as a painter. Shortly after the end of the First World War, Jean made the painful decision to leave the firm in order to procure an income that would adequately support his wife and two children. He was promptly branded a traitor by his brother André, who for a long time had been the driving force of the House of Falize. Although, like his father, André had published several articles about jewelry early in his career, he had none of Lucien's flair for design and was out of touch with current tastes and contemporary fashions. He also had none of his father's business sense, and the funds accumulated throughout the years were spent in his campaigns for the protection of animals. He commissioned Pierre to design posters to prohibit the use of blinkers on horses, and spent vast sums in trying to stop bullfighting in France. A man known for his great charm and sense of humour, he was also impetuous and extravagant. The firm had moved to 17 Rue du Faubourg Saint-Honoré in 1911, but by 1930 the shop was sold in order to gain extra funds. In inferior premises in the quickly deteriorating quarter of the Rue Saint-Lazare, money was lavished yet again in incorporating the Falize initials into all the building's balconies. The diminishing stock barely filled the showcases and André was reduced to purchasing broken pots and vases from junk markets, restoring them and placing them on the shelves for sale. The once prosperous and thriving firm that had been Falize was left with nothing more tangible than memories when André Falize died in 1936.

BOUCHERON

For more than a century, the story of Boucheron has been closely linked to the history of fine French jewelry. When the firm started in 1858, the styles that held sway were garish and excessively ornate. Eugénie de Montijo, Napoleon III's beautiful Empress, saw herself as a second Marie-Antoinette and tried to bring back into vogue the styles of Louis XVI – flowery garlands, roses, quivers, arrows, knots and intertwining ribbons. The prevailing fashion was, however, a motley mix of neo-Classical, Etruscan, Roman and Ancient Egyptian. Baudelaire wryly observed that "ordinary life can now simply be shifted into an ancient Greek setting". The archaeological digs at Cumae and Pompeii served as inspiration, as did the collection of more than a thousand pieces of ancient Greek, Roman and Etruscan jewelry owned by the Cavaliere Campana, which was installed in the Louvre in 1861. In addition, a museum of National Antiquities was opened at Saint-Germain-en-Laye, and interest in Ancient Egypt was heightened by the construction and eventual opening of the Suez Canal.

Frédéric Boucheron chose the theme of nature as a contrast to all this paste "finery". He set a new trend with designs featuring thistle-heads, plane tree leaves and rustic bouquets of flowers, which were pinned to the fronts of bodices, or made into chokers and châtelaines. He also launched designs in translucent enamels, then back in fashion, which were inspired by the writings of Benvenuto Cellini to Francis I. Frédéric was keenly interested in new ideas and inventions. A prominent specialist in diamond-engraving and gold inlay on blued steel, he combined simple materials in totally original ways; rock-crystal and wood, for instance, were matched with the rarest precious stones.

Elegant ladies of the period, eagerly seeking out the latest fashion, were quick to spot his originality. They flocked to his salons in the Palais-Royal, where you could see crowned heads, eccentrics and "demi-mondaines" toying with their fans. Royalty had the good taste to wear only one or two pieces of jewelry, preferably priceless; Boucheron was already renowned for using only the most exceptional stones. Many of the others, however, adorned themselves so extravagantly that they looked like walking jewel-boxes.

The famous Hugo, *maître d'hôtel* at Maxim's, related in his memoirs an anecdote which admirably demonstrates this contrast. One day La Belle Otéro was dining at the restaurant. Frédéric Boucheron had once created a sort of bodice for her made entirely of diamonds, and on this occasion she was "covered from head to foot in sparkling jewels. The table reserved for her rival, Liane de Pougy, was still unoccupied. Finally the latter made her majestic entrance. She was dressed in a simple, totally unadorned black velvet gown; her lady's companion followed in her wake. The diners were astonished, then absolutely stunned as Madame Liane removed the hat and cloak worn by her servant to reveal the young girl, covered in all her own priceless jewels. Amid wild applause, Madame Liane and her escort, the Comte de T., took their seats. Madame Otéro angrily rose and left the restaurant, cursing furiously in Spanish as she passed Liane's table."

A rigid system of etiquette prevailed at Boucheron's, where members of high society crossed each other's paths. One might observe the Tsar of Russia or the Grand Duchess Maria Alexandrovna pass by, ignoring with superb disdain famous actresses such as Hortense Schneider or Mlle Réjane. Her Imperial Highness Princess Mathilde took precedence over the equally renowned Sarah Bernhardt;

Left, *a poster, made by the artist Fonseca for Boucheron around 1900, which shows elegant women admiring the window display.* Private collection

Far left, *an 1895 portrait of Frédéric Boucheron by Aimé Morot.* Private collection

Left, *La Belle Otéro wearing the gem-set bodice that Boucheron designed for her.* Archives of Gilles Néret

The premises at 26 Place Vendôme where Frédéric Boucheron moved his establishment in 1893. Private collection

Encouraged by his success in Paris, Frédéric opened branches of his establishment in Moscow and New York. It was for the fabulously wealthy American Mrs Clarence Mackay that he created a magnificent diamond and sapphire necklace, which contained the biggest (159⅛ carats), purest and loveliest sapphire that had ever been seen. It long remained her favourite "armour" to wear across the Atlantic.

In 1893 Frédéric was at the height of his fame. He moved his business into luxurious premises in the Place Vendôme, five years before César Ritz opened his fabulous hotel in the same expansive square. Boucheron's had been showered with medals and decorations at the international exhibitions in Vienna, Antwerp and Philadelphia. Installed in his new domain, Frédéric promoted the Art Nouveau style, producing jewelry made to set off diamonds, as well as a whole range of objects featuring a combination of gold and ivory, bronze and precious stones: statuettes, vases, candy boxes, lorgnettes, fans, matchboxes, châtelaines and belt-buckles. These sparkled with gold and blued steel, while designs discreetly picked out in pearls and precious stones decorated rock-crystal and enamel.

Frédéric drew his inspiration from the Japanese, whom he considered "the greatest decorative artists in the world". He quickly realized, however, that Art Nouveau would be short-lived because of its extreme elaborateness. From then on, he sought to simplify settings and gradually to make them "invisible", a technique which was eventually perfected by his successors using platinum, a metal that had previously been used solely for industrial purposes.

Frédéric's son, Louis Boucheron, was an equally skilled master of "restrained extravagance". He inherited the view that the reputation of a great jeweler was made through the beauty of the stones he used. During the *années folles*, he created Art Deco jewelry which developed further the trend set by the Comtesse Greffuhle, one of the leaders of Paris society, with the diamond "wing" clips she wore in her hair. Louis was also able to capture the mood of Cubism with a toned-down *Demoiselles d'Avignon* look. Further sources of inspiration were the Ballets Russes and, in the wake of the colonial exhibition held in Paris in 1931, African art.

the Comtesse de Polignac or the Marquise de Noaille curtseyed low to Her Majesty Queen Isabella of Spain, while the wives of Barons Willi, James and Alphonse de Rothschild curtseyed to the Duchess of Sutherland. Members of the Vanderbilt family came to buy their diamonds, tiaras, aigrettes and chains, exchanging passing greetings with the gun merchant Zaharoff. Oscar Wilde, in the days before his misfortune when he was still living in lavish style, chose rings with coloured gemstones for himself and his intimate friend, together with enameled watches and tie-pins set with cut diamonds.

Above left, *a bud-shaped brooch with leaves, and a watch in the shape of a pansy hanging from it; both set with diamonds, garnets and amethysts (c. 1890–95). Private collection*

Above, *design by Paul Legrand for a necklace in sapphires and diamonds, set in silver and mounted in gold (1878).*

Left, *a châtelaine showing Apollo's chariot, and a suspended watch, the ensemble in gold, silver, sapphires, rubies, diamonds and enamel (c. 1870–80). Private collection*

Left, *a brooch in the form of a butterfly, the body composed of a ruby and a diamond, the wings of engraved diamonds, mounted in gold (c. 1894).*
Private collection

Right, *a rock-crystal scent bottle in the form of a medieval woman; rose diamonds, rubies, sapphires and emeralds mounted in gold (late 19th century).*
Boucheron collection

Below left, *a scent bottle of fluted rock-crystal; each flute is outlined with gem-set gold bands, and at each end of the bottle an emerald (c. 1900).*
Private collection

Below, *a smelling-salts bottle made of engraved rock-crystal, fitted with a gold mount (c. 1890–1900). The bottle stopper is set with a cushion-shaped amethyst surrounded by diamonds.* Private collection

Above, a boxwood clock designed and carved by Edmond-Henri Becker, with mount and chasing by Alfred Menu, originally made in 1900. The decorative details symbolize night and day. Boucheron collection

Top left, a belt-buckle designed by Lucien Hirtz, composed of two gold lionesses standing on a jade carving of a lion's head and with a cornelian between their jaws (1908). Boucheron collection

Above, a gold brooch designed by Lucien Hirtz, in the form of two symmetrical serpent's heads; the large stone is a garnet, the eyes are emeralds, and the diamonds are old-cut (c. 1900). Private collection

Right, a bow-shaped brooch made of a blackened platinum lacework pattern set with diamonds (1908). Boucheron collection

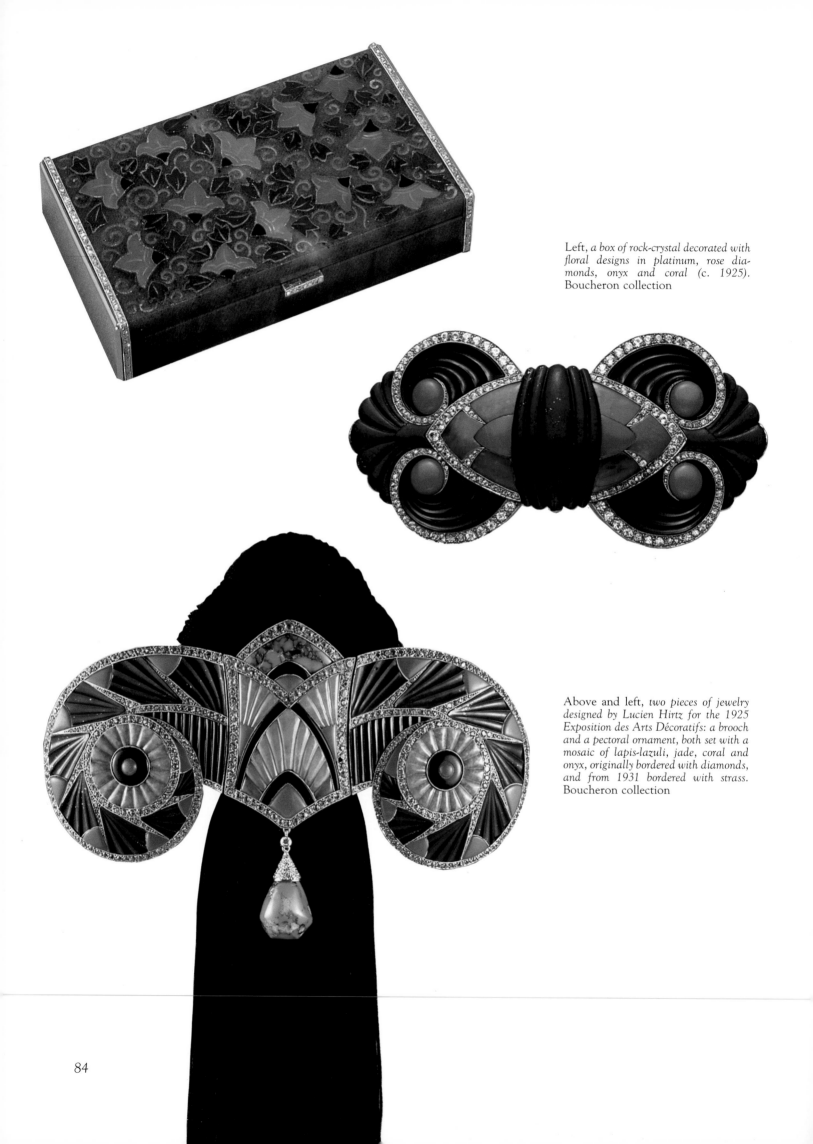

Left, *a box of rock-crystal decorated with floral designs in platinum, rose diamonds, onyx and coral (c. 1925).* Boucheron collection

Above and left, *two pieces of jewelry designed by Lucien Hirtz for the 1925 Exposition des Arts Décoratifs: a brooch and a pectoral ornament, both set with a mosaic of lapis-lazuli, jade, coral and onyx, originally bordered with diamonds, and from 1931 bordered with strass.* Boucheron collection

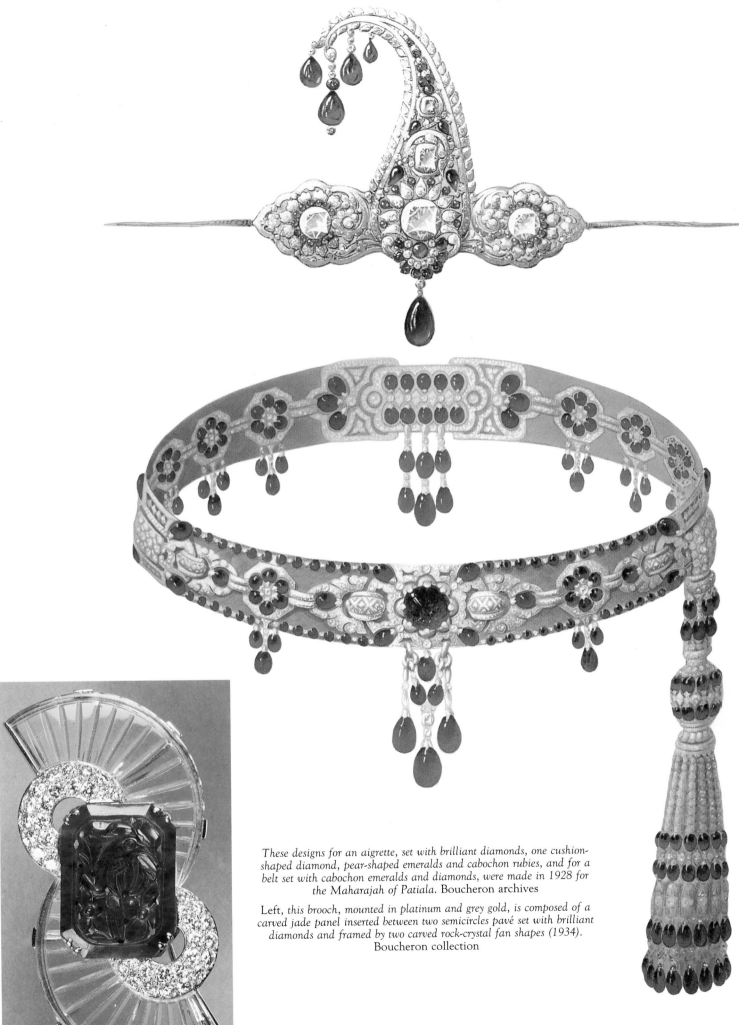

These designs for an aigrette, set with brilliant diamonds, one cushion-shaped diamond, pear-shaped emeralds and cabochon rubies, and for a belt set with cabochon emeralds and diamonds, were made in 1928 for the Maharajah of Patiala. Boucheron archives

Left, this brooch, mounted in platinum and grey gold, is composed of a carved jade panel inserted between two semicircles pavé set with brilliant diamonds and framed by two carved rock-crystal fan shapes (1934). Boucheron collection

Below, *a fan-shaped gold wrist watch set with brilliant diamonds and calibré-cut sapphires (1942). Boucheron collection*

Right, *a bracelet with tassels composed of two gold cabled chains linked together by five tubular forms of gold and platinum, set with brilliant diamonds (1946). Boucheron collection*

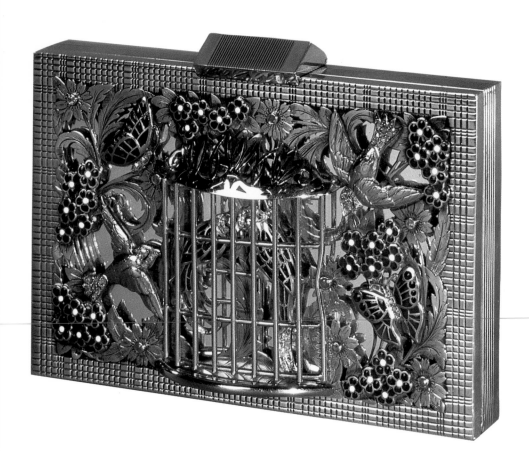

Left, *an openwork vanity case in gold and silver; the decoration of birds and a cage is applied with enamel and set with rose diamonds (1945). Private collection*

Necklace composed of two gold chains joined at the centre by an interlacing motif with a pendant in the shape of an acorn; set with sapphires and round diamonds, mounted in gold and platinum (1944). Private collection

87

Left, *a matching necklace and earrings of acacia wood, decorated with coral and brilliant diamonds, mounted in gold (1987). Boucheron archives*

Below left, *a ribbon clip of baguette diamonds, oval and round rubies framed with round and drop diamonds, set in gold and platinum (1962). Private collection*

Below right, *a flower clip, the centre made of round rubies, the petals of baguette, round and drop diamonds, the stem of baguette diamonds and the leaves of round diamonds; mounted in platinum and gold (1961). Private collection*

Drawing on his training as an engineer, Louis created an entirely new style in contemporary jewelry, which was based on technological discoveries. Stones were cut in new ways – the table-cut, the baguette, the prism and the trapezium. Solid blocks of material such as onyx, lapis-lazuli, malachite, turquoise, amber, coral and jade were used. These innovations resulted in the jewels and objects displayed at the exhibition of Arts Décoratifs et Industriales Modernes in Paris in 1925, which launched the fashion for Art Deco. They were eagerly snapped up by collectors and museums, from the Victoria and Albert Museum in London to the Musée des Arts Décoratifs in Paris.

Louis Boucheron designed a variety of accessories intended for the emancipated woman, with her sun-tanned, short-haired look and sporty stride. There were bags sewn with sequins or pearls, cigarette-holders thirty inches long, and compacts encrusted with eggshell, as well as the more important pieces which made his reputation. These included chains, diamond-studded brooches which an elegant woman might pin on to the lapels of a man's smoking-jacket, and collars set with precious stones. The firm also produced jeweled belts and bracelets which became heavier and bulkier, designed to set off the beauty of rubies and emeralds. Since the trend was for sleeveless dresses, Boucheron created cuff-like bracelets and watch-bracelets which were clasped closely round the wrist. "Fountain"-style tiaras were introduced to complement the cropped hairstyles of the period. The cascading water was marvellously represented by baguette-cut diamonds; the line of round diamonds made perfect ripples, imitating the small waves of a lake in which the water is barely touched by the wind. Necks bare of hair prompted Boucheron to bring back long earrings – so long that they almost brushed the shoulders. Hollywood stars, from Pola Negri to Gloria Swanson, from Mary Pickford to Louise Brooks, spent thousands of dollars on his tempting creations.

During this period Louis Boucheron's international reputation earned him the epithet "jeweler of the Thousand and One Nights", and indeed he was much sought after by wealthy customers from the East. For instance, the flamboyant Maharajah of Patiala, then ruler of the Punjab, arrived at Boucheron's in 1927, accompanied by a retinue of forty servants all wearing pink turbans, his twenty favourite dancing-girls and, most important of all, six caskets filled with diamonds, pearls, emeralds, sapphires and rubies of incomparable beauty. Boucheron was commissioned to transform this mass of precious stones, then valued at about eighteen hundred million francs, into tiaras, aigrettes, belts and necklaces *en cascades* and fringes to be worn under the sari. He also created a breathtaking armlet, the supreme symbol of the "Son of the Moon", which the Maharajah wore on his left arm. It had a 100-carat emerald as the centre stone, surrounded by diamonds and a cascade of pear-shaped emeralds. The Maharani's royal emblem, a diamond crescent and star, studded with large rubies, was no less eye-catching.

A few years later, in 1931, Louis Boucheron was chosen by the Shah to value and classify Iran's fabulous treasures, and was appointed by imperial decree official custodian of these riches, a privilege passed on to his descendants. The treasure included the two largest rose diamonds known to the world, together with hundreds of emeralds, each over 100 carats, one of the seven thrones of the Grand Moghul, set with 200-carat emeralds, and a globe which was almost twenty inches in diameter, decorated with 52,000 precious stones: emeralds represented the oceans, rubies and sapphires marked the continents, while parallels and meridians were picked out in diamonds.

Because of the Second World War, there was a lapse of thirty years between the initial valuation of the "treasures of Golconda" and the opening of the museum which houses them. The building, which was opened by the Shah and Empress Farah in 1960, was designed and built entirely by Boucheron. Three hundred tons of steel were used in its construction, together with bronze and glass. Its delicate mechanisms and electronic equipment were perfected in France and then shipped to Iran. It had a most elaborate alarm system. The instant one touched the side of one of the glass display-cabinets, sirens began to wail – and within seconds, heavy steel barriers clamped shut to trap any thieves.

Frédéric and Gérard (my father) were the two sons of the next Boucheron generation. The period of their activity was far from a

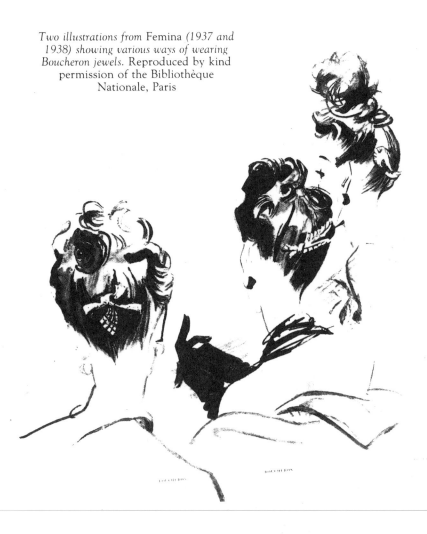

Two illustrations from Femina *(1937 and 1938) showing various ways of wearing Boucheron jewels. Reproduced by kind permission of the Bibliothèque Nationale, Paris*

happy one. It began with the international exhibition held in Paris in 1937, at which the pompous pavilions of Nazi Germany and Stalinist Russia portentously confronted each other across from the newly built Trocadéro, and extended to the postwar era, when business and creative design were slow to recover.

The jubilant mood following the Liberation was expressed at Boucheron by a return to the theme of flowers and fauna, including exotic as well as European birds. Boucheron designed jewelry meant to be worn with the "New Look", launched by Christian Dior in 1947. There were multicoloured pieces, plumes and bouquets, as well as jewelry that could be taken apart and rejoined by means of a system of concealed hinges and invisible links – thus enabling women to create several effects from a single item.

The firm also produced star-shaped brooches, brooches in the form of a question-mark, and "rosettes" made of round and baguette-cut diamonds. Other items included *coup de vent* ("gust of wind") rings, and cigarette lighters with matching lipstick cases in silver inlaid with niello and set with coloured gems, as well as gold cigarette cases engraved with a map of France, the towns picked out in a variety of different coloured stones.

Before war broke out Boucheron had become interested in the designing of watches, and now they were being created in every shape and form. Some were set in balls and in rings, and the *tête de clou* ("nail's head") watches were indeed jewels in their own right.

New methods of mounting were introduced to create the new shapes. From now on, Boucheron mounted gems on different levels, a technique known as the *style chahuté* ("high-kicking style"). To begin with, stones were arranged in shapes resembling knots, cascades or the pistils of a flower. Designs became more supple. Previously stones had been mounted on plaques, in settings arranged on bands of pierced metal; although this allowed a certain amount of movement, it was still rather heavy. Now settings were grouped together in clusters on different levels to create a unique new surface and to produce the impression of delicacy combined with depth. The method is illustrated by the little diamond sprays made by Boucheron in 1949. These featured stems so supple that when an elegant woman wore one of these brooches, the flowers quivered with her every movement.

Colour was once more an important consideration, and this gave rise to the reappearance of gold, with all its sensuousness and warmth, after its long eclipse by platinum. From then on, however, gold was to be tinged with unusual new shades – pink, red, green, white or grey. It was polished or given a satin finish, ornamented with chequering, plaited, threaded, pierced with dots, filed, twisted, faceted, "purled", arranged in lattices, shaped into lace or mesh.

In this way Boucheron managed to banish heavy, imposing styles. The use of filigree-work contributed to the new impression of delicacy. Stones took the form of silhouettes or were arranged in arabesques, looking for all the world like ribbons or some soft material. Jewelry seemed about to come to life and move of its own accord. Hard, chunky geometric designs disappeared; instead flower jewelry set off the upswept hairstyle promoted by *Vogue* and Hollywood alike, as it "showed off a pert nose".

Boucheron had never before followed a fashion so closely, or contributed so notably to its creation. The New Look wreaked havoc on an international scale. In the United States retail outlets were stuck with stocks of short skirts worth millions of dollars. In Britain the Chancellor of the Exchequer, Sir Stafford Cripps, went so far as to appeal to women to keep to shorter styles "as is consistent with common sense and current restrictions". This was all in vain.

By ignoring "reason" and economic prudence, and by doing the opposite of what might have been expected of a country ruined after years of foreign occupation, Paris regained the status it had briefly lost, and was once more the world's leader of fashion. After all, didn't women deserve some compensation after being deprived of new dresses and jewelry for four years? Dressed by Dior, wearing shoes by Roger Vivier, loaded with Boucheron jewels and sketched by Demachy or Gruau, the elegant woman was once again the true representative of French style. Like the *Normandie* just before the War, she was launched to win back national prestige.

Gérard Boucheron was hailed in Cairo, Beirut, Rio de Janeiro, Caracas, Lima and Mexico as the new ambassador of this return to beautiful jewelry after the lapse of the war years. He returned to Paris from his travels eager to resume his work with precious stones. "The back of the head is once again adorned with jewelry," stated *Vogue*, describing his barettes and hairpins set with round and baguette-cut diamonds. The new jewelry sparkled at the joyous succession of parties held in Paris; in 1949 a famous ball was known as the "Night of the Precious Stones", where "ten detectives danced fifty sambas to keep an eye on a hundred people wearing two thousand millions worth of jewels."

The most popular items of all in that period were the perforated and hand-engraved boxes, decorated with gold on a silver background and set with sapphires, diamonds and cabochon rubies. The designs, pierced into the metal, featured birds, butterflies, flowers with pistils, even elephants. The boxes contained items of a lady's toilette for a ball: compacts, lipsticks, cigarette-boxes, lighters and even cigarette-holders, all in rectangular or circular cases. There were over 40,000 examples of this "Pandora's Box": Boucheron could have paved the whole of the Place Vendôme with them several times over.

My father handed over the reins to me in the 1970s, and I became the head of the Boucheron establishment. Adopting the principle that nothing seems newer than something which has been forgotten, I reintroduced the same kind of rock-crystal my great-grandfather Frédéric had used to create his exquisite pieces in the last century. I had been inspired by the beauty of about fifty precious items, all made from rock-crystal between the 16th and 18th centuries, which I had seen exhibited in a Munich museum. Designs had to be drawn up for the new pieces, cutting processes developed and applications for patents filed. The results were peacock-clocks, horses and birds which made up a fantasy kingdom, and characters from the Commedia dell'Arte, adorned with gold and richly decorated with gems.

Every year we exhibited our most recent designs together with other French jewelry Houses. I was able to persuade a number of my distinguished fellow jewelers to join forces in relaunching the transformable brooch. Each establishment designed its own version; in the case of Boucheron, we were inspired by the crystal châtelaines designed by the founder of our House. Our creation featured two rows of baubles, decorated with a twist of cut crystal and mounted *en châtelaine* on two lapel brooches, which could be detached if desired. The matching brooches could be pinned on to a dress or suit, or worn as earrings. Just as gold may be manipulated in different ways, this combination of precious stones and rock-crystal made a piece of jewelry that could take a variety of forms. It gleamed with changing hues, and prices ranged from the most costly to the eminently affordable. The design succeeded in catering for contemporary tastes and met the requirements of the international market.

I learned my profession as managing director on Wall Street, where I also picked up the essential new knack of marketing. But when I am shown new gems, I still feel the same emotion I felt as a child when I used to dig around in my father's briefcase each evening, to find a packet of stones and jewels inside.

My predecessors all shared this emotion – but times have visibly changed. The Russian Tsars, the Aga Khans, the various royal families, the American railroad and steel tycoons, the Arab Emirs, and the Elizabeth Taylors and Sophia Lorens of this world can no longer be the sole makers of a jeweler's reputation. Neither can clients like the late Princess Grace of Monaco or Her Majesty Queen Elizabeth II, for whom Prince Philip commissioned Boucheron to make a magnificent diamond-and-ruby bracelet on the occasion of their fifth wedding anniversary. We are now living in an age of jeans, when the emancipation of women is reflected by a delightful anarchy in fashion. There is a huge variety of styles, just at a time when the number of consumers interested in fashion has greatly increased.

We have entered on the era of what I describe as "everyday jewelry". This is produced for a much wider clientele, and is more affordable. We at Boucheron feel that we spearheaded this trend in creating, for instance, the "multiple" pieces: rings, bracelets, necklaces or brooches – all mounted in gold, or in gold and diamonds, combined with different coloured stones – which can be detached, enabling the wearer to change the appearance of her jewelry as she pleases. Thus several different pieces can be had for the price of one. With similar ideas in mind, we reintroduced lapis-lazuli, coral, onyx, tiger's eye, and other less valuable materials out of the past.

Boucheron has also maintained the close connection between watches and jewelry first established by Frédéric Boucheron at the beginning of the 20th century. The new style of quartz watch can be worn in outer space or plunged into the depths of the sea, it comes in every imaginable colour and is outfitted with straps of everything conceivable from sealskin or ostrich-feather to gold and diamonds – but it remains a significant item of jewelry. All designs for the shape and decoration of watches are based on the principle of the perfect curve, which is a symbol of total femininity. Each Boucheron model has twenty-eight different variations, all made to complement the curve of a slender wrist and to reflect the graceful contours of a shoulder or a low-cut neckline.

Nowadays it is more important than ever for fine jewelry to have an international market. This means spending hundreds of hours every year in a plane, creating new sales outlets all over the world. Boucheron aims to make its designs more accessible, while retaining their splendour and prestige. The latest creation of the House is Boucheron perfume, contained in a magnificent golden ring worthy of a maharajah. Lift the stone – a blue "Burmese" cabochon – and a heavenly scent is released. It reflects the intimate link between perfume and luxury jewelry. Fashions come and go, but the creative process is eternal.

FABERGE

"The value of the work is ten times the value of the material," was the proud battle cry of Monsieur Granchez, the proprietor of Le Petit Dunkerque, the famous jewelry establishment in 18th-century Paris. It is this philosophy which young Fabergé brought to St Petersburg where, just over a hundred years later, he found an exactly contrary regime prevailing. From now on, he decreed, it was a question of the precise shade of enamel or fragment of semi-precious stone set within a modest frame of rose diamonds that was paramount, and not the number and weight of large brilliant-diamonds, frequently of questionable colour, which could be crammed into an ill-mounted, clumsy piece of jewelry.

The picture of Carl Fabergé, secreted in his private office behind the showroom of the monumental *sang de boeuf* premises he had built for his firm in Morskaya Street in St Petersburg, is one of watchful tranquillity. The famous photograph of him sorting stones, which has been used in endless publications, exactly captures this mood. The impression, however, is a little misleading. He was not merely that quiet, benign figure although, as we are told, he was invariably generous and understanding as a boss. He was something else as well, a revolutionary in the authentic sense of that word.

As is well known, young Carl, when only 24 years old, took on his ailing father's jewelry firm in 1870. He had already acquired an educated sympathy for what we used to call the applied or decorative arts throughout Europe. The appreciation of what he had seen in so many museums and collections had opened his eyes to a rich selection of visual excitements, and his curiosity ranged easily both historically and geographically. The curiosity and flexibility of appreciation were never to desert him and for that we are deeply in his debt. He was never far away from the library to which he was continually adding, and his inclination was fundamentally academic, although he proved to be a highly successful man of affairs as well. His father's business had been a modest concern, producing ordinary jewels in an ordinary St Petersburg basement which satisfied an ordinary Russian taste.

Young Carl had made up his mind that, in principle, the value of the object must be judged by its design and craftsmanship and not by the intrinsic worth of its ingredients. In reviving this philosophy at that time in that place, Fabergé was a true revolutionary, and the jewels he designed and manufactured were well ahead of what was being produced around him. He rejected anything he judged unworthy. In this pursuit of excellence he was, of course, being an élitist – inevitably, since any artist worth a second glance falls naturally into this absurdly maligned category.

Fabergé, then, was a young revolutionary élitist – no bad thing to be! His mission in life was to design confections which would reward their recipients with a *frisson* of delight when they were unwrapped and handled. They were invariably chic and afforded those fortunate enough to receive them a feeling that, like themselves, these objects were well-bred and impeccably turned out.

Often witty in conception, these objects were consistently well made. Fabergé's was not a tiny Renaissance goldsmith's workshop with two or three assistants at the bench – rather, it became an elaborate business enterprise with, in all, about 500 employees, designers, craftsmen and salesmen dedicated to the production of luxury accoutrements for the rich.

It is interesting for us today to learn of their working hours: the day started at 7 a.m. and went on until 11 p.m. On Sundays the number of hours was reduced from 8 a.m. to 1 p.m.

Top, enameled gold buckle with scrolled borders set with diamonds and six gold buttons set with brilliant and rose diamonds.

Below, a gold fur clasp, consisting of two octagonal panels which are enameled translucent pale blue over an engraved ground and overlaid with a trellis set with rose diamonds. A sherry-coloured citrine framed by rose diamonds is set at the centre of each panel, while the borders are made of red and green golds, set between lines of white enamel and chased with laurel and flowerheads.

Discussing the objects designed in St Petersburg, Terence Mullaly has pointed out that "The real key as to why Fabergé answers a widely felt need lies in the fact that [his jewels] are intensely pretty, a word of which, thanks to puritanical aesthetic theories and even what we imagine to be a social conscience, we have become frightened."

Let us put aside our social consciences when examining Fabergé's jewelry and allow ourselves to enjoy charming and stylish artifacts, which were designed simply to give pleasure to the wearer.

His profound understanding of his craft in its many manifestations enabled him to look forward to new horizons, and he espoused interesting new movements with enthusiasm, including Art Nouveau when it was launched in Europe. As he was very much a man of his time, many of the designs he made around 1900 were to serve as models for several of the leading European Houses right up to the present day. Thus in this second sense, too, Fabergé was a revolutionary, for he was not satisfied to rest exclusively upon laurels long since won. As Alexander von Solodkoff has reminded us in his 1988 book on Fabergé, "there are some jewellery pieces – brooches and pendants – that look as though they were made by Cartier in Paris during the 1920's, although they are in Hölmstrom's stockbooks as early as 1913."

One of Fabergé's most significant achievements lay in his ability to allow well-tried techniques to express new forms. His lapidaries were invited to carve stones for jewels in shapes not previously visualized; the enamelers adopted a wide range of different manners; and his metal-workers, the chasers and engravers, were encouraged to employ different colours of gold in startlingly new designs. The delight he felt in exploiting the shining dark green beauty of his native jade – Siberian nephrite – is well illustrated in many of his amusing designs.

Above all, he never forgot Aristotle's wise dictum that "everything desires to retain its own nature" and never allowed the medium to be abused. The most appropriate material was religiously selected for the job in hand.

There is an illuminating parallel to be drawn between the initial success with which Fabergé's products were greeted when they were introduced to an astonished and delighted Russian aristocracy and the enthusiasm demonstrated by serious collectors today. The jewels designed in St Petersburg were offered to those Russians at a time when they were particularly susceptible to just such an injection of glamour and novelty – they were a bored and disenchanted society. Under Nicholas II especially, the Imperial family was living on borrowed time, the Tsarina huddled in her Palace quarters, under the thrall of a corrupt and mangey divine. All this was far removed from any idea of a glittering court. The Dowager Empress, for her part, lived a far more active social life with a great deal more ceremony. Nevertheless, the family – at least the more percipient among them – were apprehensive about the future of their country.

Opposite: upper level, *a gold pendant by Carl Fabergé in the Old Russian taste made to celebrate the Romanoff tercentenary (1693–1913). The jewel centres on a chased gold Romanoff eagle beneath the Imperial crown designed by Jeremie Pauzié and from it hangs a rectangular frame in which the Monomach crown of Ivan the Terrible, the first Romanoff Tsar, is seen. The jewel incorporates the dates of the tercentenary, is set with brilliant-cut Siberian amethysts, and is signed with the initials of the chief jewelry workmaster Albert Holmström. It is contained within its original blue leather case emblazoned with the Romanoff eagle. The final watercolour for this jewel is contained in Holmström's record book, against which it is shown here together with the written confirmation that it was made on the Imperial command for the Royal cabinet.*
A diamond and fugitive "pink" sapphire cluster pendant fitted in its case with a rarely seen London lid-lining of Allan Bowe, who was Fabergé's partner from 1887 when the Moscow branch was founded. The partnership broke up in 1906 and Bowe clearly conducted business independently at a later date in London and sold jewels by Fabergé. This pendant has been photographed on the page next to the original design.
Lower level, *carved orletz (rhodonite) pendant mounted in platinum and set with brilliant and rose diamonds, shown resting on the page with the original design in ink and watercolour dated 12 May 1914. It was not necessary to stamp any hallmarks on platinum and the owners of this unmarked object had no idea that it was by Fabergé until the discovery of the record books.*
Mecca stone brooch mounted in platinum and set with diamonds. Fitted in its original holly box with the sketch in ink and watercolour dated 27 May 1911, and a note in Russian which gives the cost of polishing the Mecca stone (stained chalcedony) as 1.50 roubles.

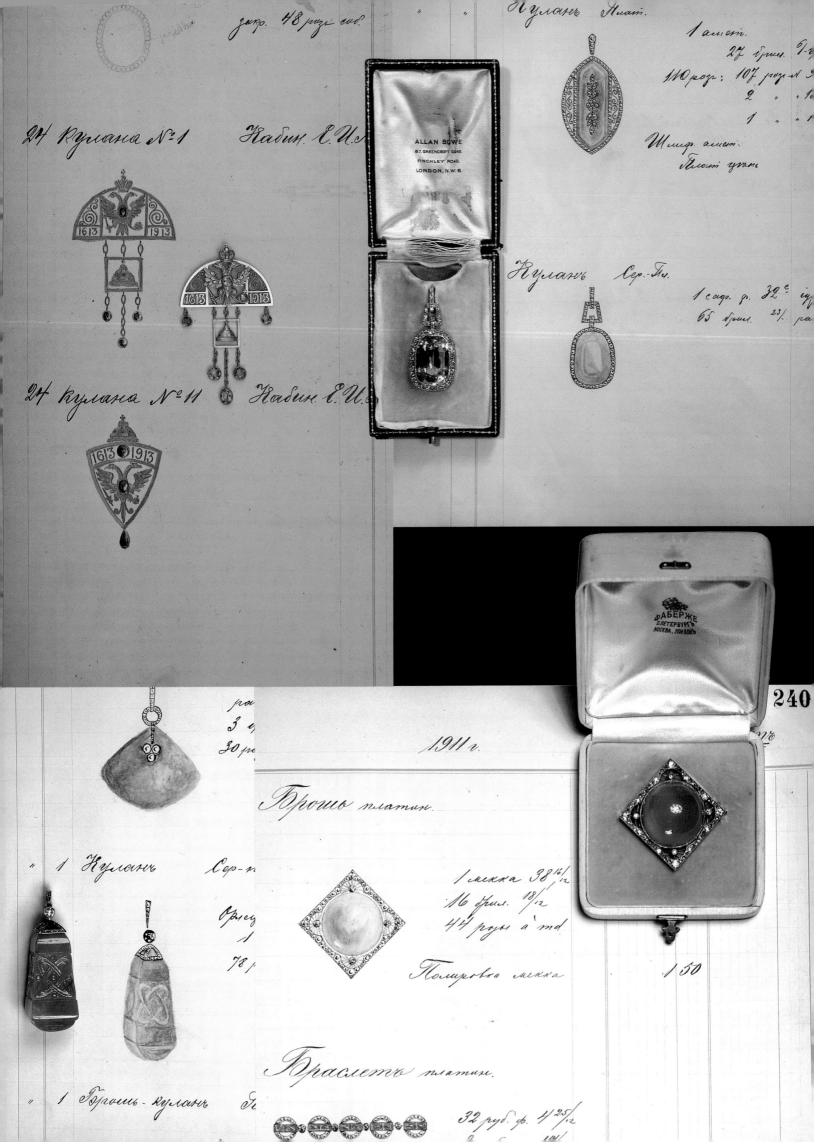

закр. 48 розъ сер.

Кулонъ Плат.

24 Кулона № 1   Кабин. Е.И.В.

24 Кулона № 11   Кабин. Е.И.В.

1 амет.
27 брил. 5-8
110 розъ: 107 розъ
2
1
Шлиф. амет.
Плоск. гуан.

Кулонъ   Сер-Пл.

1 сафир р. 32° ....
65 брил. 23/ ра

ALLAN BOWE
87. GREENCROFT GDNS.
FINCHLEY ROAD.
LONDON, N.W. 6.

ФАБЕРЖЕ
С.ПЕТЕРБУРГЪ
МОСКВА, ЛОНДОНЪ

240

1911 г.

Брошь платин.

1 мекка 38 15/12
16 брил. 18/12
44 розы à ...

Полировка мекка   150

ра
3
30 р

1 Кулонъ   Сер-п...

1 Брошь-кулонъ

Браслетъ платин.

32 руб. ф. 4 25/

Above, *cabochon Siberian amethyst and gold brooch by Gustav Fabergé, the father of Carl, who established himself in Bolshaya Morskaya Street, St Petersburg, in 1842. This rare jewel is fitted in its original case.*

Above right, *a pair of blue chalcedony cufflinks mounted in red and yellow golds, enameled opaque white with ribbon ties.*

Right, *aquamarine brooch pendant in a broad red gold trellised frame set with brilliant and rose diamonds following the canted contour of the stone. Fitted in its original holly box.*

Top, *a group of jewels incorporating the use of translucent, opalescent and opaque enamels with diamonds, rubies, amethyst and aquamarines.*

Above, *a square openwork brooch in gold applied with diamond-set Cyrillic initials forming the word POMNI (Remember) with a conventionalized fleur-de-lis at each corner. Moscow, c. 1880. Centre, a large pear-shaped diamond hanging freely from a diamond and calibré ruby frame mounted in gold. Right, shaped oval brooch enameled pale translucent blue over a guilloché sunburst with diamond border and a central diamond motif of crossed torches and leaves.*

Above, *a yellow gold dress watch, the back enameled opalescent oyster with a hint of flame over a wavy sunburst engraving, edged with rose diamonds within opaque white-enameled borders and, at the centre, an embossed dull green gold rosette on a granulated ground.*

Above right, *a star sapphire pendant set within a diamond border and surmounted by a bow knot.*

Above, *a gold brooch in the form of a knotted bow of broad ribbon enameled translucent pink over a moiré ground and bordered with rose diamonds set in silver.*

Below, *a pair of yellow gold cufflinks of bombé form, enameled in opalescent tones of apricot to pink on sunray backgrounds, with rose diamond borders and brilliant diamond centres.*

An articulated bowenite carving of a Pagoda by Carl Fabergé, the gold cuffs in red translucent enamel and set with rose diamonds, the belt and collar similarly decorated and each hung with a large rose diamond and oriental pearls. The eyes of the figure are set with cabochon rubies and diamonds and the gold earrings with similar rubies and pearls. The tongue is carved from a single ruby. The hands and tongue of the figure are delicately balanced and the slightest movement sets them in rocking motion. The carving is contained within its original fitted holly wood case. St Petersburg, 1903–15.

The origin of this chinoiserie figure type is to be found in Meissen porcelain in the mid-18th century.

Opposite above, *a diamond-set court tiara known as a Kokoshnik fitted in its original holly box.*
Below, *a diadem, convertible to a necklace, of silver and gold set with brilliant and rose diamonds
in the form of cyclamen, made in the workshop of Albert Holmström, 1908–17.*

Below, *the Mosaic Egg presented to the Tsarina, Alexandra Feodorovna, by Nicholas II on Easter
morning 1914. Shown resting on the page of the Fabergé record books next to the watercolour
drawing by Alma Theresia Pihl, dated 24 July 1913, from which the Imperial Egg derives.*
Reproduced by Gracious Permission of Her Majesty Queen Elizabeth II

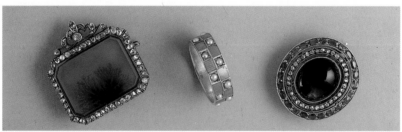

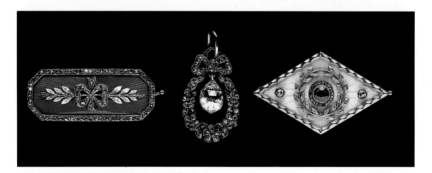

Top, *a group comprising four miniature Easter Eggs, one an amusingly simplified owl carved from purpurine set with tiny brilliant diamond eyes; another in gold enameled with translucent pale green, brown and rose stripes over guilloché fields culminating, at its base, in a blue agate carved as a heart; and two in platinum set with rose diamonds and one brilliant. A carved gold-mounted turn-of-the-century lapis-lazuli pendant of an abstract design some twenty-five years ahead of its time, and a gold horse-shoe brooch enameled translucent pale blue with a brilliant diamond trefoil.*

Centre, *a moss agate and rose diamond brooch, a gold hoop ring chequered with translucent pale blue enameled squares and half pearls, an oval cluster brooch set with a cabochon amethyst, rose diamonds and an outer border of alexandrites.*

Bottom left, *an octagonal panel brooch enameled translucent scarlet over an engraved ground with rose diamond set bow and leaf spray.* Centre, *a diamond briolet swinging freely in a rose diamond and ruby frame surmounted by a bow-knot. From the collection of a close friend of Carl Fabergé, Max Othmar Neuscheller.* Right, *a diamond-shaped brooch enameled opalescent white with gold and sapphire and rose diamond decorative motifs.*

There does exist in these Fabergé jewels a feeling of perfectionism, an impression of battles won rather than battles being waged, which somehow suggests a note of despair. It is almost as if they presage, in their minute isolation, the bloody horrors which followed. From a technical point of view, they nevertheless represent an apogee reached by goldsmiths, lapidaries, jewelers and enamelers in the long history of a noble craft.

Reaction in this field, as in others, is historically inevitable. Having been restricted in artistic endeavour by our didactic forebears a century ago, we have since that time been conducting ourselves rather like a mob of unruly schoolchildren let loose in a candy store, grabbing and devouring without criticism everything within reach. This has led to an aesthetic permissiveness which is finally even more tedious than the unnecessarily solemn and claustrophobic art sometimes imposed by the Victorians.

Our present attitude in the matter of realism is reflected in our renewed and welcome respect for anything which shows evidence of work well done. Another page of the art historian's handbook of volteface in taste has been turned yet again!

One of the hazards attendant upon any proposed effort to produce a useful history of an artist or group of artists who functioned comparatively recently – say within two or three generations – is the possibility, by no means remote, of vital material turning up after the great effort has been made and laboriously set down and published. This is exactly what has happened on several occasions in the matter of Fabergé research during the last few years. The sales ledgers of the London branch, diligently kept and written from 6 October 1907 to 9 January 1917, every entry dated with the name of the buyer, the description of the object, the inventory or stock number, the selling price in sterling and the cost expressed in roubles, have turned up. The immaculate handwriting, from the year 1908, is that of Henry Bainbridge, a splendid gentleman who perfectly reflected, as London Manager, Carl Fabergé's own magnanimity and imagination. It is fascinating, at our end of the century, to delve into these pages and discover who was buying what for whom and when, and for how much.

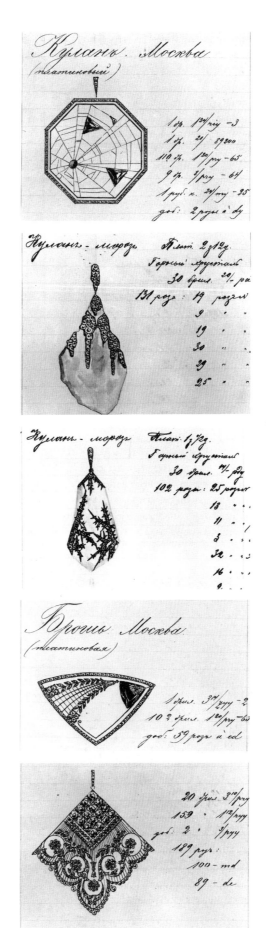

A group of ink drawings from the two Fabergé record books which extend from 1909 to 1915.
The octagonal spider's web pendant and the brooch in the form of a curved wedge are dated 1910 and the pendant of lace design (bottom) 1911. All were to be carried out in platinum set with diamonds and coloured gemstones. The two rock-crystal and platinum icicle pendants (second and third from the top) were to be set with diamond frost flowers for Dr Emanuel Nobel as gifts for the ladies invited to his dinner parties. These drawings are dated 1913.

Among the most required jewels of the Edwardian era was the jabot brooch; necessarily quite small, it served a practical purpose in addition to its intrinsic beauty. This explains the proliferation of what are usually described as "small brooches" by Fabergé. They were, in fact, exactly what was wanted when correctly worn.

Sheets of original jewelry designs, some signed, have turned up at intervals in auction rooms and each one somehow increases our understanding of the sheer scale of this extraordinary St Petersburg enterprise.

In addition, as far as the jewels of Fabergé are concerned, perhaps the most important of these recent discoveries are the two noble volumes of drawings and watercolour designs, records of what appears to be the entire output of the chief workmaster Albert Holmström's St Petersburg jewelry workshops from 6 March 1909 until 20 March 1915.

Each item, drawn or painted with the loving and meticulous care characteristic of the spirit of the House, is dated and very often furnished with further details regarding weight of stones used in a particular item, notes of any incidental expenses (such as lapidary work) and the names of clients to whom the jewel was sold or for whom, in many cases, it was designed and made.

Apart from diamonds, which Fabergé used in both rose-cut and brilliant form, his workshops popularized the use of coloured stones both precious and semi-precious. The range of materials was thus greatly widened and this in itself encouraged the development of more unusual and original designs. Fabergé was so faithful to his dictum concerning the relative importance of craft over materials, that it is in no way surprising to find him attracted to what was called the Mecca stone – in fact a translucent pale blue-green chalcedony cut cabochon and artificially stained to impart a rose-coloured glow. Mecca stones are sometimes confused with natural moonstones.

Aquamarines were a great favourite of the House and these stones mined in Russia, with their authentic colour of the sea, are preferred by many, including the present writer, to the unrelenting rasping shade of blue of contemporary examples imported from the Santa Maria Mines in South America.

The gems found in Russia range from the most valuable of all – Siberian emeralds are recognized as the finest in the world – to some of the more modest, notably the amethyst from the same region; both were consistently used in Fabergé jewelry.

The only stones which the Imperial family were traditionally said to view with a

Albert Holmström sitting at his desk in his office, c. 1912. The books of original designs, some of which are illustrated in this chapter, are lying on the desk.

certain disfavour were rubies, which evidently symbolized for them the shedding of innocent Royal blood. It has to be noted, however, that in spite of this alleged caveat we know of numerous Imperial jewels unashamedly glowing with splendid examples of the offending gem.

One finds very few rings signed by Fabergé. When one does appear the marks are usually stamped on the outside of the bottom of the shank. These marks have often disappeared either through wear over many years or more simply if the size of the ring had to be altered. A hoop ring enameled and set with pearls is illustrated on page 104; necessarily the marks on this ring were struck on the inside and may be clearly read. The other examples that have been found are generally quite conventional.

The tercentenary of Romanoff rule was commemorated in 1913 and Fabergé made

a variety of brooches and pendants incorporating carefully enameled models of Peter the Great's sable-trimmed *Shapka* or Cap of Monomach to be presented to each of the Grand Duchesses and ladies of the Court. One page of designs, we are told by Henry Bainbridge, was based on drawings made by the Tsarina Alexandra Feodorovna herself.

While the House continued to fulfil orders for quantities of conventional items of high quality which were clearly in regular demand, an impressive number of jewels were made which must have seemed extremely *avant garde* when they first appeared. Perhaps the most enthusiastic and loyal of the collectors of this latter category was Dr Emanuel Nobel, whose uncle Alfred's name will remain forever green as a result of his prize and his gunpowder. His nephew distinguished himself in a particularly engaging way. Every lady invited to his

Above: left, *Empress Alexandra Feodorovna, the last Tsarina.* Right, *Prince Youssoupoff.*

FABERGÉ

justly famed dinner parties, when seated, discovered carefully concealed in her table napkin a jewel by Fabergé cleverly designed as a piece of rock-crystal set with tiny diamonds depicting frost. These icicle pendants and brooches, so generously and imaginatively offered, must have ensured a thoroughly successful evening.

Another item of adornment supplied by the firm in a bewildering variety of patterns was the belt buckle. The classic model was in silver and enamel, though gold and plain examples are not unknown. Carried out in every possible colour and technique, they were often bordered by chased mounts, sometimes set with rose diamonds or pearls.

Haircombs of tortoiseshell usually set with diamonds provided handsome head ornaments less formal and brilliant than the tiaras which were available at Fabergé's for those attending at Court and important parties where they were *de rigueur*.

The vast bulk of jewelry produced was of course designed for the embellishment of women, whether their coiffed heads, slender necks and ears, shapely bosoms or their slim wrists and fingers; but a small quantity was meant for men. Stick-pins, waistcoat buttons, shirt-studs and sleeve-links were made by the House of Fabergé in a wide multiplicity of designs and materials.

Even the "run of the mill" items were always exquisitely designed and made, which is hardly surprising when it is remembered what particular mill they were run from. Many, however, were quite unconventional — we know of a watercolour sketch for a pair of sleeve-links in the form of small elephants carved from rhodonite, the warm rose-coloured stone mined in Ekaterinberg which the Russians call *orletz*. The links most often found, however, are composed of translucent enamels combined with gems of colour and rose diamonds.

A stick-pin was an appropriate gift for a member of the Imperial family — for example, to bestow when the need arose for some special recognition of service rendered. The number of Romanoff double-headed eagles carried out in diamonds, often of mixed brilliant- and rose-cut, each one perched on its pin, must be legion.

There is a gentleman's gold dress-watch, enameled and set with rose diamonds, which appears to be the only example by Fabergé to have been recorded, but there can be no doubt that a number must have been made for the fashionable man-about-town.

Finally, it seems reasonable to emphasize that, although the name of Carl Fabergé will always be most immediately connected in the public's mind with spectacularly fashioned objects of vertu in precious metals, stones and enamels, the jewelry we have been discussing and which illustrates these notes, designed and put together with the same devoted care for detail, was by no means a merely peripheral activity — it forms a significant spring contributing to the mainstream of Fabergé's creativity.

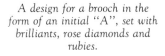

A design for a brooch in the form of an initial "A", set with brilliants, rose diamonds and rubies.

TILLANDER

The Soviet Union in the age of *glasnost* is so full of surprises that a Fabergé exhibition in the Leningrad Elagin Palace is no longer a shocking event. But for the Helsinki company of A. Tillander Jewelers the exhibition of 1989 brought back memories of times past though never forgotten. It recalled the triumphs and setbacks of a four-generation-old company of goldsmiths and jewelers, of the joys and misfortunes of a family saga, of tenacity in the face of adversity.

The story begins in 1837 with the birth of Alexander Tillander into a family of poor tenant farmers near Helsinki. As the farm was too small to support another mouth, at the age of 11 Alexander was put on a cart carrying produce to St Petersburg, told to contact his brother there and to get himself apprenticed to a barber. There was nothing unusual in this; hundreds of 10- to 13-year-old boys and girls left Finland every year to seek their fortunes in St Petersburg, the rapidly expanding capital of Russia, a mecca for aspiring craftsmen from all over Europe.

The young Alexander took an immediate dislike to barbering and managed to get himself apprenticed to Fredrik Adolf Holstenius, a Finnish master goldsmith at Tsarskoe Selo. After the compulsory seven years, he qualified as a journeyman and returned to St Petersburg as journeyman to the German master Carl Becks, maker of Imperial orders and decorations. Capable, industrious and thrifty, he decided by 1860, with savings of 200 roubles (about £1200 in today's money), to start out on his own. Renting a modest room with workbench and tools, his capital invested in gold, Alexander began producing simple gold bangles, at that time in vogue and easy to sell. These he worked on eighteen hours a day, spending what free time he had teaching himself to read and write.

In the 1860s St Petersburg had well over three hundred goldsmiths' workshops employing some 3,000 people, a good quarter of them Finns. Alexander's business slowly increased, apprentices were taken on – even a journeyman – and a private clientele was acquired in addition to the great stores on the Nevski Prospekt. The way ahead was to concentrate on fashionable yet simple articles, well designed, carefully made, modestly priced, above all appealing to Russian taste. Russian jewelry possessed a certain naivety and nostalgia, a deep and patriotic humanity; it was characterized by vivid colour and naturalism, and an almost excessive decorativeness. Alexander made bangles from gold tube set with pearls or Russian gems, rings, brooches with matching earrings, cufflinks and studs. His bar-shaped brooches set with pearl-studded anchors symbolized Peter the Great's naval city. He also made lily-of-the-valley sprays and even a fleur-de-lis set with diamonds. Without departing from this basic style, Alexander's jewelry gradually acquired a reputation for quality workmanship.

As the business grew and more workers were taken on, Alexander found time to explore new ideas, to master the Russian, French and German languages – and even to get married. (Here, however, he dispensed with courtship by marrying his Finnish housekeeper Mathilda Ingman.) More important private customers were acquired, among them the nobleman Tulinoff who was to rescue the company from impending bankruptcy that resulted from Alexander's disastrous venture into the diamond business.

Above, A. Tillander's workshop in St Petersburg at 28 Bolshaya Morskaya Street, c. 1900.
On the right, Alexander Tillander Jr at his bench.

Below, *the business-card of the House in French and Russian around the turn of the century.*

Fabricant-Joallier & Bijoutier

A. TILLANDER

St PÉTERSBOURG

Morskaia ²⁸/₁₃.

Fondée en 1860

ЮВЕЛИРЪ
и ЗОЛОТЫХЪ ДѢЛЪ
МАСТЕРЪ

А. Тилландеръ

С. Петербургъ

Морская ²⁸/₁₃, уголъ Гороховой ул.

Тел. 215 70.

With both business and family expanding – Alexander Theodor was born in 1870 – new premises were found on the corner of Bolshaya Morskaya Street and Gorohovaya. These included the workshop, living quarters for the family, and a granite-columned showroom that provided a suitable background for the company's illustrious customers.

By 1874 Alexander Tillander made his first trip abroad, to the Exposition Universelle in Paris, the most important venue for new ideas from European jewelers. At home, Fabergé's copies of the sensational Scythian finds at Kerch received widespread publicity, and before long replica jewelry also became a best-selling item at Tillander's. These included tubular gold bangles and bar brooches set with snake heads and bead terminals, and with filigree or granulation finish. Alexander Tillander's workmanship was recognized with the award of silver medals at the St Petersburg and Ekaterinburg arts and crafts shows in the mid-1880s.

New articles gradually came into production. Commemorative badges in gold and silver, decorated with enamel, were made in their hundreds for associations and societies. So important were these, and so limited the capacity of the workshop, that sub-contractors were resorted to, small workshops working exclusively for Tillander.

Then came the "egg business", as it was called in the ledgers. In the Orthodox tradition, it was obligatory to give an egg to each female member of the family on Easter morning. Fabergé's famous and imaginative eggs were eagerly emulated by other jewelers in St Petersburg.

The production of gold, silver and hardstone objects of a practical or decorative nature acquired an increasing importance. Photograph frames sold well, and many fine examples in gold and silver have survived privately or in museums. An enameled silver frame in the Louis XV style is on display at the State Historical Museum in Moscow, another is in the collection of the Baron Thyssen-Bornemisza in Lugano. What these have in common is a wavy-patterned guilloché enamel in the vivid scarlet so characteristic of Alexander Tillander's palette. Siberian nephrite was much favoured by Tillander and a number of *objets de vitrine* were made from it, often gold-mounted and set with gems.

Around 1887, the younger Alexander left the German School he had been attending in order to spend a short apprenticeship with his father's company before being sent abroad. His three-year sojourn was spent in Paris with Smets & Fournier, in London with Gugenheim and White, and finally in Dresden with Kämpffs. He returned home in 1891 as representative of L. Coulard, the Paris manufacturer of diamond jewelry, and achieved a success in Moscow with the display of their jewelry. Burning with an enthusiasm fed by new ideas, he viewed the family business as basically sound, but too modest and limited.

Back in St Petersburg, Alexander Junior assumed partial responsibility for the running of the company and introduced two new profitable lines of business: the sole agency for the export of demantoid garnets from the Urals that became so popular in Russia and late Victorian England, and commission trading in privately owned second-hand pieces of jewelry and *objets d'art*. By the turn of the century he had assumed full control of the company. From 1901 to 1917 he chronicled its fortunes in a series of highly personal reports detailing output, sales, customers – even employees' lives. These reports provide a unique insight into the goldsmiths' trade in pre-revolutionary St Petersburg.

By 1902 the company had 17 journeymen, 2 apprentices, a salesman, *dvornik* or houseboy, and a designer Luedke "with whom we are well pleased". "We have made 724 custom-made pieces and 752 other pieces for stock . . . [and] 971 badges for various associations and organizations." Among the illustrious customers listed were the Grand Dukes Vladimir and Alexis, the Grand Duchess Marie Pavlovna, and the Grand Dukes Andrew and Boris. There was reference to a number of pieces being made in the "new style": this was the Edwardian style inspired by the future Queen Alexandra of England, who was a sister of the Tsarina Marie Feodorovna.

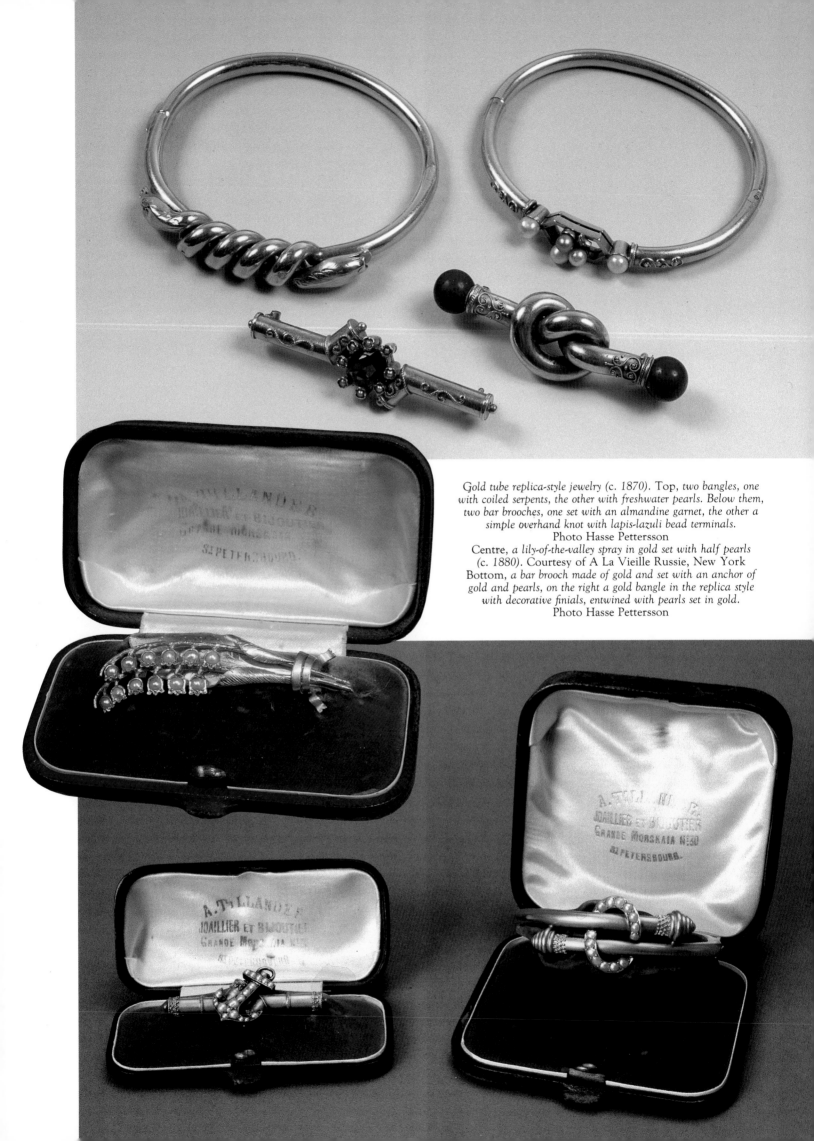

Gold tube replica-style jewelry (c. 1870). Top, two bangles, one with coiled serpents, the other with freshwater pearls. Below them, two bar brooches, one set with an almandine garnet, the other a simple overhand knot with lapis-lazuli bead terminals.
Photo Hasse Pettersson
Centre, a lily-of-the-valley spray in gold set with half pearls (c. 1880). Courtesy of A La Vieille Russie, New York
Bottom, a bar brooch made of gold and set with an anchor of gold and pearls, on the right a gold bangle in the replica style with decorative finials, entwined with pearls set in gold.
Photo Hasse Pettersson

Above, *fin-de-siècle jewelry in the Russian style. On the left a pearl and diamond ring, on the right a diamond brooch with suspended pink and bluish beryls.*
Photo Hasse Pettersson
Opposite, *a silver-gilt and enamel miniature frame in the Louis XV style, with scarlet waved guilloché enamel (c. 1890). State Historical Museum, Moscow*
(photo Rauno Träskelin)
A gold jeweled and enameled charka or cup, with bombé sides, the handle in the form of a curling snake, the upper rim set with emeralds, enameled in the vivid translucent red typical of Tillander (c. 1890). Photo Hasse Pettersson

Above, *a diamond-set platinum pendant in the Louis XVI style (c. 1900).*
Photo Hannu Männynoksa
A circular gold presentation brooch set with diamonds and sapphires; commissioned by the Imperial Cabinet in 1913 in honour of the Romanoff Tercentenary and presented to Marie, wife of King Ferdinand I of Roumania. In the centre are the crowned initials M A. Photo Hannu Männynoksa
A rosé and green gold locket on a long gold chain in the Art Nouveau style, the trefoil-shaped flower set with cabochon emeralds and a half pearl.
Photo Hannu Männynoksa
Below, *commemorative badges in gold and silver decorated with enamel.*
Photo Hasse Pettersson

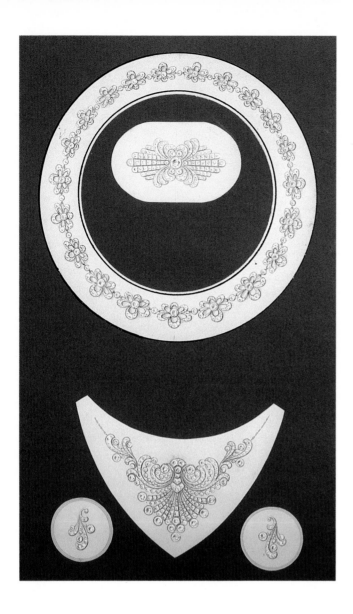

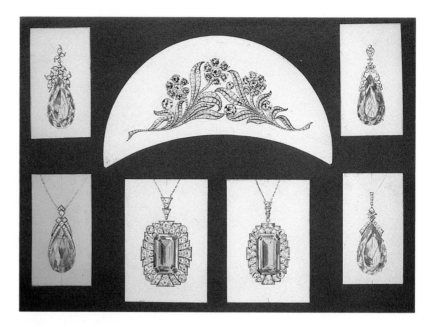

Various jewelry designs from the sketchbooks of Oskar Pihl, ranging from the 1920s to the early 1940s.

Opposite above, *a gold cigarette case and lighter set with a freshwater pearl and enameled in an opaque matt black enamel; designed and enameled by Oskar Pihl in 1934. Below, a platinum diamond-set necklace and earrings designed by Pihl and made at A. Tillander around 1950. Photos Hasse Pettersson*

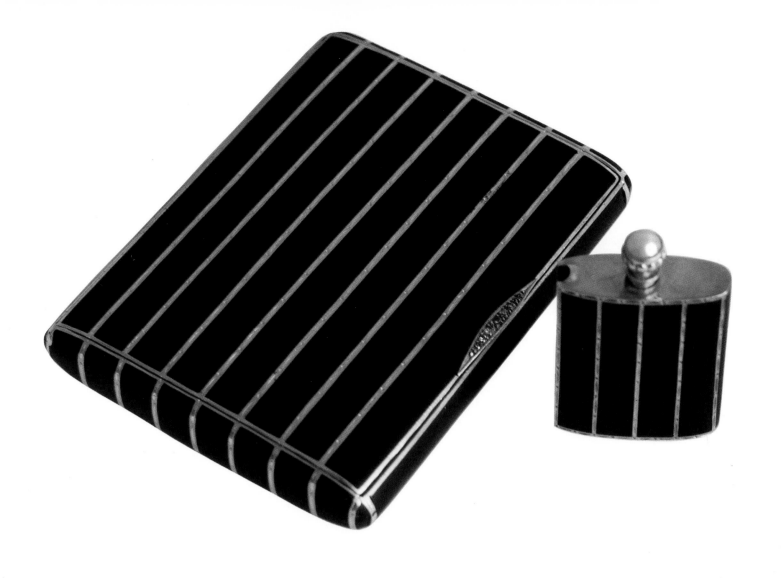

Above, *a large gold circular brooch inspired by Viking jewelry, designed by Lotta Orkomies and cast in the cire-perdue method in the late 1960s. Below it, another Orkomies design of the 1960s, a cast gold brooch set with coral beads and diamonds.*
Photos U. J. Pettersson

Opposite, *a yellow and white gold necklace with an octagonal pendant, pavé set with diamonds, designed and made by Raimo Nieminen at A. Tillander in 1984.*
Photo Veijo Autio

In 1899 the younger Alexander married a Finnish girl, Edith Gallén. He had avowed his love for her when she was only a baby and he ten years old. At the age of thirteen she declared her desire to learn foreign languages, and thus came to lodge with the Tillanders. Like his father before him, Alexander saw the good sense of marrying a girl with whom he was already familiar. Leo, their first born, arrived in 1899 and Herbert and Viktor in the first decade of the new century.

Family life was concentrated around the business. One or two annual business trips were made, and there was time now for extended summer holidays. All the Tillanders became converts to Dr Sebastian Kneipp's health cures and the older generation in particular spent long periods at Kneipp's spa in Wörishofen (Germany). The younger generation preferred sailing in the Gulf of Finland.

The first blow to this otherwise typical bourgeois success story came in 1905 with the outbreak of the first Russian revolution. Yet even then, bad times had their bright side, as Alexander Junior happily remarked in his annual report: "Although costs have risen by 10 per cent, at least hardly anyone left this year." Tillander's workers had to join in the general strike, which won them a nine-hour day. Sales of demantoid garnets to Boucheron in Paris and London doubled, more than a hundred miniature eggs were made, and the firm even indulged in a primitive form of industrial espionage in Paris to obtain new designs.

The Tillanders, especially Alexander Junior, were active in the Finnish community in St Petersburg. Most of their employees were Finns and an increasing number of pieces were being sent to Helsinki jewelers for sale on commission. Apart from holidaying in Finland, Alexander Junior also became an ardent nationalist and a member of one of the independence parties. He taught his three sons Swedish and Finnish, and also supervised Leo's appren-

ticeship in goldsmithing and jewelry. Even the family servants were Finns.

During the years of peace and prosperity that followed the aborted revolution, in addition to making large quantities of gold jewelry (brooches, rings, chains, miniature eggs, and other pieces for stock), Tillander fulfilled a number of special commissions. Among these were a silver writing set for the Ministry of Roads and Waterways, a silver garland for the Glinka monument, and two magnificent diamond *colliers de chien*.

The company also produced cigarette cases, bowls, *kovshes* or scoops, cups, dinner bells, and photograph frames.

From 1907 onwards A. Tillander had the patronage of Marie Feodorovna and from 1909 of the Tsar and Tsarina, as well as the Tsar's sister, the Grand Duchess Olga. This illustrious clientele was in due course swelled by members of the cabinet, bankers and other wealthy patrons. Unfortunately, there are few records of what was actually made for the Imperial family, but the pieces varied in value from £100 to £7,800.

There exists a fine cigarette case in gold, enameled in a brilliant translucent rust, made for Tsar Alexander III and given to his son, the Tsarevich (later Tsar Nicholas II), at Gatchina Palace on Christmas Day 1893. The engraved Imperial Romanoff double-headed eagles on both sides of the case appear through the enamel. The case also has a match compartment and tinder cord attachment. The message inside, engraved over the Tsar's handwriting, reads: "From Papa, 25th Dec. 1893, Gatchina."

In 1910 the 50th anniversary of the company was celebrated with great pomp and expense (6,000 roubles or £30,000, including generous gratuities to the staff) at the Hôtel l'Europe on the Nevski Prospekt. The staff presented Alexander Senior with a miniature silver statue of himself at the anvil. The following year they took over the premises of the jewelers Hahn at 26 Nevski Prospekt.

A gold pendant on a blue silk ribbon, set with gold nuggets from Lemmenjoki in Lapland and with cabochon cut iolites; by Jaana Lehtinen at A. Tillander. Matching gold bracelet with iolites, designed by Jaana Lehtinen and made by Raimo Nieminen at A. Tillander. The set was commissioned by Wärtsilä Helsinki Shipyard in 1984 and presented to HRH the Princess of Wales at the launching of the luxury cruiser Princess Royal. *Photo Mikko Hyytiäinen*

A Tillander family portrait
(1911). Left to right: Leo,
Mathilda (Alexander Sr's wife),
Herbert, Alexander Sr, Viktor,
Alexander Jr and his wife.

In 1905 Boucheron's representative and his son were murdered while returning to Moscow by train from Baku. The company closed their Moscow shop and Tillander took over the sole agency for Russia. Though business continuously improved, these new moves incurred colossal debts. Moreover, bribery and corruption in government circles led to the loss of a foothold in the Dowager Empress's cabinet.

The celebration in 1913 of the tercentenary of the Romanoff dynasty was a major event for the luxury trade of St Petersburg, especially jewelers. The House of Tillander received a number of substantial commissions from members of the Imperial family and cabinet. These were mainly for small but nevertheless luxurious pieces in gold, presentation brooches, pendants, bracelets, cufflinks and tie-pins. The Imperial crown provided one important decorative element, others were the initials of the donator or recipient. They were all delivered in the special red leather cases, intended for Imperial presentation pieces,

that were manufactured by the Finnish case-maker Ampuja.

Although the outbreak of the First World War reduced sales substantially, inflation had the effect of increasing income if not volume. Alexander Junior's reports for the war years reflect the general tragedy experienced throughout Europe, but also the increasing prosperity of the company. The year 1916 was so good financially that he did not dare to reveal the true situation in his report. Prices, however, continued to rise, shortages grew worse, and workers were mobilized or imprisoned (there were many German craftsmen in the city). Indeed, most of the major jewelers along the Nevski Prospekt were forced to close down, some to be replaced in time by commission stores selling antiques and jewelry. Finally, there was the fear of the enemy's reaching Petrograd (St Petersburg renamed and de-Germanized) or of another revolution. Though Tillander kept going, the future looked very bleak indeed. In October 1917 the Bolshevik Revolution provided the final blow.

The family were by no means taken by surprise when the Bolshevik Revolution took place; early in 1917 plans had been laid to avert total disaster. Choice pieces of jewelry had been sent to Finland and buried in the family's summerhouse garden. Considerable funds were transferred to banks abroad, but Tillander's other assets were frozen. In Petrograd, robberies became a daily event, inflation was out of hand, food, fuel, everything was in short supply. By September, with only one apprentice remaining, the business closed down. In November six bandits, led by a former journeyman, attacked and shot Alexander Senior outside his home. Although the wound was not fatal and the valuable pearls he was carrying not stolen, he never fully recovered from the shock. In December 1918, at the age of 81, he died in the city where he had spent 55 years of his life.

In the autumn of 1917 Alexander Junior and his family did not return from their holiday in Luumäki. Finland had declared itself an independent state and civil war had broken out to decide who would rule the new Russia. Because of their White sympathies, the family decided it was more prudent to hide out in Luumäki. A party of foraging Reds threatened to shoot Alexander, but before this could be carried out he managed to escape and met up with a band of White troops, among them his son Leo.

By spring 1918 the Whites had won and a new life could begin. The first years were extremely difficult and, to start with, Alexander went into partnership with the jeweler Viktor Lindman. In 1921 the company of A. Tillander Jewelers was re-established in Helsinki and initially survived by placing jewelry bought from émigrés on the international market.

Alexander set about rekindling the company workshop in order to continue the tradition of craft production. His workers, though Finns, were themselves emigré craftsmen from St Petersburg. All had been trained in Russia, in Russian techniques and in Russian taste; even their common

The interior of the A. Tillander shop in Helsinki in the late 1920s. The group of three men in the back are Oskar Woldemar Pihl (son óf Fabergé's Moscow manager Knut Oskar Pihl and grandson of August Holmström), Herbert Tillander, and Alexander Tillander Jr.

TILLANDER

language was Russian. Through them, the company managed to maintain the continuity of the St Petersburg image. It was not until 1979 that the last of the original Russian-trained craftsmen retired.

Until the Revolution, Finnish goldsmith and enamelist Oskar Pihl (son of Fabergé's Moscow master) had looked forward to a promising career as a Fabergé designer in his uncle's workshop. But he too had to leave Russia, and from 1923 to his death in 1957 he was Tillander's chief designer. He was the essential link with the St Petersburg style of design and technique. A child of the Edwardian period, his designs blend the lightness and elegance of that style with the naturalistic decorativeness of Russian jewelry.

Oskar Pihl favoured the simple and beautiful gems of his two native lands, Russia and Finland. His sketches blaze and glow with Russian gemstones and decorative Finnish quartzes. If his designs possess nostalgia for a past era, there is no indication of stagnating into a St Petersburg mould, for they led effortlessly into something quite new.

When Finland emerged bruised but not defeated from the Second World War, it faced the twin problems of reconstruction and geopolitical reorientation. As prosperity returned, the leading industrialist families began to commission and buy fine jewelry. Here the House of Tillander and its workers played an important role, helping to create Finland's new image. The sketchbooks of Oskar Pihl and the ledgers of the company give evidence of the fine hand-made platinum and palladium jewelry produced in those post-war years.

The approach of the Helsinki Olympics urged Tillander to hold a Souvenir Competition in 1948 to seek out new and original designs. Among the discoveries were Tapio Wirkkala, Birgit Rydman and Kirsti Ilvessalo, all of whom went on to conquer the world. In all respects, except for the weather, the 1952 Helsinki Olympics were a success. It rained throughout the Games and A. Tillander's best-selling item was a silver box with an enameled umbrella on top.

Within the company, a new generation of designers was being prepared under the tutelage of Oskar Pihl. One of those whose talents he nurtured was Lotta Orkomies. Her cast-gold jewelry using the *cire perdue* method was inspired by nature, something of great importance to all Finns. She has also found inspiration in Viking archaeological finds. Her creations were among those that took the world by storm in the 1960s with the phenomenal success of Finnish design. This tradition of the older master training and guiding the next generation has created what they themselves call the Tillander style. In the 1980s the company still has its own workshop and shop in central Helsinki, and still makes everything by hand.

In this spirit Lotta Orkomies herself has trained, guided and inspired A. Tillander's younger generation of designers, including the talented Raimo Nieminen and Jaana Lehtinen. It was Jaana Lehtinen who in 1984 designed a delightful necklace and bracelet set with blue iolites cut in cabochon for the Princess of Wales. The works of these young designers possess an originality in materials, a simplicity of style, quality craftsmanship, and an overall charm – just those elements that Alexander Tillander had in mind when he set up his own company in the St Petersburg of 1860.

A rectangular silver cigarette case in the Art Nouveau style set with a sapphire push button. Photo Hannu Männynoksa

LALIQUE

ené Lalique (1860–1945) was the undisputed genius of Art Nouveau jewelry and arguably the greatest artist-jeweler ever known. A leader of the Art Nouveau movement as a whole, he was a man of exceptional talent, imagination and versatility. In 1900 the French critic Léonce Bénédite described him as "the true innovator . . . the one who tore down old barriers, overturned entrenched traditions and created a new language." Single-handed he broke through the established conventions of 19th-century jewelry design and manufacture, and used the skills in which he had been trained to create instead an entirely new expression for the art of the jeweler.

By the year 1900, as one century was gently turning into the next, women too were changing from toys into temptresses and Lalique was transforming their jewels from trivial trinkets into great works of art. As the new century emerged, metamorphosis was in the air; things were not always what they appeared to be. The seemingly riotous Belle Epoque was rocked by an undercurrent of sadness and pessimism. The *fin de siècle* atmosphere was filled with nostalgia for the dying century, mixed with fear and hope for the new age. This theme of turbulent change and transformation is one of the most important and bewitching features of Lalique's Art Nouveau jewelry.

It was in 1900 that Lalique triumphed at the great Exposition Universelle in Paris. Crowds flocked to Lalique's showcase at the Exposition to press their noses against the window and gaze in amazement at the fantasy creatures and dream objects that were causing such a stir in Paris and all around the world. His display was eerie, erotic and eye-catching. Black velvet bats swooped against a grey gauze star-studded night sky. Below this a semicircular grille was formed by five patinated bronze figures, a tribute to femininity and perhaps at the same time to the American dancer Loïe Fuller, who also had a triumph at the Exposition Universelle. With her free-form serpentine dances, in which she seemed to change into one of Lalique's winged jewels, a strange, hybrid creature with floating incandescent wings, she personified both the swirling Art Nouveau line and the theme of metamorphosis.

Lalique was hailed by art critics as the emancipator and master of modern French jewelry. He became a national hero, compared to the greatest artists of all time. Lalique won a Grand Prix, was awarded the rosette of the Légion d'Honneur; and orders for jewels and objects poured in from rich and famous admirers all over the world. His future was secured. But like all overnight sensations, he had been struggling with his creations and their acceptance for many years, trying to find fresh and exciting ways to express his imagination and to break completely with the past.

Born on 6 April 1860 in the little town of Ay in the Marne region of France, René Lalique was the only child of a merchant of novelty goods. The family moved to the suburbs of Paris in 1862, but returned to the countryside for holidays, thus giving Lalique the chance to study the flowers, birds and insects that were to provide the dominating theme of his jewelry. Details of Lalique's life are scarce. In his definitive work on 19th-century French jewelry, the jeweler and historian Henri Vever tells us that Lalique first showed signs of mixing artistry with entrepreneurial talent when, at 15, he began painting gouache flower miniatures on thin ivory plaques, which he later sold.

A photograph of the Lalique stand at the Exposition Universelle of 1900, where the jeweler's imaginative creations enjoyed a great success. On the right of the Lalique stand is that of Vever. Musée des Arts Décoratifs (photo Fonds Vever)

When his father died in 1876, Lalique was forced to leave school to earn a living and was apprenticed to the Paris jeweler Louis Aucoc. After two years he went to London to study at the Sydenham college in South London, at a time when art schools in England were far more progressive than in France and involved with the thriving Arts and Crafts movement. The college was probably the Sydenham School of Art which had been established in the original Crystal Palace, and moved to Sydenham in 1854.

Returning to Paris in 1880, Lalique would naturally have been immersed in the reawakening of artistic interest that led up to Art Nouveau. He worked for various manufacturers, then as a free-lance designer, all the time teaching himself, extending his own talents, particularly by studying sculpture and drawing. During the early 1880s, he went into business with a family friend, M. Varenne, at 84 Rue de Vaugirard. Lalique created the designs and Varenne sold them to various jewelers. They were painted in bright yellow, to look like goldwork, on a black background. This association lasted for two years. Lalique's early designs of the 1880s, as illustrated in Vever's book, were basically traditional, diamond set jewels of the type in demand by his customers, the leading manufacturers and retailers of Paris such as Vever, Cartier and Boucheron. He made diamond set roses, brooches designed as lively, twittering birds on branches, or a simple ear of corn. Even at this stage, his work showed a lightness and vitality that set it apart from the rest.

In 1884 he exhibited his own jewels for the first time at an exhibition of the Crown Jewels in the Louvre. To extend the show, a display of industrial arts was added, in which Lalique was invited to take part. His display was modest but it did succeed in attracting the attention of Alphonse Fouquet, the leading Paris jeweler whose firm was later to create spectacular Art Nouveau jewels.

An important year for Lalique was 1885. At that time he took over the Place Gaillon workshops of Jules Destape, one of his customers, and became independent for the first time. His success was such that in 1887 he took over another workshop in the Rue Quatre Septembre. Then in 1890 he moved his entire operation to 20 Rue Thérèse, at the corner of the Avenue de l'Opéra, where he lived above the shop with his new wife, the daughter of the sculptor Auguste Ledru. In this new building he was able to decorate his atelier and his home to his own liking, and this secure environment helped his imagination to flow more freely. Here too he began his experiments with glass, presumably as an extension of his work with enameling techniques, since enamel is a form of glass.

It was not until 1895 that Lalique publicly exhibited his jewels (as opposed to designs) under his own name, at the Salon of the Société des Artistes Français where the decorative arts were allowed for the first time. Here he showed a cloak clasp in the prevailing Renaissance manner, its seemingly conventional format contradicted by the addition of a naked female form that caused much comment and controversy. It was the first sign of Lalique's famous "shock" tactic, always delivered in a deceptively seductive package of line, colour and composition.

Opposite: top row, a wooded landscape haircomb of horn, gold and enamel (c. 1899–1900), enclosing a luminous moonlit enameled landscape of trees and a distant lake. This was exhibited at Agnew's, London, in 1905.
Next to it, a speedwell bracelet of gold, glass, enamel (c. 1900–02), in which the thick flowering plants are made of moulded lavender blue glass, tapering into gold and enamel buds, stems and leafy borders.
Below it, an owls bracelet of gold, chalcedony, enamel and glass (c. 1900–01), in which five plaques form a frieze of moulded frosted glass owls, each sitting on an enameled branch of a pine tree set against a moonlit sky of plique-à-jour enamel. All three pieces by courtesy of the Calouste Gulbenkian Museum, Lisbon
Bottom row, a flower and bee haircomb of horn, gold, enamel, opal and glass (c. 1902–05). A carved opal bee hovers on one of the three luscious, umbelliferous blooms; the comb's teeth are shaped as the stems of the flowers. Ulf Breede, Munich
Next to it, a pair of Medusa head cufflinks in foiled glass and metal (c. 1920). John Jesse and Irina Laski, London
Below it, a rose corsage ornament of gold, glass, amethyst and enamel (c. 1905–10). The roses are of moulded rose pink glass, their thorny stems of enameled gold. The Calouste Gulbenkian Museum, Lisbon

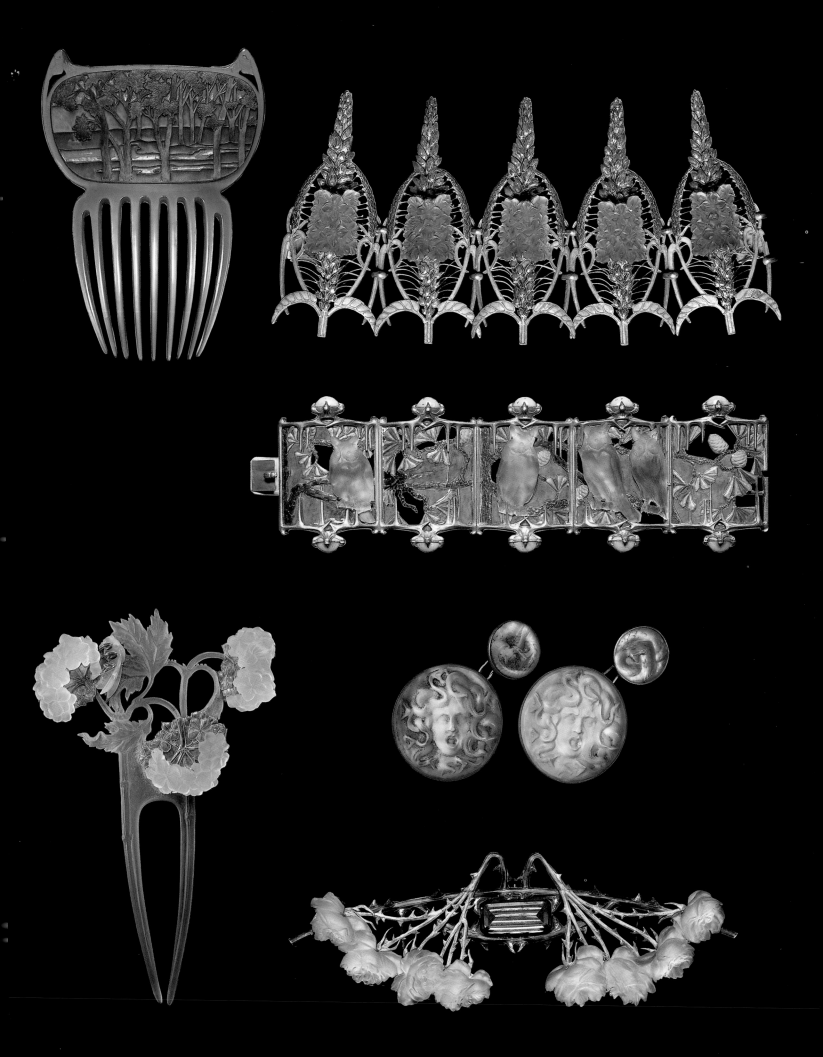

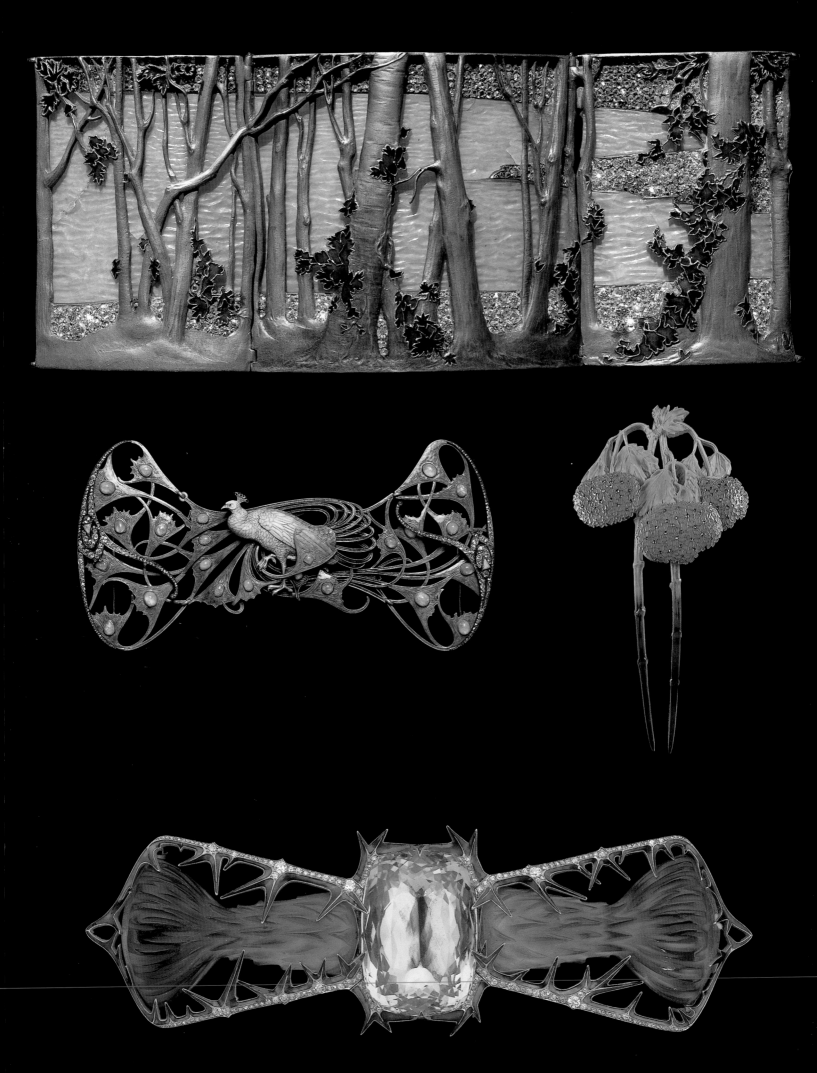

Opposite: top, *a wooded landscape dog collar plaque of gold, opals, enamel and diamonds*
(c. 1898). A lake of carved opal shimmers between gold trees wound around with green enameled
leaves.
Centre, *this peacock corsage ornament of gold, opal, enamel and diamonds (c. 1898–99) is a*
quintessential Art Nouveau jewel.
Next to it, *a guelder rose haircomb of horn, gold, enamel and diamonds (c. 1902–03). The*
patinated horn is carved with softly hanging leaves and three heavy snowball-shaped plants.
The Calouste Gulbenkian Museum, Lisbon
Below, *a thistle corsage ornament of gold, enamel, glass, diamonds and aquamarine (c. 1905–07),*
in which the thistles are of moulded glass, stained blue-green, and set in a spiky frame of enamel
and diamond foliage. Silver, London

Above, *a dragonfly corsage ornament of gold, enamel, chrysoprase, moonstones and diamonds*
(c. 1897–98). This spectacular hybrid dragonfly of immense proportions and striking allusions to
metamorphosis and female sexuality is perhaps the most memorable of Lalique's jewels.
The Calouste Gulbenkian Museum, Lisbon

Right, *this wasps pin in gold, enamel, opal and diamonds (c. 1899–1900) was shown at the 1900 Exposition Universelle, Paris.* The Danish Museum of Decorative Art, Copenhagen

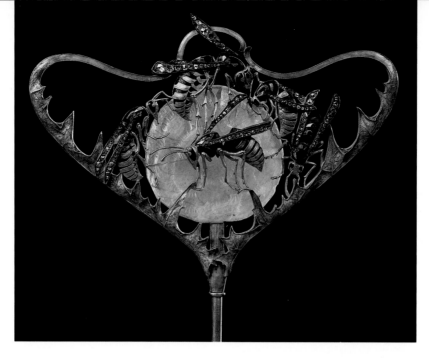

Below, *wood nymph cloak clasp of gold, glass and enamel, which was widely illustrated in contemporary journals after it appeared at the Paris Salon d'Automne in 1905.* Ulf Breede, Munich

Below left, *a grape and vine diadem of gold, horn, enamel, rock-crystal and mother-of-pearl, which captures the* fin de siècle *mood of melancholy so forceful in Lalique's jewels.* Silver, London

Bottom right, *an insect and corn haircomb of carved horn and enameled glass, suggesting a strong Japanese influence.* Ulf Breede, Munich

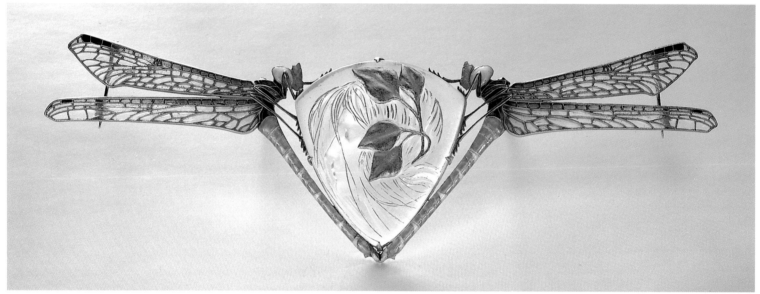

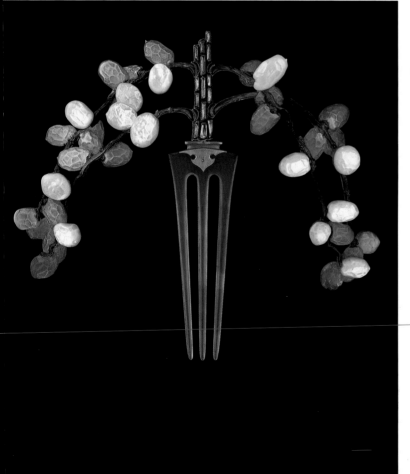

A damselflies necklace of gold, enamel, aquamarines and diamonds (c. 1900–02). The delicate hovering insects are entwined to form curvilinear Art Nouveau shapes. Private collection

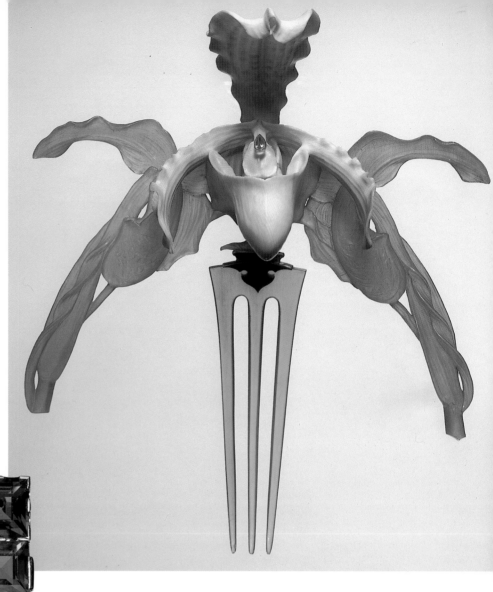

Right, *an orchid diadem of gold, horn, ivory and topaz (c. 1903–04). The exotic hothouse orchid, a symbol of the aesthetic movement of the late 19th century, was treated realistically by Lalique with the stress on its sexuality.* The Calouste Gulbenkian Museum, Lisbon

Below, *a geometric brooch of gold and citrines (1904–05), an early prediction of Art Deco form.* Schmuckmuseum, Pforzheim

Right, *a cherries haircomb of horn, enamel, gold and diamonds. Some of the cherries are of carved stained horn, others overlaid with enamel, their stems set with diamonds. Shown at the Paris Salon in 1903.* Private collection

134

A grasshopper necklace of horn and pearls (c. 1902–04). Each of the graduated motifs is composed of two grasshoppers, head to head, of carved and stained horn, with natural baroque pearls held between their front and back feet. The Calouste Gulbenkian Museum, Lisbon

From the mid-1890s his jewelry began to show a strong sculptural element, combining classicism with the sinuous movement of Art Nouveau. Nymphs and sea maidens carved in ivory fight against the currents of the ocean, or their own sensuality, in their struggle towards a new century and new freedom. In 1894, Lalique adapted the technique of *tour à réduire*, a process familiar to engravers and medallists and widely used for making coins. It involved a machine for reducing or scaling down a design so that the complex detailing carved on a large master model could then be transferred to much smaller surfaces, without sacrificing fine definition. Lalique was the first to apply this technique to jewelry, working initially on ivory reliefs. The experiment was a great success, immediately copied by leading Paris jewelers.

By the 1890s Lalique's gold work was also showing distinctive signs of a new sculptural fluidity. An important characteristic of his jewels and of the best Art Nouveau jewelry is the tendency of the materials towards deliquescence: he was able to turn gold into a substance that seemed almost liquid, flowing like life's blood or sap in constantly moving lines that suggested energy and growth. At this time he was also gradually adding more unusual, acutely observed motifs from nature. He was fascinated by curious aspects of plant or animal life and concentrated on intriguing specimens, whether exotic or everyday, from the surreal orchid and luscious lily or iris, to the thistle, hazelnut branch or willow catkin. In tune with all Art Nouveau designers, he took an interest in plant structure, in stems, leaves and in the bud, a charming allusion to the springtime of artistic fervour. He focused also on the decay and rebirth of the natural world, choosing wilting leaves and petals, world-weary anemones or poppies, overblown roses, or the humblest field flowers, like cow parsley or thistles, so light and ephemeral with their soft seedheads about

to disintegrate with the next breath of wind. Lalique used his fluid gold work, alive with enamels, to convey the dynamic forces of organic life: crisp and curling autumn leaves, rippling water, trailing branches, budding stems, gnarled and knotty roots of trees.

Lalique's vision of nature was closely linked to prevailing symbolist ideas and thought. His art depicted what the poet Mallarmé referred to as a "veiled essence of reality", with a highly disciplined emotional intensity that became achingly life-like, compelling and often uncomfortably decadent.

Lalique was a master at spotting the potential of techniques from other areas of the decorative arts, and adapting and improving them for use in jewelry manufacture. He was never a slave to the tyranny of the diamond, never intimidated by the intrinsic value of gems. He chose materials only for their artistic worth, for their value to his compositions and portrayal of nature. Taking advantage of the progressive art glass movement in France at the time, Lalique became gradually more involved with glassmaking, in a renewed effort to create an entirely new form of jewel. His early one-off glass objects were made using the *cire perdue* or "lost wax" method of casting, a process borrowed from his goldsmithing techniques or from sculpture. From the late 1890s he began to incorporate glass motifs into his jewelry, daring to mix a valueless material with precious metals and gems. He developed his own special glass, a *demi-crystal* that was sparkling yet malleable. The shapes were cast in moulds and then finished by hand and wheel-carved to obtain a high degree of definition. Often they were painted with enamels, or stained to produce the effect of a patina.

Alongside his glass experiments, Lalique's use of enamels became more adventurous and an integral part of almost every jewel that came out of his workshop.

Opposite top, *a pendant of two peacocks on a prunus branch in gold and enamel, facing each other above an opal (c. 1902–03).*
Centre, *a winter woodland pendant of gold, glass, enamel and pearl (c. 1899–1900). The central moulded intaglio glass panel shows a frosty lakeside scene within a frame of enameled gold trees.*
Bottom, *a poppy maiden pendant of silver, glass, enamel and hanging pearl (c. 1898–1900). The trance-like face of cast glass contrasts with the swirling hair of oxidized silver, the open poppies symbolizing sleep and oblivion.* The Calouste Gulbenkian Museum, Lisbon
Left, *a willow catkins corsage ornament of gold, glass and opals (c. 1904–05). In this exquisite study from nature, Lalique has created the effect of light shining through the opal and casting a blue-green glow on the catkins.* Silver, London

His use of colour and texture to suit his subject matter is unrivalled, his techniques masterful, in particular the open-backed translucent or *plique-à-jour* enamel, the most spectacular and complicated of enameling effects. In this process, metal cloisons were fixed to a base which would either not adhere to the enamel when fired, or which could be dissolved easily by acid after firing. Lalique improved the method by using saw-pierced sheets of gold for cloisons, usually with an acid-soluble copper backing, making a much sturdier framework. His striking application of *plique-à-jour* is seen to perfection on his most macabre and memorable jewel, the monumental dragonfly corsage ornament, now in the Gulbenkian Museum, Lisbon. The creature's wings of blue-green *plique-à-jour* are like thin membranes, fragile and veined, gleaming with foiled enamels.

In 1896 Lalique exhibited his first horn jewel, a bracelet, followed in the next few years by a series of sensational horn ornaments, mostly haircombs, modeled into extraordinary organic motifs, glistening softly with gems, enamels, or with patination. Horn is an organic substance akin to plastic, an intransigent material, difficult to work. Lalique experimented tirelessly with techniques of carving and pressing the horn into moulds when it was heated and therefore malleable. The use of such a humble material marked another important break with tradition, as the material had been used in previous eras for small objects but not for important jewelry. Lalique was attracted by the natural colours and texture of the tactile material with its shifting clouds of misty translucency which he coloured, stained and carved to varying degrees of thickness to obtain different effects of simulating nature. Once again he was able to turn this tough material into a seemingly soft, floating substance, like the gossamer silver-coated wings of butterflies, velvet-soft clusters of spent petals. Perhaps the most entrancing technique associated with Lalique's horn jewelry was the "bloom" or iridescent coating he introduced, a patina which looked like an organic, sometimes ghostly skin.

In 1895 Lalique contributed jewels to the opening exhibition of S. Bing's Paris shop "La Maison de l'Art Nouveau", which gave the movement its name. Bing had been a leading Paris dealer in Oriental objects at a time of enormous interest in everything Japanese, when indeed Japonisme became the single most important contributing factor to Art Nouveau. The leaders of the incipient movement were captivated by the simplicity of Japanese design, the economy of line that produced the most striking effects, the asymmetrical compositions and, above all, the deep reverence for nature. Japanese artists were able to portray nature with intimacy and drama, but without actually copying every surface detail. For Lalique, nature occupied a place of equal importance in life and art, and his transition from Japanese influence to Art Nouveau was particularly smooth. He understood the Japanese fascination with random patterns of nature, the curling planes of the iris petals, the haphazard design of fallen sycamore seeds. In his moody, nightmarish designs Lalique also interpreted the tendency of the Japanese to frighten themselves with images of the supernatural, the spirits that might haunt their dark pine forests, majestic mountains, and cascading waters.

Like the Japanese, Lalique was a brilliant master of atmosphere. He created a series of jewels depicting seasons such as winter woodlands sparkling in icy stillness, and jewels evoking different times of day: bright sunlight rippling on carved opal water, and gleaming on diamond studded shores, moonlight shining through a veil of cloud onto dusky owls. Lalique's perfection of cloisonné and *plique-à-jour* enamel was a further tribute to a great Japanese skill, while the large number of haircombs in his output paid homage to these decorative ornaments that played such an important role in femininity and daily life in Japan.

It was in the mid 1890s that Lalique began working with the great actress Sarah Bernhardt. Her flamboyant and adventurous personality acted as a catalyst on Lalique's fertile imagination at a crucial point in his career. He was probably introduced to Bernhardt by Robert de Montesquiou, the aesthete and critic. Montesquiou was very encouraging to young artists, and both he and Bernhardt commissioned from Lalique rings set with star sapphires, which they exchanged. Lalique made Bernhardt's stage jewels between 1891 and 1894 for her roles as Iseyl

and Gismonde and designed jewels for
various productions of *Théodora*, which
may or may not have been made up. An
accomplished artist and sculptress herself,
Bernhardt was both patroness and inspiration to the artists and designers around her.
Undoubtedly Lalique's work for Bernhardt and for the theatre encouraged his
own impulse towards drama and fantasy in
jewels, and freed him from the usual inhibi-
tions of size, cost and materials.

Lalique's portrayal of the female face and
figure in his jewelry not only reflects the
cult of femininity that dominated the age,
but illustrates particular characteristics,
including a bizarre blend of sexuality and
death. The symbolists were similarly ob-
sessed with woman as a symbol of nature,
of fertility, also of predatory seduction.
The Belle Epoque fell under the spell of its
luscious females, singers, actresses, dan-
cers, courtesans.

In Lalique's jewels, sinuously graceful
yet classical bodies, always shown in writh-
ing Rodin-like movement, suggest unbri-
dled sensuality, yet the faces are always
curiously passive, androgynous, mask-like.
To compound this vision, Lalique chose
unexpected materials for his female faces,
moulded glass shrouded in a ghostly patina
of opalescent enamel, or deep turquoise
scarred with matrix.

It was probably Bernhardt who introduced Lalique to Calouste Gulbenkian, the
gifted and discerning millionaire-collector
of fine art and objects. Around 1895
Gulbenkian commissioned from Lalique a
series of 145 jewels and objects, giving the
artist a free hand and providing the kind of
patronage every artist must dream of. The
Gulbenkian jewels made from 1895 to 1910
or 1912 were the most fantastic, original
jewels of Lalique's career, and arguably of
any age. They marked the high point of
Lalique's work and of Art Nouveau jewelry
in general. The Gulbenkian jewels were
shown by Lalique at various exhibitions at
the turn of the century, and are now housed
permanently at the Museum of the
Calouste Gulbenkian Foundation in Lisbon. Although they could all be worn, they
were certainly never intended as wearable
accessories; they were *objets de vitrine*, sheer
flights of fantasy expressed with consum-
mate skill and artistry, and they represent
every aspect of Lalique's talent and imagination from macabre and decadent images

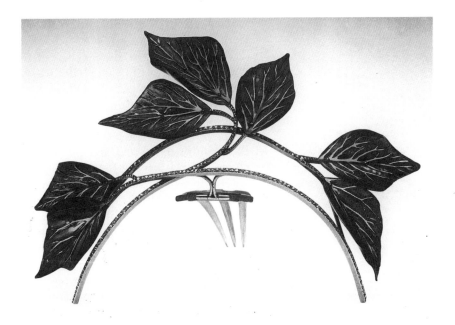

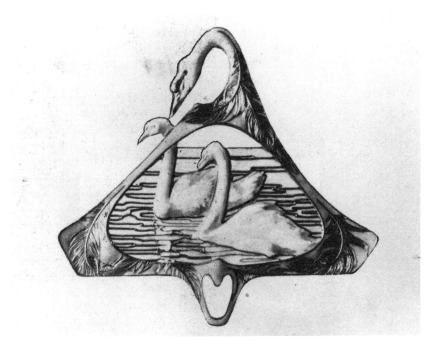

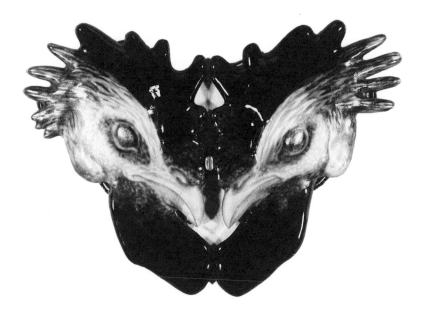

LALIQUE

to serene and brilliantly observed representations of nature.

The themes of the Gulbenkian jewels illustrate the range of Lalique's decorative vocabulary. Flowers and plant life include soft full-blown roses, the lusciousness of hanging wisteria, heavy, ripe cherries, the Oriental charm of the *prunus* branch, the exoticism of the orchid and the humble charm of field flowers. Reptiles, fish and sea creatures recall the continuous swaying movements of water and suggest prehistoric life, the repulsive elegance of strange animals that dwell at the bottom of the ocean. Insects like grasshoppers look shimmering and translucent, hovering mayflies become magical and ethereal, beetles are black and menacing. Lalique made much use of bats, while his bird motifs range from the proud peacock, the gliding swan (symbol of pride and metamorphosis), and cockerel (symbol of France and dawn), through owls and plump doves, to vultures and terrifying eagles in shadowy silhouette. The peacock was the quintessential motif of Art Nouveau jewelry, symbol of nature's magnificence and also of the narcissistic quality of the Art Nouveau movement in general.

After 1900 and his overwhelming success at the Exposition Universelle, Lalique was flooded with orders from all over the world. He took part in further major international exhibitions in Europe and in the United States: Turin 1902, Berlin 1903, St Louis 1904. With the world-wide revival of interest in the applied and decorative arts, newly established art schools and museums were eager to acquire the finest examples to encourage pupils with talent and potential in their own countries. The Hamburg Museum, directed at the time by Justus Brinckmann, acquired several examples of Lalique's work at the 1900 Exposition Universelle; and in the United States, industrialist Henry Walters purchased a number of jewels directly from Lalique at St Louis in 1904. The latter are now in the Walters Art Gallery, Baltimore.

Each new unveiling of Lalique's jewels and objects at the various Salons and Exhibitions was an eagerly awaited event, the subject of lengthy critical articles in contemporary art journals. He was invited to exhibit jewels in London at the Grafton Galleries in 1903 and then at Agnews in 1905. Since Gulbenkian was a client of Agnews, the exhibition included a section devoted to the Gulbenkian jewels and was also honoured with the presence of a jewel, a swan pendant with a border of peacock feathers, belonging to Queen Alexandra. The jewels were expensive: the costliest diadem was priced at £1,000, a sum of money which would certainly have purchased a good conventional diamond equivalent. On the whole, those with sufficiently adventurous, avant-garde taste could not afford Lalique's creations; as a result the sales at Agnews were not very good. A critic writing of the exhibition in *The Studio* in 1905 accused Lalique of concentrating "on the imitation of beautiful natural forms in unnatural looking materials, which suggest sometimes an unpleasant decadence".

In 1902 Lalique moved premises again to 40 Cours la Reine (now Cours Albert Ie), a five-storey town house designed specially to his requirements. The doors were made of panels of glass with pine cone motifs, echoed in the masonry and wrought-iron balconies. In 1905 he worked briefly with the sculptor Gaston Lachaise, expanding his team of colleagues. However, his jewels were entirely his own creations, and he designed every piece himself. Also in 1905 he opened a shop at 24 Place Vendôme and it was from this boutique that he began to sell the famous perfume bottles and glass objects that were gradually taking more of his time and attention.

Probably disillusioned with the vast flood of second-rate imitations that his jewels had inspired, and anticipating a lack of suitable patrons for his work, Lalique turned his attention entirely to glassmaking around 1910, when he bought the glassworks he had previously rented at Combs-La-Ville. His first glass exhibition was held at the Place Vendôme shop in 1912. His fame as a master glassmaker unfortunately eclipsed his genius as a jeweler and goldsmith. Upon his death in 1945, Calouste Gulbenkian expressed his conviction that Lalique had not yet received full credit for his contribution to the history of art. "I feel, I am absolutely convinced, that justice has not been done him yet. He ranks among the greatest figures in the history of art of all time, and his masterful touch, as well as his exquisite imagination, will excite the admiration of future cognoscenti."

VEVER

"Two names may be sufficient by themselves to represent the art of jewelry design, as seen on display at the Exposition Universelle: Lalique and Vever." Léonce Bénédite's pronouncement on the exhibition held in 1900 expressed a view largely shared by his contemporaries, and in particular by the panel judging the jewelry design category, who awarded a Grand Prix to each of these two jewelers.

Although René Lalique's creations are internationally recognized and admired, it is a different story for Henri Vever, whose name and jewels are known only to a handful of enthusiasts, and mainly through his masterly history of 19th-century jewelry, a peerless work of reference even today.

Vever was born into the third generation of a family of jewelers and goldsmiths. His grandfather Pierre Paul Vever (1794–1853), the son of a hotel-keeper, set up his business in Metz in 1821. After serving a long apprenticeship and living in Hanau and Vienna, his son Jean Jacques Ernest (1823–84) took over the business in 1848.

When the World Fair was held in Metz in 1861, Ernest Vever, by then established at 6 Rue Fabert, exhibited several designs from his workshops: "Gothic holy-water stoup in silver, Byzantine chalice in vermeil, Renaissance chalice in vermeil, bracelets, brooches, jewelry sets and necklaces in gold set with brilliants."

This succinctly worded list shows us that Ernest took his inspiration from the past and, like many of his contemporaries, made his name with what we now term historicism. Today a bracelet and a few silver charms are the only known surviving examples of the House of Vever's work during that period.

The Franco-Prussian War and the Treaty of Frankfurt which ended hostilities on 10 May 1871 soon forced the Vever family to flee their native Metz, which now became part of the German Empire. Ernest chose to establish himself in Paris where he bought up the business of Baugrand, who had died during the siege, and thus combined his old provincial factory with the workshops of a famous Parisian jeweler who had been one of Napoleon III's foremost suppliers. Cordially welcomed by his fellow jewelers in Paris, Ernest was appointed in 1874 judge of the Tribunal de Commerce in the Seine region, and then in 1875 he was made President of the Jewelers and Goldsmiths Trade Association, an important position he was to occupy until 1881, the year in which he retired from business.

Ernest was accompanied to Paris by his two sons, Paul and Henri, who were aged 20 and 17 respectively. Paul was admitted to the Ecole Polytechnique, while Henri received a technical and artistic education. He was apprenticed in the jewelry workshops of the Loguet brothers at 94 Rue du Temple; then, when he attained the status of craftsman, he began work with Hallet at 95 Rue des Petits-Champs, where he learned the crafts of jewelry-making and stone-setting. At the same time he embarked upon the study of professional design under Dufoug and later attended evening classes at the Ecole des Arts Décoratifs. In February 1873 he passed the entrance examination for the Ecole des Beaux-Arts, where he studied painting for two years under Millet and Gérôme.

In 1874 Paul and Henri became their father's partners. In accordance with their respective educations, Paul assisted his father with the administrative and commercial aspects of the business, while Henri helped to manage the artistic side. In their separate capacities both took part in the preparations for the next Exposition Universelle, which was to be held in Paris in 1878. Although Ernest, being a member of the panel of judges, could not enter the competition, he did present a display

A typical group of delicate pieces from the House of Vever in the turn-of-the-century Art Nouveau style, using diamonds, gold, pearls and precious gems. Below is a dog collar, "Pois de Senteur" (1900), composed of diamonds, rubies and enamel on a base of gold or silver.
Musée des Arts Décoratifs, Paris (photo Fonds Vever)

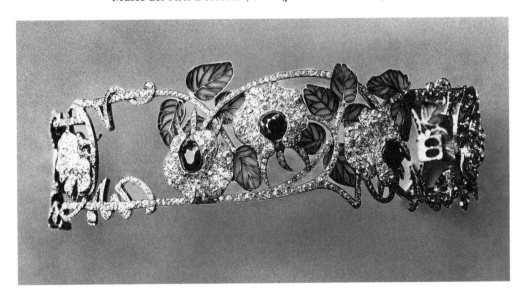

A necklace, or collar, in the Assyrian style in chased gold, designed by Ernest Vever and shown at the Paris Exposition Universelle in 1878. Musée des Arts Décoratifs, Paris

which caught the attention of professional craftsmen and public alike. He exhibited jeweled bouquets, a parure in the classical style studded with emeralds, and a necklace in the Greek style, set with pearls and brilliants. Most noteworthy of all, and showing great originality in an exhibition where the Renaissance style was predominant, was an Assyrian necklace in chased gold. Inspired by Oriental design, it had a triple interwoven chain hung with palms and lotus flowers, in alternation with rectangular tablets resembling cylindrical seals, each decorated with an animal, for example an ox, a lion, a wild boar, or an insect. These gradually decreased in size towards the clasp at the back.

In 1881 Ernest handed over the management of the family firm to his two sons. They were both to impart to the business fresh impetus which, in just a few years, resulted in their being among the finest jewelers in Paris. This rise to fame was confirmed at the Exposition Universelle of 1889 when Vever was awarded one of the two Grands Prix for jewelry design, the other prize going to Boucheron.

Vever's presentation brought together the richest and rarest jewels. There was a parure set with diamonds of every possible hue and a tiara with a 54-carat golden diamond as the centre stone, surrounded by diamond "sun-rays". The display also included a shell featuring an extremely rare rose brilliant and a Louis XVI "knot" with a 165-grain black pearl in the centre. For these exceptional stones, Vever designed classic settings; for less spectacular gems his settings had a floral theme in a naturalistic style: "Branches of rose trees, almond trees and strawberry plants in blossom, as well as orchids and all kinds of flowers, [are] set with such daintiness and so natural a movement that they might have been picked in the fields one beautiful frosty morning."

Opposite, a Renaissance style châtelaine and watch in gold, designed by Henri Vever in 1895.
To its right, a Renaissance pendant of gold, enamel, rose-cut diamonds and a hanging pearl
(1895). Below, a gilt bronze box with cameos in the Antique style and enamel (1889). Musée des
Arts Décoratifs, Paris (photos Georges Fessy)

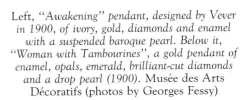

Left, "Awakening" pendant, designed by Vever in 1900, of ivory, gold, diamonds and enamel with a suspended baroque pearl. Below it, "Woman with Tambourines", a gold pendant of enamel, opals, emerald, brilliant-cut diamonds and a drop pearl (1900). Musée des Arts Décoratifs (photos by Georges Fessy)

Below, the "Perfume" pendant of 1900, designed by René Rozet in partially enameled gold, opals, brilliant-cut diamonds and a suspended pearl. Musée des Arts Décoratifs (photo Georges Fessy)

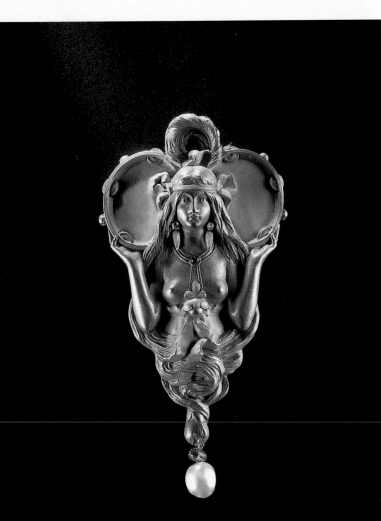

Opposite, the "Omphale" necklace designed by Eugène Grasset in 1900; gold, silver, enamel, red jasper, rubies, turquoises, emeralds and brilliant-cut diamonds. Musée des Arts Décoratifs (photo Georges Fessy)

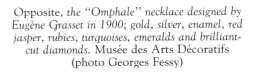

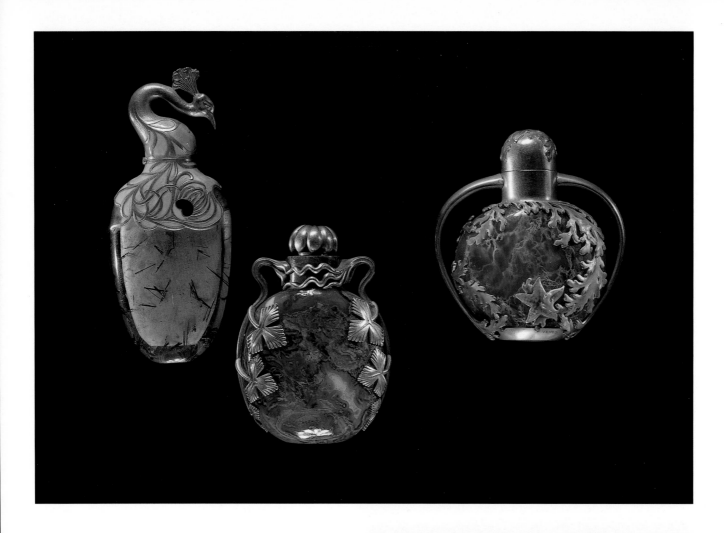

Above, *three Vever bottles of 1900 in gold,*
agate and crystal. Musée des Arts Décoratifs
(photo Georges Fessy)
Right, *an elaborate bottle of 1900 in rock-crystal*
with enameled gold decoration. Musée des Arts
Décoratifs (photo Georges Fessy)

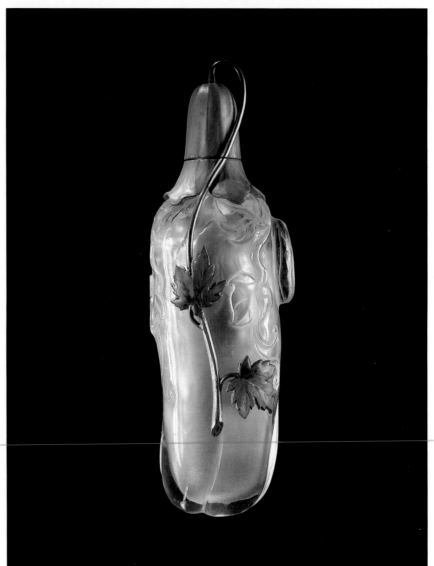

148

Two combs of 1900. Above, mistletoe, composed of gold, enamel, tortoiseshell and pearls. Right, an owl, made of horn, gold, translucent enamel à jour, cabochon emeralds and rose-cut diamonds.
Musée des Arts Décoratifs
(photo L. Sully-Jaulmes)
Above right, a 1900 pendant called "La Bretonne", made of gold, enamel, opals, diamonds and amethysts. Private collection

Left, *a brooch of 1900 called "Apparitions", designed by Grasset and made of gold, ivory and enamel.* Musée des Arts Décoratifs (photo Georges Fessy)

Left, *a "peacock" belt-buckle design of 1900 by Grasset, of gold, enamel and cabochon cornelians.* Musée des Arts Décoratifs (photo Georges Fessy)

An elaborate pendant of 1900 called "Silvia": gold, agate, ruby, enamel and brilliant-cut diamonds. Musée des Arts Décoratifs (photo Georges Fessy)

Above, *a belt-buckle design of hornets (1907): carved gold and enamel. Musée des Arts Décoratifs* (photo L. Sully-Jaulmes)

Above, *a belt-buckle of 1897 with an iris design, made of gold and translucent enamel à jour.* Musée de l'Horlogerie et d'Emaillerie, Genève (photo Jean-Marc Yersin)

The "Syracuse" belt-buckle (1900), made of gold, enamel and cabochon emerald. Musée des Arts Décoratifs (photo Georges Fessy)

Vever also used flowers as a source of inspiration for his work as a goldsmith, which won him the compliments of the critic Roger Marx: "M. Vever has had the happy notion of rebelling; he has opened his windows wide onto the countryside, fashioning mimosa blossoms and newly gathered roses in silver repoussé-work." Among the items in its collections the Musée des Arts Décoratifs in Paris has a silver sugar bowl and coffee pot decorated with eucalyptus leaves, Virginia creeper, convolvulus flowers and roses, all executed in repoussé.

The House of Vever became equally famous in the field of new techniques, including the different methods of applying enamel; for instance, translucent enamel *à jour* enhanced an Oriental-style lamp, while enamel painted in the Limoges style was used for a portrait of Vittoria Colonna by Paul Grandhomme and *basse-taille* enameling was applied to a small, round mirror, which bore a scene in the medieval style.

The Vever brothers' choice of themes shows considerable eclecticism. They took their inspiration from classical times for mirrors and a casket decorated with antique cameos linked with enameled tracery-work. They were also inspired by the Middle Ages and the East, while the French 18th century exerted an equally strong influence, as is evident from the bracelets decorated with pastoral scenes or the fables of La Fontaine, and a silver powder box adorned with a circle of putti, a work which may be attributed to the engraver Jules Brateau. He was known principally as a pewterer, although he worked for several jewelers, including Falize, Vever and Boucheron, and was himself a jewelry-maker.

In 1891 a French exhibition was organized in Moscow amid the climate of the new diplomatic relationship between France and Russia, which was to culminate in the famous Franco-Russian alliance of 1893. The exhibition, held in Petrovski Park, was much admired by the élite of Russian high society, and the House of Vever's display was undoubtedly one of the main attractions. In the centre were six parures, all of exceptional rarity. One was adorned with white pearls, while the others were studded with sapphires, rubies or emeralds; finally, one featured black pearls

mounted with clusters of brilliants. Alongside some items which had already been exhibited in 1889 were displayed new creations from the House of Vever, including *bonbonnières* in rock-crystal set with enamel and diamonds, flagons of hard stones and a series of flowers and butterflies in gold and silver covered with semi-transparent, iridescent enamel.

The new trend which took the theme of nature and the humblest plants as a source of inspiration was already reflected in certain Vever creations from 1889, as is evident from the House's display for the Exposition Universelle of that year. The movement appeared for the first time in 1889 in the work of jewelers like Vever and Falize and gained in popularity until it triumphed in 1900 as "Art Nouveau", in which the principal themes of flora and fauna became linked with the female form.

It was from 1895, however, on the occasion of René Lalique's exhibition at the Salon des Artistes Français, that the most perfect examples of Art Nouveau in the field of jewelry design were seen. Now precious metals, combined with other materials, took pride of place, in contrast to the art of mounting stones, where settings were overshadowed by the gems.

It cannot be disputed that Lalique influenced Vever in some measure, although Vever certainly forged his own personal style. Whereas Lalique rejected all categories and hierarchies to win artistic freedom, Vever wanted to bring about changes and developments within the confines of tradition. It was not his practice to combine processes and he mixed materials only in the most discreet ways. As a jeweler, he always attached great importance to the beauty and worth of gems and retained what some describe as "a bias in favour of precious stones". But if he did always use precious stones, he at least endeavoured to find new ways of magnifying their splendour. He abandoned the ubiquitous bouquets of wild flowers beloved by Oscar Massin in favour of the materials and flowers which Lalique had brought back into fashion: honesty, mistletoe, thistle, eucalyptus leaves, fuchsia, nasturtiums and cyclamen, which he fashioned in opal, ivory and enamel. Henri Vever himself encapsulated this new trend: ". . . On the occasion of the impressive industrial exhibition of 1900, the House of Vever's chief

Design by Eugène Grasset for a pendant "Poésie" (1900) to be produced by Vever. Cooper Hewitt Museum, New York

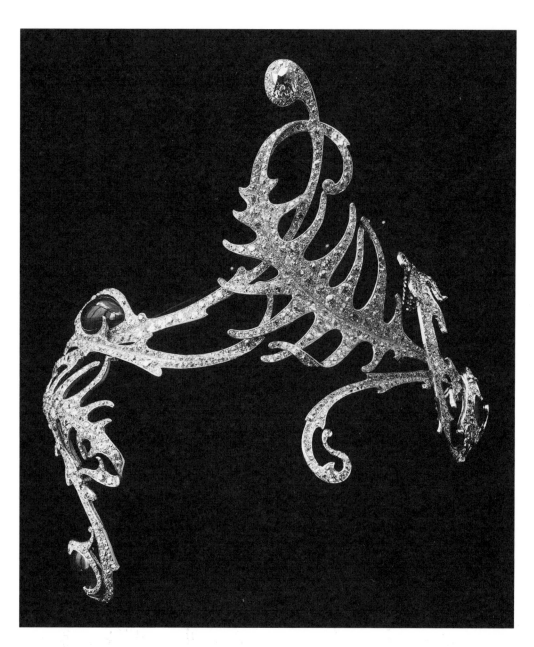

A *fern tiara of diamonds and gems (1900)*. Musée des Arts Décoratifs (photo Fonds Vever)

aim was to create only items which had an especial character of novelty, while remaining subject to the unchanging laws of balance and harmony essential to all fine composition."

It is certainly true that the House of Vever's presentation at the Exposition Universelle of 1900 revealed exceptional creative power not only in the number, but also in the quality, of the items on display: "Contrary to what is usually the case, these glass display cabinets do not contain a few important pieces intended for competition emerging from a flood of pieces which form part of everyday production. There are innumerable interesting themes, on which the jeweler wished to impress his personality. Each piece gives evidence of research

and has its own special fascination." The House of Vever's display was divided into two separate categories: one a personal contribution, the other creations based on the designs of Eugène Grasset.

Vever's greatest efforts were devoted to making jewelry set with gems, among which were a series of tiaras, each outstandingly original and showing perfect harmony of composition. These included a "fern" tiara, which had jagged diamond-studded "leaves" that encircled the temples and then curled upwards from the forehead, where they were decorated with a large yellow diamond. Another consisted of a simple circlet of diamonds above which waved a peacock-plume. The eye was made of opal, surrounded by diamond feathers. A third circlet featured a spray of honesty which adorned the front of the wearer's coiffure; some were set with diamonds, others made up of a series of opals. Several combs, which combined diamonds and enamel with horn, tortoiseshell or ivory, also drew on the floral theme for their designs; they form a group of exceptional quality and originality. One comb has five teeth in pale tortoiseshell, its upper part adorned with a coil of green enameled mistletoe leaves, spangled with pearls. In another model, the artist has created with opal-encrusted ivory two cyclamen leaves surmounted by flowers in translucent enamel faintly veined in gold. Others are decorated with hydrangea, thistles, carnations or parsley. The human form appears as a tenderly embracing couple, sculpted in ivory, while the animal kingdom is also represented by the head of an owl made of horn, its emerald eyes encircled with gold.

The metal jewelry comprised items in chased and enameled gold. There were pendants set with medals by Roty or Bottée, brooches and buckles where flowers and women played their decorative roles in accordance with the tastes of the day, with a great deal of ingenuity as well as restraint in design. For example, one pendant which attracted considerable attention was prettily decorated with the profile of a Breton girl wearing a traditional headdress. It is fashioned in ivory, opal and enamel against a background of flowering broom.

Together with these items which show such grace and harmony of composition, the House of Vever also presented about twenty pieces which were the result of a working partnership with the designer Eugène Grasset (1845–1917), who had already been active in the field of decorative arts before Vever asked him to design jewelry. Vever had certainly met Grasset through Charles Guillot, a printer who shared Vever's enthusiasms as a collector. Their first joint project was the binding for Launette's book *Quatre fils Aymon* (1883). Vever commissioned Grasset to produce a large design which was to be executed by Tourette in cloisonné enamel on gold and mounted on the front of the binding. This work, which was carried out from 1892 to 1894, was displayed at the Exposition Universelle of 1900, where it was much admired.

Henri Vever was not the only jeweler to call upon an artist outside the profession to design new pieces. That same year, Georges Fouquet entered into collaboration with the painter Alphonse Mucha. Although each designed very different creations, all their pieces may be described as "painters' jewels", for their effects were achieved as if by brush-strokes, with enamels or by colouring gold. The stones served solely as accessories, and the focal point of these jewels was their composition and the harmony of the colours used. Grasset, in fact, favoured more sombre hues. One set was described by Gustave Geffroy as being somewhat archaic and severe in appearance: "The workmanship was all very distinctive, the appearance magnificent yet deliberately austere. If a comparison had to be made, it could be likened to examples of Merovingian art, which remains an inimitable model, both for the soft, muted richness of its colours and the uncluttered amplitude of its form." Grasset decorated his jewelry, which was frequently described as "barbaric", with mythical female figures, animals or flowers. Nymphs swimming among the waves appear on a brooch or the upper part of a comb. On one impressive necklace Omphale, standing on a lionskin, holds Hercules' club on her shoulder; she is flanked by two cupids on clouds of opaque enamel studded with cabochon emeralds. The most successful pieces are a brooch in the form of a woman's head in profile, her hair adorned with a daisy, together with the motto, "Un peu, beaucoup, passionnément, pas du tout", and also a pendant called *Poésie*, the most feminine among these somewhat unpolished designs, which depicts in ivory the head and shoulders of a young woman with long blonde hair, playing the lyre. In the case of other creations, Grasset adapted the decoration to fit the purpose of the jewelry: on a belt buckle, for example, the head of a peacock joins up with the tip of its tail, thus forming a circle into which the bird's body is blended.

When the awards were presented, the House of Vever was given a Grand Prix for its display, but in particular for its setting of stones. Vever achieved first place because of the House's success in combining tradition with the new naturalistic trends. As Roger Marx explained, "M. Henri Vever appears to be the goldsmith destined to

A bookbinding produced by Vever in gold and enamel after a design by Eugène Grasset (c. 1883). Musée des Arts Décoratifs (photo Fonds Vever)

establish the transition between the old and new schools, between stone setting and decorative jewelry, between M. Massin and M. René Lalique.''

The success of Art Nouveau was, however, to be short-lived. From 1902, signs of exhaustion became apparent, and the young artists Maurice Dufrêne and Paul Follot tended towards less cluttered designs; shapes became more geometric, moving towards a stylized look. It was during this period that René Lalique gradually abandoned jewelry for glass design, and although certain jewelers, such as Feuillâtre and Gaillard, continued to work in the Art Nouveau tradition, others like Fouquet and Vever adapted their work to changing tastes.

This step proved particularly easy, as the move towards geometric shapes and more neutral tonality made the role of jewelry increasingly significant.

In 1907 the Vever brothers transferred their business from 19 Rue de la Paix to No. 14, a building they had commissioned on the site of the old Béral pharmacy. To coincide with the opening of their new establishment they presented a new collection of jewelry which strongly reflected the changes initiated over the past few years. The use of platinum instead of silver for jewelry mounts made it possible to fashion extremely fine threads, which were then pierced so that stones could be inserted. Although these creations were still inspired by floral themes, they were simpler and more geometric in design, as well as more synthesized in form.

On the death of his brother Paul, on 13 May 1915, Henri was left sole director of the family concern, but business suffered in the unfavourable conditions of wartime. In 1921 Henri, then aged 67, handed his share of the business to his nephews André and Pierre, Paul's sons. But it appears that they were unable to maintain the reputation of their House at the level it had reached under the direction of Paul and Henri Vever. The critic Emile Sedeyn wrote in 1923 that "their contribution to the business is still effective, but seems to be cautious and reserved". At the 1925 Exposition, several Vever pieces were noticed: bracelets with a cloud motif after the drawings of Jules Chadel, and a series of jewels made of precious stones and inspired by Persian miniatures.

André and Pierre Vever continued to run the firm until 1960, having enlarged it in 1924–25 by acquiring the House of Linzeler, to whom they were related. After 1927 the workshops no longer existed at 14 Rue de la Paix, and the execution of jewelry was entrusted to two or three studios that worked for Vever. In 1960 the House was taken over by Jean Vever, a grandson of Paul, who had worked with his uncles since 1934; then in 1982 all activities ceased.

Whenever Art Nouveau jewelry is mentioned, the name of Lalique immediately springs to mind. His current popularity frequently overshadows certain other jewelers of the same period, even though they would have been acknowledged by their contemporaries as his equals. Today, it is high time they were recognized as such. In the development of the new artistic movement that they all sought to foster, Lalique was undisputed master of decorative jewelry, but it was Vever who, by his harmonious and original creations, turned the setting of gems into a form of art.

FOUQUET

When the House of Fouquet received a prize at the Paris Exposition Universelle of 1900, it had already existed for forty years with a reputation well established by its founder Alphonse Fouquet. It was during the years after the First World War, under the management of his son Georges Fouquet, that the firm was to acquire international fame and become recognized as one of the leading jewelers in Paris. The name of Georges's son Jean, who later entered the business as well, eventually became associated with its most innovative creations. Unfortunately the 1929 crash proved to be catastrophic for the House of Fouquet; bankruptcy was unavoidable and in 1936 the shop in the Rue Royale was finally forced to close its doors.

Born in 1828 into a family of tradesmen established at Alençon, Alphonse Fouquet moved to Paris in 1838. Since his parents were financially unable to pay for his studies, he was apprenticed, at the age of 11, to a manufacturer of novelty jewelry. His master had premises in the Marais, traditionally the neighbourhood of jewelers, goldsmiths, clockmakers, engravers and gem-setters.

After a five-year apprenticeship, he left his master and worked for various manufacturers in turn. Starting out in workshops which produced inexpensive items, he was later employed by such jewelers as Charles Murat, Alexis Falize and Jules Chaise. By nature studious, he constantly sought to improve himself. He was an assiduous worker and was generally highly rated by his various employers, although circumstances and his own needs led him to change jobs frequently.

In 1855 he began to work for Rouvenat, where he first learned the techniques of jewelry making and was quickly caught up in the competitive atmosphere which prevailed on the eve of the first Exposition Universelle in Paris. He committed himself to the competition for a headdress to figure among the wedding presents of Ismail Pasha of Egypt, and created a spray of wild flowers arranged on a woman's profile, life size and modeled in wax. Rouvenat, who had never previously made jewelry using naturalistic flowers, was greatly attracted by Fouquet's project, which was chosen in preference to the other entries.

Encouraged by this first success, Alphonse began to teach himself, without any formal lessons, decorative design and flower drawing from life, and to create wax models for engraved jewelry. From 1854 he made designs which were sold to manufacturers by his brother, a jewelry sales agent.

In 1860 Alphonse joined forces with Eugène Deshayes and set up business at 176 Rue du Temple. Two years later they separated and Fouquet moved to the Rue aux Ours, first to no. 36 and subsequently to no. 53. It was only after his success at the Exposition Universelle of 1878 that he was able to leave the Marais and establish himself at 35 Avenue de l'Opéra.

From 1862 to 1868 he created jewelry decorated with interlacing motifs, delicately executed in pierced gold, and mounted with engraved gems, cameos, miniatures and paintings on enamel. Then in 1868 he began to specialize in "fantasy creations" in onyx set with rose-cut diamonds. He also produced jewels which combined cut turquoises with diamonds and pearls.

From the very beginning he employed about thirty workers, producing items for export to other European countries and as far afield as South America, where he sent "rich extravaganzas" made in what he termed "the finest style".

Top, *a photograph of the Fouquet shop in the Rue Royale which was designed for the firm by Alphonse Mucha. Musée des Arts Décoratifs, Paris*

Below, *various brooches and pendants designed by Alphonse Fouquet in 1866, consisting of engraved gems, cameos and enamel. Musée des Arts Décoratifs, Paris*

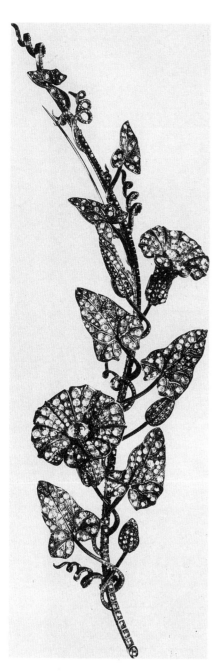

A bodice-clip by Alphonse Fouquet based on convolvulus flowers set with diamonds. Museum für Kunsthandwerk, Frankfurt (photo Rudolf Nagel)

Once his business was well established, he could turn his attention to the exhibition of 1878. He applied himself to this with great enthusiasm, but not without problems; creating outstanding pieces for the exhibition meant adding more work to an already heavy load. He presented various items of jewelry at the exhibition, some of them inspired by lace, such as a bracelet imitating Venetian point-lace and a necklace in the form of a "Medici ruff". Other pieces were inspired by the ancient world, notably an "Egyptian" necklace with two sphinxes and a diadem featuring a pair of chimeras confronting each other on both sides of a sapphire.

The jewels set with precious stones have disappeared, but the items made of gold still exist. Four of the surviving pieces are now owned by the Musée des Arts Décoratifs in Paris: a châtelaine in the form of a sphinx, a bracelet decorated with a figure of Diana, a "Renaissance" brooch featuring a portrait of Elizabeth of Austria after Clouet, and a châtelaine adorned with a portrait of the beautiful Florentine Bianca Capello. Designed by Alphonse, they were made in collaboration with the sculptor Carrier-Belleuse, the engravers Honoré Bourdoncle and Michaut, and the enameler Grandhomme.

A few years later, at the 1883 World's Fair in Amsterdam, Fouquet exhibited diamond necklaces which could also be worn as tiaras; their central motif was the head and shoulders of a winged woman. They were realistically modeled in the round, and no longer painted like miniatures as on the jewels of 1878. Although the necklaces themselves have disappeared, they are known to us through photographs and two drawings.

Although Froment-Meurice and his son, Jules Wiese and the Fannière brothers had, long before Fouquet, introduced the representation of the human figure into jewelry on cameos, medals, and bas- and high-reliefs, and François Désiré Froment-Meurice had even depicted female nudes on a pendant of 1854 showing the "toilet of Venus", Massin's remarks on the subject are always taken as a reference to the jewelry made by Fouquet in 1883. Massin, who shared the opinions of Charles Blanc, author of *L'Art et la Parure dans le Vêtement* (1875), considered that it was contrary to the rules of good taste for a woman to wear a reproduction of the human form on her head, neck or bosom. The matter was to be viewed quite differently a few years later by the creators of Art Nouveau, Lalique and Vever chief among them.

True to his concept of jewelry with finely designed representational subjects, Alphonse retained his preference for using mythical animals as a decorative motif right up to the end of his career. He produced bracelets in which the central motifs were dolphins or swans facing one another. Foliated scrolls and chimeras with coiled tails were used to decorate bangles. One of his favourite themes, which appeared on belt-buckles, brooches and cufflinks, was that of a chimera locked in combat with a serpent. It even formed the centrepiece of an impressive necklace, a wax model of which was exhibited at the Exposition Universelle of 1889. In Yvon's portrait of Madame Alphonse Fouquet, painted in 1887, she is wearing a brooch, pinned to her bodice, fashioned in the form of a pinecone with a rearing chimera.

Like the other jewelers of his time, Fouquet was interested in floral themes, as is shown by the designs he produced from 1880 to 1895, among them a bodice-clip in the form of convolvulus flowers, owned by the Kunsthandwerk Museum in Frankfurt. Lack of financial resources, however, prevented the creations of the House of Fouquet from approaching the splendour of those masterpieces of naturalistic jewelry which were being made during the same period by Boucheron and Vever.

ALPHONSE FOUQUET: opposite: top, *two gold châtelaines, one in the form of a sphinx, which were displayed at the 1878 Exposition. The portrait in enamel of Bianca Capello was painted on mother-of-pearl by E. Bérenger and P. Grandhomme.* Both courtesy of the
Musée des Arts Décoratifs, Paris
Below, *gouache design for a diadem with two chimeras. The diadem, which featured diamonds set in gold-plated silver and a central sapphire, was shown at the Exposition Universelle of 1878.*
Musée des Arts Décoratifs, Paris
Above it, *a design in gouache for a diadem or bracelet, the central motif consisting of the head and shoulders of a winged woman (1883).* Musée des Arts Décoratifs, Paris

GEORGES FOUQUET: opposite, *a gold corsage ornament in the form of a winged sea serpent, decorated with cloisonné enamel à jour, emeralds and baroque pearls (1902).* Private collection

Right, *"fuchsia" necklace (c. 1905). The portion encircling the wearer's neck is made of translucent enamel à jour, while the cascade of flowers is set with opals, pearls and brilliants.* Musée du Petit Palais, Paris

Below it is a *"thistle leaf" bracelet (1905–09) in gold and transparent enamel on coloured* paillons *with matrix opal.* Musée du Petit Palais, Paris

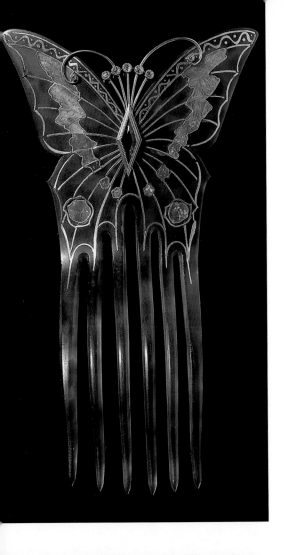

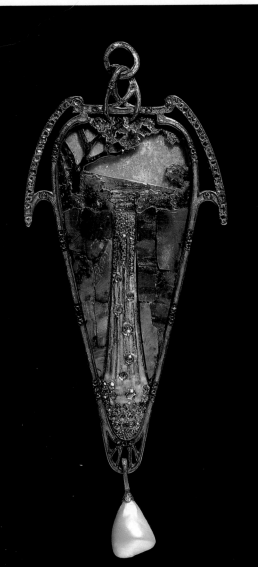

GEORGES FOUQUET: opposite: above, a "bramble" necklace (1912), fashioned from gold, enamel à jour on gold paillons, and rose-coloured pearls. Musée des Arts Décoratifs, Paris

Below it, a gold and glass paste pendant, decorated with rubies and a cabochon sapphire, in the form of a woman's profile against a swirling, trefoiled background (1899). Photo Sotheby's

Centre: above, butterfly haircomb (1899) of mottled tortoiseshell encrusted with opals mounted in gold, a lozenge-shaped amethyst and diamonds. Musée du Petit Palais, Paris

Beneath it, the "cascade" pendant. The setting of 1900 was originally used for a corsage clip designed by Alphonse Mucha, and then altered (probably in 1910) to introduce a waterfall. The materials used are gold, black opals, translucent enamel sur paillons and diamonds. Musée du Petit Palais, Paris

Above, the gold serpent bracelet, set with a mosaic of opals, enamel, rubies and diamonds, which was made for Sarah Bernhardt and based on Alphonse Mucha's design (1899). Photo Christie's

Inset, a gold and opal ring made after a design by Mucha (1900). Private collection

165

GEORGES FOUQUET: above, *the diadem's modern setting preserves the original arrangement of the five aquamarines within their openwork surrounds composed of small arches. In the original diadem, these surrounds were set into a bandeau of translucent enamel à jour.* Wartski, London

Right, *a dress ornament (1920–25) in the form of a Chinese mask. The face is of enamel, the eyes and hair of onyx, pearls and jade, while the framework is set with diamonds.* Private collection (photo Tomas Heuer)

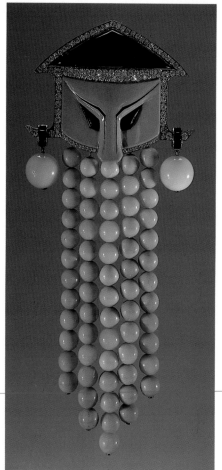

JEAN FOUQUET: opposite: above, *a necklace (1925–30) of gold, platinum, black lacquer and aquamarine.* Private collection (photo Tomas Heuer)

Below centre, *ring and bracelet of rock-crystal set with amethysts and moonstones in platinum (c. 1930).* Private collection (photo Tomas Heuer)

Far right, *ring and bracelet in gold and topaz (c. 1937).* Musée des Arts Décoratifs, Paris

166

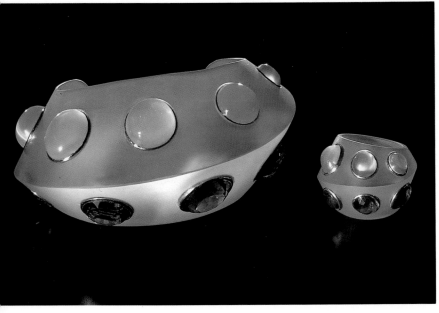

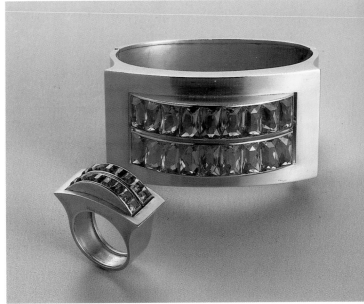

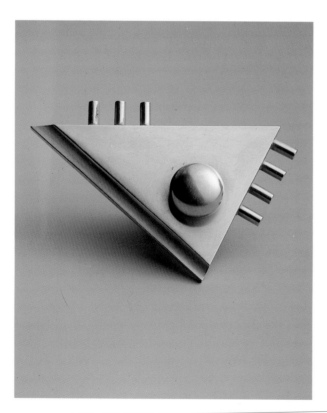

GEORGES FOUQUET:
Top left, *ivory and coral fibula brooch (c. 1923)*. Musée des
Arts Décoratifs, Paris
Left, *gold clip brooch based on a design by Lambert-Rucki
(1936–37)*. Musée des Arts Décoratifs, Paris
Above, *platinum brooch set with diamonds (1924). The disc
is of onyx, the cabochon and pendant stones coral.*
Private collection (photo Tomas Heuer)

In 1895, Alphonse handed over the running of the business to his son Georges, then aged thirty-three; but far from forsaking his interest in the jewelry trade, he took advantage of his retirement to write *Histoire de ma Vie Industrielle* (1898). This not only charts Alphonse's own career from 1839, but also describes the organization and development of the profession in Paris during the second half of the 19th century, explaining the hierarchy that existed within the workshops, the system according to which tasks were assigned, the relationship between the small specialist manufacturers and the well-known big companies, and also the organization of sales through agents.

Georges Fouquet had been working for his father's firm since 1880, learning the craft in the workshops and becoming familiar with the profession. Determined to secure the reputation of the family business, he was clearly interested in new ideas and was fortunate in becoming head of the firm in the key year of 1895, when all the elements which were to characterize Art Nouveau coalesced. That same year industrial art was finally permitted to appear alongside examples of decorative art at the Salon des Artistes Français in the Champs-Elysées. It was also in 1895 that Lalique exhibited his jewelry under his own name for the first time: previously he had used agents to present his creations to wholesalers. His work attracted the attention of critics and public alike, who found his designs innovative not only in their inspiration, but also in their execution. Lalique combined with metals and precious stones materials chosen for their decorative effect rather than their intrinsic worth, which punctured the whole notion of value linked to the possession of jewelry.

From that time onwards Lalique, Vever and Fouquet made art jewelry along with their settings of precious stones, and revived the tradition of fine, well-designed gold and enamel jewelry for which France had once been famous. These new items proved so popular that craftsmen and manufacturers began to produce them in increasing quantities. Consequently many inferior examples were bought by the public; the critics, however, were more discerning and recognized Lalique as the leading figure, followed by Vever and then Fouquet – whose creations were always singled out for "their perfect taste", as Henri Vever put it in his *La Bijouterie française au XIXème Siècle*.

Georges presented his first creations in 1898. Among other items, there was a brooch in the form of a lady's-slipper orchid and a tortoiseshell comb shaped like a butterfly, its wings veined in gold and encrusted with opals. His own style was already defined. The object of his jewels was not to imitate nature, but to draw on the world of flora and fauna for inspiration, to interpret and stylize its models.

Georges always maintained that creativity involved team effort, and he chose as his designer Charles Desrosiers, a former pupil of the painter Luc-Olivier Merson and of Eugène Grasset. Desrosiers, a teacher at a drawing school in Paris, was not connected with any commercial firm and designed jewelry only for the House of Fouquet. He met with Georges twice a week to discuss ideas and orders, and would then sketch the designs in his own workshop. His surviving drawings are undated, but their identification indicates that he designed all the models from 1898 to 1914.

In order to mount the most spectacular display possible at the Exposition Universelle of 1900, Georges sought the services of the Czech painter Alphonse Mucha to add to Desrosiers' contribution. The collaboration with Mucha was probably encouraged by Sarah Bernhardt at the time Fouquet was making her famous snake bracelet. It was usually Lalique who provided Bernhardt's theatre and private jewelry, while Mucha designed those she wore in the posters advertising her plays. In 1889 she asked Fouquet to make a bracelet for her based on drawings by Mucha. It was fashioned as a serpent coiled around the wrist with its head resting on her hand, and was joined by chains, as in some antique jewelry, to a finger-ring also in the form of a snake's head. The craftsmanship of the piece was remarkable not only for Fouquet's work with gold, enamel and opals, but also for the system of hinges which gave it its suppleness.

The pieces which Georges based on Mucha's drawings for the Exposition of 1900 were a departure from his usual style. There were imposing parures, consisting of jewels to adorn the hair or bodice, with chains linking their various components. All that remains of these eye-catching en-

A pendant designed by Georges Fouquet set with diamonds, mother-of-pearl, gems and hard stones (1927). Musée des Arts Décoratifs, Archives Fouquet

sembles are some old photographs showing them in glass display cases, also designed by Mucha. Some of the elements, however, still exist, among them a large bodice-clip with a centrepiece featuring the face of a woman in ivory, her hair fashioned from chased gold and surrounded by a halo set with opals. The central ornament of a large necklace also survives: a miniature of a seated young woman lost in reverie, her hair billowing loosely around her like a wave. Other fragments have been detached from their settings and dispersed; some were later remounted in different settings. The workmanship of these parures is always flawless, whatever material Fouquet was using: different shades of engraved gold, baroque pearls and stones shaped into charms, combined with miniatures painted on ivory or mother-of-pearl, cloisonné à jour enamels, opals or pale-coloured horn.

The critics were either admiring of the inventiveness which evoked a Byzantine ostentation of goddesses with bare arms and breasts, the "eternal feminine", or else they were shocked by these "dreadful harnesses".

While preparing for the exhibition of 1900, Georges was also thinking of moving to new premises with a modern, fashionable decor that would attract and impress new clients. He chose a location in the Rue Royale opposite Maxim's restaurant, not far from the shop opened by Sandoz in 1895, and commissioned Mucha to design the window displays and the layout of the interior.

For the centre of the façade between the two windows, Mucha designed a bronze bas-relief nearly ten feet high, which depicted a veiled female nude holding out jewelry similar to the pieces he himself had drawn. The salesroom itself was even more elaborate with its counters, decorative wood panelling and sculpture. Some years later, when Art Nouveau was no longer in fashion, this remarkable decor was to be dismounted; and just after the 1914–18 war it was replaced by a more ordinary design. The original has, however, recently been reassembled and installed by the Paris City Council in the Hôtel Le Peletier de Saint Fargeau, the new extension of the Musée Carnavalet.

In the Rue Royale workshop all the jewelry which was to make Fouquet's repu-

tation was created under the management of the foreman, Louis Fertey. The numerous designs by Desrosiers, old photographs, and illustrations in contemporary journals, all give a clear idea of the genre and style of these pieces. Those which survive demonstrate the high quality of their workmanship: the way the gold is treated, the use of unusual stones like opals and baroque pearls, and in particular the skill in cloisonné à jour enamel.

The enameler Georges used was Etienne Tourette, who had studied under the famous Louis Houillon. Tourette presented his first enamel appliqués for jewels in 1897, and from then on he worked for Fouquet, who wrote: "I particularly liked the way enamel gave a jewel its bright colour. Tourette and I studied ways in which we could improve the vivid enamels to catch and reflect the light." For this purpose, a background of worked gold would be covered with a fine layer of translucent enamel. Another technique was also devised to create a transparent effect in metal cloisons without a background for the petals of flowers and insects' wings. This was more suitable for earrings or hair-ornaments. Tourette, however, sought to increase the possible range by the use of translucent enamels. In the case of jewels to be worn against the skin or on clothing, he would scatter small fragments of metal (paillons) into the enamel, or engrave it with ripples of acid, in order to make it sparkle when it caught the light.

The workshop produced the various types of jewels popular at that time; diadems, brooches, belt-buckles, bracelets, rings, combs of pale-coloured horn and choker-style necklaces known as "dog-collars", which generally consisted of a small plaque held in place by rows of pearls. There were also pendants, necklaces decorated with a central motif, and chains which were worn knotted and which had a small metal tag at each end. Bodice-clips, triangular in shape, were intended to be worn in the middle of the bust.

The themes of nature, both flora and fauna, were frequently exploited and their various elements combined: for example, a large bodice-clip which featured a winged serpent and a bundle of seaweed. Fouquet used the wavy lines popular in the period to suggest a woman's hair, the plumes of a bird's tail, or the stem of a flower.

Mostly, the motifs were symmetrically divided by an axis at various points and set in a frame of small diamonds. Nature was not imitated; unlike Lalique, Fouquet did not reproduce "real" flowers. Nor were there examples of symbolism, as in the pieces designed by Grasset for Vever.

At the Brussels Exhibition in 1910, Fouquet presented jewels of a new type: circular pendants and a diadem in the form of a bandeau consisting of five oval motifs. In the centre of each of these ovals was a large aquamarine surrounded by an openwork design made up of small arches set with lines of diamonds. Georges had such a strong predilection for this blue stone that dealers dubbed him "the father of aquamarine".

The changing style in jewelry beginning around 1910 was linked to developments in women's fashion, which underwent a revolution after the First World War. Long cumbersome dresses were replaced by new designs made up in soft materials. Skirts became shorter, revealing first the ankles, then the legs. The waist was either very slightly accentuated, or else not at all. The neck, shoulders and arms were left bare. Choker-style necklaces were replaced by strings of pearls, tassels on chains or strands of braiding. Fibula brooches were worn as clips or belt-buckles and caught in folds of drapery. Bare arms were adorned with bracelets.

Hairstyles also changed. There were no more chignons to be embellished with combs or diadems. Instead, hair was cut short and worn with a headband. Long, dangling earrings were *de rigueur* and hats were adorned with decorative pins.

As new colours and colour combinations became fashionable, so new materials were brought into use by jewelers. The vogue for black and white, for instance, was reflected in black onyx jewelry set with diamonds. This austere combination was later enlivened by the addition of coral, jade and lapis-lazuli, and semi-precious stones like aquamarine, amethyst and topaz. Georges particularly admired large stones and anything out of the ordinary, for instance old engraved jade and matrix turquoise. He also favoured as an elegant setting for stones rock-crystal which had had the polish removed.

In 1925, when there was a question of mounting an Exposition Internationale des Arts Décoratifs, Georges played a significant role in convincing the exhibitors that they must be bolder and freshen up their objectives. In 1906, Georges had been secretary and recorder of the Exposition Internationale in Milan; the position he held in 1925 as President of the Jewelry Section was even more important, and the book he coordinated after the event, *La Bijouterie, la Joaillerie, la Bijouterie Fantaisie au XXème Siècle*, which described all the works featured in the exhibition, remains a most useful document.

During this period, Louis Fertey was the principal designer of models produced in the workshop, but for the display at the 1925 Exposition Georges Fouquet also called on artists such as the architect Eric Bagge, whom he had asked, in his capacity

Top, a tiara with aquamarines and enamel designed by Georges Fouquet in 1908. Musée des Arts Décoratifs, Archives Fouquet

Below, a brooch in the form of a mask based by Georges Fouquet on a design by A. Léveillé (1925). Musée des Arts Décoratifs, Archives Fouquet

FOUQUET

A pendant and chain designed
by Jean Fouquet (1929);
polished platinum, cabochon
sapphire and diamonds.
Musée des Arts Décoratifs,
Archives Fouquet

as president, to plan the hall for the jewelry design section. In addition he commissioned work from the painter André Léveillé and the poster-artist Cassandre (André Mouron), and the pieces based on their designs attracted a good deal of attention. They are well known to us from photographs and various glowing accounts that appeared in the press. A few surviving examples enable us to appreciate their beauty, originality and superb workmanship.

A new style was born with the effort of each of the thirty jewelers invited to show "only pieces of genuine originality, drawing on new sources of inspiration." Jewelry, like all the other sections of decorative art, bore the stamp of the times; shapes were simplified, even made geometric, and reduced under the influence of Cubism to a juxtaposition of abstract motifs. The exhibition had the merit of familiarizing the public with the new production, and over the next few years costume jewelers were to show the effects of this change.

Georges Fouquet never tired of repeating that a jewel should "be in harmony with the personality of the woman who wears it" and that "it forms part of her toilette". At one point, he might have convinced himself that his ideas were to be realized, so well matched were *haute couture* and jewelry; and in 1927 he even persuaded the couturier Jean Patou to feature jewelry from the House of Fouquet in presenting his collections. But in the years that followed, the two types of design became separated again. The idea of linking jewelry and fashion was possible when the jewels were of only moderate value, composed of inexpensive stones. During the 1930s, however, the use of extremely valuable gems made jewelry a speculative investment, and as a result settings became less original. Couturiers individualized their styles and created their own collections of accessories and jewelry, while clothing manufacturers produced standardized streetwear in bulk.

In 1929 Georges took the initiative in arranging an exhibition devoted to jewelry and goldsmiths' work at which he re-stated his views on design: "Every piece of jewelry must be based on an idea, those made of a single, costly stone as well as those made up of several gems. A jewel should not give the impression of a company badge through the repeated uniformity of its setting."

The name of Jean Fouquet first appeared at the exhibition of 1925. In 1926, 1927 and 1928 he went on to design necklaces and pendants, bracelets and rings of marked originality. All were large pieces, their workmanship and materials in harmony with their bold design. Most were made of white gold, their surfaces treated with a flat tint alternating with lacquered areas. The creative spirit behind these jewels links them with those of the young artists of that generation: Raymond Templier, Paul Brandt and Gérard Sandoz. In 1931 Jean published *Bijoux et Orfèvrerie*, in which he set forth his creed: "A jewel should consist of pieces visible from afar; miniatures are loathsome." And he expressed his personal view on the ultimate aim of creation: "Jewels and pieces of goldwork should constitute works of art while meeting the requirements of industrial items."

It was during this period that geometric designs were being succeeded by curved lines: Jean Fouquet created the first ring in this style in 1931, and a bracelet and a ring that figured in the 1937 Exposition testify to its culmination. Although the House of Fouquet had by then been forced to close, it participated in the exhibition with pieces created by independent manufacturers after models by Jean Fouquet and the sculptor Jean Lambert-Rucki.

After the Second World War, Jean Fouquet continued to take on private commissions, and the work was done for him by Charles and Pierre Fertey, son and grandson of Georges's foreman. In the 1950s he created jewels made of rounded wires moulded into either brooches in the form of a kind of loop decorated with gems, or rings shaped like a spring. Working with the enameler Gaston Richet, a former pupil of Tourette, he brought back into fashion translucent enamel, which was used to create palm designs, waves or leaves.

The Fouquets held an important position in Paris, mainly between 1878 and 1930, a highly creative period. Individually Alphonse, Georges and Jean made significant and original contributions to the development of fashion and taste. Through drawings and old photographs we are able to appreciate their entire production, and we recognize their originality by means of the great number of their jewels that survive.

Emperors, kings, queens, presidents, captains of industry and theatrical stars have all passed through the portals of Tiffany & Co. Although there is no American equivalent to "By Royal Appointment", the firm has been designated jeweler and silversmith to many royal houses throughout the world, thus achieving that status even without official sanction. When President Abraham Lincoln wished to present a special gift to his wife to wear at his inauguration, he turned to Tiffany's. Many years later, when Jacqueline Kennedy became First Lady, the President-elect ordered a strawberry clip for her, designed by Jean Schlumberger for Tiffany.

The glamour of Tiffany jewels has tempted European royalty as well as American dignitaries. Empress Eugénie of France, famous for her sumptuous jewels, added the "Queen Pearl", a fine American pearl weighing 93 grains, to her collection. Such famous personalities as Lillie Langtry, Diamond Jim Brady, Lillian Russell, and Sarah Bernhardt bedecked themselves with diamond-and-pearl jewelry by Tiffany.

The birth of the firm dates to 21 September 1837 when Charles L. Tiffany and John B. Young opened the first store, known as Tiffany & Young, at 259 Broadway in New York City. Stationery and fancy goods, including fans, Chinese goods, umbrellas, pottery, and "curiosities of every description" filled their shelves. In 1841, Jabez L. Ellis joined the firm and the name was changed to Tiffany, Young & Ellis. With a new partner and added capital, John Young was able to travel abroad to secure the latest European merchandise, initially imitation jewelry from France and Germany and, in 1844, gold jewelry. The firm's first catalogue, published the following year, advertised "a new style of bracelets, hair pins, dress combs, head ornaments, chatelaines, scarf pins, brooches, shawl pins, chains, etc. in gold and imitation" from London, Paris, and Rome. In the year 1848 the firm began the manufacture of gold jewelry, which quickly became one of the most important branches of their business.

Charles Tiffany, a businessman and entrepreneur of genius, relied upon the expertise of others. His brilliance lay in promotion and he seized every opportunity to promote the name of the store. During the political disturbances in Paris in 1848, when the value of diamonds declined by 50 per cent, John Young, who had arrived there to buy jewelry and European novelties, decided to divert the funds at his disposal to invest in diamonds. This first large purchase of gems was followed by many others, such as the acquisition of the girdle of diamonds reputedly once owned by Marie-Antoinette, and diamonds from the estate of the Hungarian Prince Esterhazy.

Gideon F.T. Reed, formerly of the Boston jewelers Lincoln, Reed & Co., became a partner in 1850. He established a branch in Paris, at 79 Rue Richelieu, which became known as Tiffany & Reed. Operating from this store, he purchased precious stones and was able to secure select merchandise for the "diamond parlor" at the New York establishment.

Steady expansion of the business prompted several moves uptown, to 271 Broadway in 1847, and to 550 Broadway in 1854. When Young and Ellis retired on 1 May 1853, the name of the firm was changed to Tiffany & Co., as it remains today.

The firm was incorporated on 1 May 1868, with Charles Tiffany designated president and treasurer. The same year, a branch was established in London with offices at 29 Argyll Street. The first Geneva office was opened at 7 Rue Leverrier in 1868, and it was followed a few years later with a salesroom for watches, jewelry and

Above, an extraordinary tiara of diamonds and turquoise exhibited at the 1900 Exposition
Universelle in Paris. The centre section can be detached and worn as a corsage ornament.

Below, a flexible collar or neck ornament, composed of 547 Montana sapphires and 299
diamonds, which took 1,800 hours to produce. It, too, was exhibited in Paris in 1900.

This peacock feather aigrette features a 30-carat canary diamond which was once part of the Duke of Brunswick Collection. It was exhibited in the 1876 Philadelphia Centennial and this engraving appeared in Jeweler's Circular, 1877.

diamonds. In 1872, Tiffany's started a watch factory in the Place Cornavin in Geneva; however, "the conditions surrounding European labor were found to be wholly inapplicable to American methods" and it was closed a few years later.

In 1870, Tiffany's moved its New York headquarters to Union Square, commissioning one of the first fireproof buildings in the city, with a stock of jewelry, silver, watches, diamonds, fancy goods, leather goods, and stationery that was expanded to include displays of art works in bronze, statuary, bric-a-brac, clocks, mantel sets, lamps, curios, reproductions of ancient armour, porcelain, and glassware. Before public museums became widely available to the general public in America, Tiffany's was regarded as an "Art Emporium", a museum of industrial art, and advertised itself as such. One reviewer noted that "seeing Tiffany's in an afternoon is like seeing Europe in three months."

Tiffany's participated in major expositions in the latter half of the 19th century, winning numerous awards and honours. These world fairs elevated Tiffany's from a small company into an international house with world-wide recognition. At their first venture, the New York Crystal Palace Exhibition of 1853, the firm showed several examples of strung pearl work which were considered as precious as diamonds in cost and beauty.

At the 1876 Philadelphia Centennial, Tiffany's displayed unmounted stones – diamonds, emeralds, rubies, sapphires, opals, cat's eyes – as well as a four-string necklace of Oriental pearls and a ring set with an American pearl, the only example of its kind in the exhibition. Conch shell jewelry, the latest fashion in Paris, was shown along with gemstone jewelry.

Upon the opening of the diamond mines in South Africa in the early 1870s, diamonds had become more plentiful, and Tiffany's display at the Centennial was the first opportunity for many Americans to view the glittering stones. One of the most remarkable specimens of diamond setting, according to a review at the time, was a "perfect imitation of a full blown rose, every leaf is detached and crusted with small white diamonds of the very purest

water." The highlight of the exhibition was a "Peacock Feather" hair ornament. The centre of the feather consisted of a 30-carat lemon-yellow diamond, purchased at the Duke of Brunswick auction in Geneva in 1874, surrounded by over six hundred diamonds, the ensemble fashioned in such a way as to quiver at the slightest movement. The quill was supported by a light platinum structure, a metal that Tiffany's was starting to use in jewelry and also to adorn their Japanesque silverware.

Herman Marcus represented Tiffany's at the 1878 Paris Exposition Universelle. Marcus had worked with Tiffany's in the 1850s when he first arrived in the US from Germany, and returned to the firm in 1877 after his own company, Starr & Marcus, was dissolved. Notable jewelry exhibited at this exposition included examples in the Japanesque style as well as reproductions of the Curium treasures that were discovered by the American Consul in Cyprus, General Luigi Palma di Cesnola. The firm did not show any pieces specially designed for the exhibition, but preferred to send examples from their stock which, they believed, would "give a fairer average view of their capabilities."

Tiffany's received many awards at the Paris Exposition, especially for its innovative Japanesque silver, decorated with metal alloys, as well as a gold medal for jewelry. Charles Tiffany was named a Chevalier of the Légion d'Honneur and received the Gold Medal "Praemia Digno" from the Emperor of Russia. There followed numerous appointments as jeweler and silversmith to many of the monarchs throughout the world, including Queen Victoria of England, the Emperor of Germany, the Grand Dukes Alexis, Paul, and Sergius of Russia, and the Khédive of Egypt.

The mines of South Africa were yielding not only large quantities of diamonds but also fancy coloured stones. Perhaps the best known example, the Tiffany Diamond, weighed 287.42 carats in the rough when it was discovered in 1878 in the Kimberley Mines. The largest and finest canary diamond in existence at the time, it was transferred to Paris and cut into a cushion shape of 128.54 carats with ninety facets to maximize its brilliance.

A selection of six enameled orchid brooches, set with precious stones. These were exhibited at Tiffany's stand in the Paris Exposition Universelle of 1889. Collection of Ruth and Joseph Sataloff

Below, *the gold corsage ornament in the form of a life-size iris is set with 139 sapphires from Montana, as well as demantoid garnets, topaz and diamonds. It was exhibited at the Paris Exposition Universelle of 1900 and was bought by the railroad magnate and art collector Henry Walters. Walters Art Gallery, Baltimore*

Below right, *a gold and platinum corsage ornament in the shape of a chrysanthemum, the flower composed of American freshwater pearls, and the leaves set with diamonds (c. 1900). Photo courtesy Wartski, London*

177

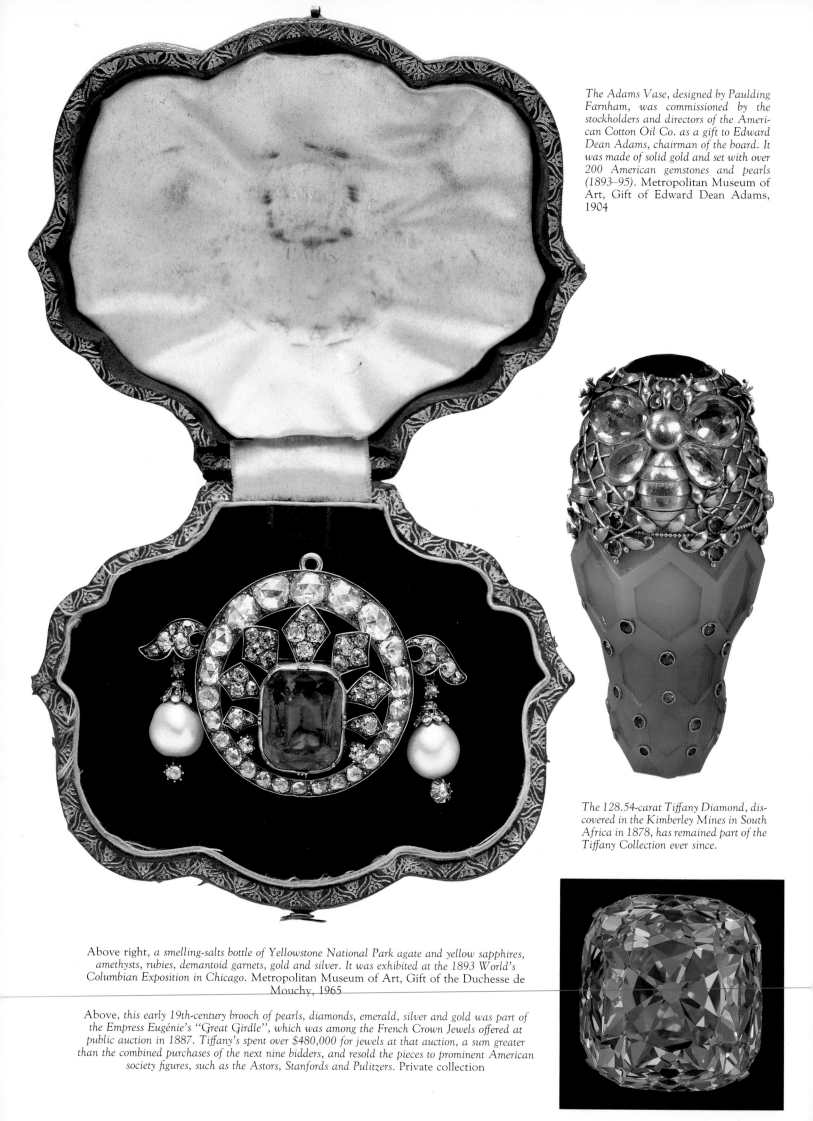

The Adams Vase, designed by Paulding Farnham, was commissioned by the stockholders and directors of the American Cotton Oil Co. as a gift to Edward Dean Adams, chairman of the board. It was made of solid gold and set with over 200 American gemstones and pearls (1893–95). Metropolitan Museum of Art, Gift of Edward Dean Adams, 1904

The 128.54-carat Tiffany Diamond, discovered in the Kimberley Mines in South Africa in 1878, has remained part of the Tiffany Collection ever since.

Above right, *a smelling-salts bottle of Yellowstone National Park agate and yellow sapphires, amethysts, rubies, demantoid garnets, gold and silver. It was exhibited at the 1893 World's Columbian Exposition in Chicago. Metropolitan Museum of Art, Gift of the Duchesse de Mouchy, 1965*

Above, *this early 19th-century brooch of pearls, diamonds, emerald, silver and gold was part of the Empress Eugénie's "Great Girdle", which was among the French Crown Jewels offered at public auction in 1887. Tiffany's spent over $480,000 for jewels at that auction, a sum greater than the combined purchases of the next nine bidders, and resold the pieces to prominent American society figures, such as the Astors, Stanfords and Pulitzers. Private collection*

Opposite, *an enameled necklace designed by Louis Comfort Tiffany, set with Mexican opals and pearls (c. 1905). Virginia Museum of Fine Arts, Gift of Sydney and Frances Lewis*

Above, *the enameled "Peacock" necklace designed by Louis Comfort Tiffany, set with opals, amethysts, sapphires, demantoid garnets, rubies and emeralds (c. 1905). Charles Hosmer Morse Museum of American Art, Winter Park, FL*

Left, *a pendant/brooch set with pink topaz, amethysts, fancy coloured sapphires and pearls; designed around 1910 by Louis Comfort Tiffany and produced at Tiffany & Co. Tiffany Collection*

Above, *designs by Jean Schlumberger: the "Scarf" necklace set with diamonds, emeralds and sapphires (1956), and an elephant clip of transparent paillonè enamel, emeralds, diamonds, cabochon rubies, pear-shaped turquoise drop, grey spinels and white onyx (1967).*
Below, a dragon brooch designed by Donald Claflin, with diamond pavé body, emeralds, ruby, cabochon turquoise (1968). Tiffany Collection
Opposite, a necklace with a 106-carat tanzanite and diamonds in a twisted knot setting, designed by Angela Cummings (1982).
A brooch with a fancy yellow diamond of 107 carats, surrounded by 23 pear-shaped marquise diamonds (1988).
The clip of a 75-carat emerald, surrounded by 138 diamonds (1950), is known as the "Hooker" emerald after its original owner, Janet Annenberg Hooker. Smithsonian Institution, Gift of Janet Annenberg Hooker

Paloma Picasso wearing an elaborate Tiffany set of necklace and earrings, set with a wide selection of precious and semi-precious stones. (From Tiffany: 150 Years, published by Doubleday & Co.)

The traditional setting of diamond solitaires used bezel mountings, which encased the lower part, or pavilion, of the stone. In 1886, Tiffany's introduced the "Tiffany setting" which lifted the diamond away from the shank by supporting prongs, thus permitting light to penetrate from below to enhance the brilliance of the gem. This setting has become the standard for engagement rings.

The association of the Tiffany name with diamonds was due in large part to the acquisition at public auction in 1887 of a major share of the French Crown Jewels. These were part of the collection Empress Eugénie was forced to leave behind when she fled Paris in 1870. Tiffany's bought twenty-four lots for $480,000, a sum greater than the combined purchases of the nine next largest buyers. Among the articles acquired were five diamonds presumed to be from the Mazarin collection. Tiffany's sold the jewels either in their original mountings or in more modern settings. According to an 1887 estimate, Tiffany's vaults held over $40 million in precious stones. Some of the stones from this sale became part of the elaborate jewelry display of Tiffany's at the 1889 Paris Exposition Universelle. One diamond, weighing 25 carats, was the centre stone of a diamond necklace, valued at $175,000.

The Tiffany exhibit featured exotic subjects and material from the Americas, and was the first attempt at a purely "American art in jewel work". Some of the jewelry designs were derived from Native American artifacts created by the Navajo and Zuñi Indians of New Mexico, the Hupa Indians of North Carolina, and the Sitka and Chillkat Indians in Alaska. One piece, a brooch in the shape of a carved wooden mask used by medicine men of the Chillkat Indians, was set with rare brown pearls from Tennessee.

Also exhibited were twenty-five enameled orchids, perfect reproductions of nature, modeled after varieties found in New Mexico, Brazil, Guatemala, East India, and the Philippine Islands. The enameling technique for these orchids was perfected under the direction of Edward C. Moore, chief designer and director of the silver manufacturing division. Colours, true to nature in minute detail, were executed in hard, dull enamels. At the exposi-

tion, the orchids, suspended from the top of the display case, formed a canopy over the glittering diamond jewelry below. Before their journey to Paris, Tiffany's displayed the orchids in the New York store and sold them to individual customers, among them Jay Gould, who added several pieces to his natural orchid collection.

Paulding Farnham is credited with designing the jeweled articles exhibited at the 1889 exposition. He was the nephew of Charles T. Cook, who became president of the firm in 1902. Beginning at Tiffany's as a youth, Farnham received his art instruction at the "Tiffany School" under the tutelage of Edward Moore. This apprenticeship, together with his training as a sculptor, inspired and enabled him to transform decorative objects into works of art. Some of the finest Tiffany jeweled objects were created under his direction.

On 1 September 1879, George Frederick Kunz joined Tiffany's jewelry department. His expertise lay not in design or in gem setting but in gem selection. He travelled the world in search of mineral treasures, wrote prolifically of his findings, and was instrumental in placing Tiffany's at the forefront of discoveries in coloured gemstones and freshwater pearls. For the 1889 exposition, Kunz assembled a collection of native American gems, minerals and ornamental stones, among them sapphires from North Carolina, beryls and tourmalines from Maine, garnets from Arizona and New Mexico, an Oregon opal, arrowheads of quartz crystal, blocks of amber and jet, and the first samples of pectolite and wollastonite ever cut. This assemblage, known as the Tiffany Collection, as well as another collection of Kunz-gathered gemstones exhibited at the 1900 Paris Exposition, were purchased by J. Pierpont Morgan for the American Museum of Natural History in New York, and formed the nucleus of the museum's gem collection, known at the time as the Morgan Collection. In recognition of these eminent individuals, two stones were named for them: a violet pink variety of spodumene was called *kunzite* and a pink variety of beryl, *morganite*.

By 1893, Paulding Farnham had assumed the position of chief designer and director of the jewelry division. For the jewelry displayed at the 1893 Chicago Columbian Exposition, he turned to the artistic work

The original drawing (detail) made in 1886 of the "Tiffany setting"

of earlier periods such as 14th- and 15th-century Italian, old Hungarian, Russian, Portuguese, Turkish, Spanish, Egyptian, Greek, East Indian, Japanese and French. For this eclectic collection, Farnham collaborated with Kunz on the selection of appropriate diamonds and coloured gemstones for each article. One piece, a foulard or epaulette based on Spanish lace, contained 9 yellow sapphires, 861 emeralds and 1,072 diamonds. The lapidary arts were evident in such pieces as an East Indian bottle of carved jade and a smelling bottle of Yellowstone National Park agate, both set with coloured gemstones. Tiffany's also displayed a representative selection of every gem used in jewelry manufacture, a collection of American pearls, and a practical display of cutting and polishing diamonds.

Paulding Farnham transformed the art of jewelry into hollow-ware design by creating works of art in silver and gold that were jewel-like in appearance. Unusual stones such as hessonites, zircons, and spessartites were juxtaposed with another jewelers' technique, enameling. One example, the Adams Vase, is a *tour de force* of Renaissance inspiration. Solid gold and set with over 200 American gemstones, pearls and rock-crystal, the vase typifies the thoroughness of research that characterized Farnham's designs. Every detail was carefully examined from living plants and animals brought to the design studio.

At the 1900 Paris Exposition Universelle, Farnham, by then chief designer of both the jewelry and silver departments, received two gold medals. One piece from this exposition, the iris brooch, the most magnificent Tiffany jewel in existence, was fashioned out of 139 Montana sapphires. At $9\frac{1}{2}$ inches in length, this jewel would be difficult, if not uncomfortable, to wear. Another object, a life-size swallow Tiffany's exhibited in the 1901 Buffalo Pan-American Exposition, had a wing span of $7\frac{1}{2}$ inches. Beginning with the orchids displayed in the 1889 Paris Exposition, some Tiffany exhibits increased in size as they decreased in their usefulness as wearable pieces of jewelry. The iris and the swallow brooches are only two of the many pieces Farnham designed formally as jewelry, but intended as works of art.

For the 1904 St Louis Exposition, Farnham contributed silverware in the Renaissance style as well as an ornate diamond necklace with enameled figures in imitation of 16th-century Spanish jewelry. In the same display, Louis Comfort Tiffany exhibited examples of his jewelry, such as the medusa brooch and sprays of American wild flowers, enameled and set with gemstones.

Louis Comfort Tiffany, son of the firm's founder, became Vice President and Art Director of Tiffany's when his father died in 1902. His lamps, Favrile glass, pottery, and enamels, as well as his early experiments in jewelry, were retailed at the Tiffany store. Executed by Julia Munson at the Tiffany Furnaces, these early pieces, such as the peacock necklace, have a "hand wrought" appearance. On 3 May 1907, upon taking over the jewelry division of Tiffany Furnaces, Tiffany & Co. established a special "Art Jewelry" department for the manufacture and sale of Louis Tiffany's jewelry on the sixth floor of the store, which had moved in 1905 to the corner of Fifth Avenue and 37th Street. After 1907, all his jewelry bears the Tiffany & Co. stamp.

Louis Tiffany endeavoured to produce simple and practical jewelry that featured remarkable colour effects by combining gold, enamel and precious and coloured gemstones, unlike Tiffany & Co. jewelry which incorporated precious stones into sophisticated and elaborate settings. An accomplished artist, Louis Tiffany trans-

Louis Comfort Tiffany (1848–1933).

ferred the palette of his Impressionistic paintings into the muted colour tones of his jewelry by juxtaposing gemstones, such as opals, with enameling and *plique-à-jour*. The earlier "hand wrought" jewelry was freer and more organic, naturalistic in feeling, while his later pieces, made at Tiffany & Co., tend to be symmetrical and smaller in scale – wearable designs for the average person.

When Charles Cook died in 1907, John C. Moore, son of Edward C. Moore, became president of the firm. For whatever reason, Paulding Farnham resigned from Tiffany's in 1908. Although some magnificent jewelry designs continued to be produced, the creative impetus that existed while Farnham was at the helm of the design department began to wane. Although Louis Tiffany remained as Art Director until 1918, very little of his influence can be seen in Tiffany & Co. jewelry other than those pieces designed and sold in the "Art Jewelry" department.

By the time of the 1939 New York World's Fair, jewelry had evolved into larger, geometric conceptions. Tiffany's exhibited a selection of necklaces, brooches, bracelets, rings and tiaras which reflected the dramatic use of gemstones in sculptural settings. One example, a diamond and ruby orchid brooch, had been transformed from its enameled predecessors at the 1889 Paris Exposition into the new style influenced by the machine age with its spirals, domes, rectangles and scrolls. Along with modernistic jewelry, Tiffany's exhibited two strands of Oriental pearls. The firm staunchly resisted selling cultured pearls, preferring to continue offering the natural variety to their customers.

In 1940, Tiffany's moved to their present premises at the corner of 57th Street and Fifth Avenue. The Paris and London branch stores were forced to close during the Second World War; a new store in Bond Street, London, was not opened until 1986. (A branch was introduced to Munich in 1987, and the following year new Tiffany shops were established in Zurich and Hong Kong.) Walter Hoving, who had been the president of Bonwit Teller, the department store located next door to Tiffany's, took over the reins of the company in 1955. Like Charles Tiffany before him, he invited talented individuals, such as Jean Schlumberger, to join the firm.

A swallow corsage ornament, set with diamonds and Montana sapphires to represent the blue sheen of the wings. This piece was shown in the 1901 Pan-American Exposition in Buffalo.

TIFFANY

Schlumberger breathed new life into Tiffany's designs, transforming jewelry from flat, two-dimensional objects into works of art. In the 1930s, he had worked with Elsa Schiaparelli, designing costume jewelry and buttons, and in 1941 he opened his own shop with Nicolas Bongard in New York. During the late 1940s and '50s, his well-known repertory of jewelry was formulated, drawing upon nature for images of animals, sea creatures, fish, birds, and flowers.

Schlumberger's creations, whether a piece of jewelry or an *objet d'art*, pulsate with life. In his own words, "I try to make everything look as if it were growing, uneven, at random, organic, in motion. I want to capture the irregularity of the universe. I observe nature and find verve." This is the essence of his jewelry.

Schlumberger revived the art of enameling, and combined precious and coloured gemstones within the total design. He revived jewelry techniques which had lain dormant since the turn of the century. His designs are characterized not by their abundant use of costly materials, but by their attention to detail and intricate workmanship. He has often been compared to Fabergé and Cellini. Tiffany's gave special recognition to his talents by signing his name to his jewelry designs.

In 1965, Hoving enticed Donald Claflin, who had worked for David Webb, Inc., to join the firm. Claflin introduced a new line of jewelry that combined gemstones with hardstones, conceived a new Tiffany setting in which two bands cross with the diamond set at the intersection, and designed fanciful jewelry based on story book characters and imaginary creatures.

In 1967, a young designer by the name of Angela Cummings became Claflin's assistant. Six years later, Tiffany's introduced her first collection and she soon became known for her unusual combinations of materials and for her nature-inspired designs. Knots are twisted, and rose petals, elm leaves, spider-webs and dragonfly wings appear frozen in gold, iced with diamonds.

In 1974, Elsa Peretti became the second signature designer to join the Tiffany design team. Her idea of creating jewelry with simple, softer, sculptural shapes was revolutionary; she changed the conception of jewelry to one of design rather than decoration. Her shapes derive from interpretations of popular symbols such as hearts, letters of the alphabet, and signs of the zodiac, or are abstracted from animal anatomy such as bones. Her designs are created in both gold and silver, making the latter metal acceptable as a jewelry material.

Not often does an offspring of a famous person establish a name for themselves; however, Paloma Picasso, daughter of the most celebrated artist of the twentieth century, has done just that. Tiffany's first introduced her jewelry line in 1980. Utilizing unexpected colour contrasts with highly polished surfaces, together with large gemstones, mounted into amply proportioned settings, her jewelry exudes the exuberance of contemporary life.

Under the helm of the current chairman, William R. Chaney, Tiffany's celebrated its first 150 years in 1987. For this special anniversary, Paloma Picasso designed a necklace, mounted with a 396 carat kunzite, in homage to George Kunz. The recent introduction of a new line of diamond jewelry, highlighted by a brooch set with a 107 carat canary diamond, continues a tradition of excellence in a manner that would make Charles Tiffany proud of his successors.

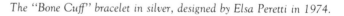

The "Bone Cuff" bracelet in silver, designed by Elsa Peretti in 1974.

The Grand Duchess Vladimir in a native Boyar costume, wearing her rectangular emerald of 107.72 carats in a brooch (centre, opposite), formerly in the collection of Catherine the Great, which she received as a wedding present from Tsar Alexander II. The stone was reputed to be the second most beautiful large emerald in the world, surpassed only in weight by another emerald owned by Catherine the Great. Upon his mother's death, Grand Duke Boris sold the emerald to Cartier in 1927.

In 1947, Raphael Esmerian, the New York lapidary and dealer, and Pierre Cartier agreed to re-mount the emerald as a pendant to a necklace that Esmerian had purchased from the Payne Whitney family (opposite, above left).

On Esmerian's recommendation in 1954 to remove a natural flaw in the stone, Cartier consented to have him re-cut the emerald into a pear shape. The stone ended at 75.63 carats and was restored to the necklace which had been made larger with the addition of another square emerald (opposite, above right).

That same year John D. Rockefeller Jr bought the necklace from Cartier. Its final appearance was at a Sotheby's auction in November 1971, when Raphael Esmerian repurchased an old friend.

Opposite, below, the Cartier clan in 1922. From left to right: Pierre, Louis, Alfred (the father) and Jacques.

During the 19th and 20th centuries, in both Europe and the United States, there was a marked proliferation of retail jewelers and manufacturers who served the appetite for luxury of the surviving aristocracy and the newly developed industrial middle class. Most jewelers traditionally worked at a local level, rarely emerging beyond the limits of their immediate city. Only for a special few, national boundaries did not exist, and as travel and communications improved, even the most remote client became more accessible to them. These international jewelers were also enabled by these changing circumstances to produce new pieces reflecting foreign motifs.

Family leadership was the foundation of a jewelry enterprise. Maintaining a tradition and passing on a reputation to succeeding generations were essential for a continuing success, but these were never to be taken for granted. Within the history of a jewelry family, there is invariably a certain period, presided over by one or more individuals, during which great design and production set unique standards for the House.

For nearly half a century, from 1900 to 1940, the House of Cartier eclipsed all its past and future achievements. Its combination of superb stones, exotic design, skilled production, and global merchandising in jewels, clocks, watches, boxes and *objets* set the supreme example for world jewelers. Although these extraordinary years were marked by war, prosperity and depression, Cartier maintained a consistent standard of excellence. The human element was responsible for the firm's successful activity. Three brothers – Louis, Pierre and Jacques Cartier – inherited a strong family establishment which had been built during the last half of the 19th century on vision, organization and a sense of fashion. They were able to divide the world among themselves. Alone, each assumed, enjoyed and excelled at his individual responsibilities; together, their teamwork created a jewelry empire that remains the model to this day.

In 1847, when Louis-François Cartier opened his small jewelry store in Paris, he was satisfying mercantile instincts, not creative design talents. In 19th-century European society, and particularly in Paris, there was a surging growth of a new middle class whose power extended into business and politics. Cartier quickly understood that a successful jeweler had to cater to the opulent tastes of the new wealth and not limit himself to the production and retailing of traditional jewels such as cameo parures and pearl ensembles. Cartier extended the range of his stock to include ivory pieces, fans, Wedgwood and Sèvres porcelain, Christofle silver, and watches.

Alfred Cartier joined his father in the 1870s, assuming leadership of the store and organizing the first international exhibition in London, which attracted a new clientele. European taste was being transformed by a spate of archaeological and scientific discoveries. Digs in Assyria, Egypt, Greece, and Italy were revealing ancient artifacts that jewelers were adapting and reproducing in the "archaeological style". This was also the period when scientific expeditions to Africa, South America, and Asia brought back to Europe unfamiliar fauna and flora – shapes and colours that inspired jewelers to mimic nature and produce lizards, birds, and flowers with appropriate stones and enamel.

Although few 19th-century Cartier jewels survive, designs and sales records from the House archives reveal fashionable pieces dictated by contemporary taste. In addition to the jewels imitating nature and drawing their inspiration from ancient Egypt and Rome, Cartier also created the overstated diamond pieces that the new middle class demanded. Certainly the Louvre exhibition of the French Crown Jewels in 1884 and their subsequent public auction sale in 1887 reinforced the appetite for ostentation. The discovery of diamond mines in South Africa and the organization of De Beers in 1880 assured European jewelers of a steady supply of this most precious decorative material.

Concurrently, the imaginative design and workmanship of Lalique jewelry offered a dramatic break with tradition. Established Houses in Paris like Fouquet, Vever, and Aucoc followed the creative genius of Lalique. In the world of painting, the Salons and academies were being challenged in a similar fashion by the Impressionists. For Cartier, however, the "Art Nouveau" look, with its exaggeration of nature's themes and abundant use of such materials as ivory and horn, was deemed totally inappropriate for the firm's image.

At the approach of the new century, Cartier was respected as a successful fine jeweler with an international clientele. But it was also apparent that changes would come about with the emergence of a new (third) family generation. In 1898 Louis Cartier, the twenty-three-year-old eldest son of Alfred, joined his father in business. By 1906 his younger brothers, Pierre and Jacques, followed Louis to create the team that would establish Cartier as the preeminent jeweler in the world. In 1899 the Paris store completed its fourth and final move – to 13 Rue de la Paix, a fitting address for its growing reputation. In 1906

Jacques moved to London and in 1909 he organized the present Cartier store in New Bond Street. During that same year, Pierre travelled to New York, married an American socialite, and opened a store at 712 Fifth Avenue. The move to the present American headquarters at 653 Fifth Avenue, which was brought about by an exchange for a famous Oriental pearl necklace, occurred in 1917.

Each brother exercised independent management and creativity within his own store. Paris, London and New York had their respective designers, workshops and merchandising facilities. The brothers had very different interests and abilities, but the propagation of the Cartier image and jewelry was paramount. Louis, Pierre and Jacques were all great world travellers, either visiting clients, seeking aesthetic inspiration from foreign cultures, or combing primitive market places for stones and pearls. But in the end they always returned to Paris, the creative centre.

Louis was the one most concerned with design and production. When he joined the store at the turn of the century, the grand tradition of Versailles and Louis XVI dominated the Cartier look. In creating dog collars and tiaras, the eight House designers drew upon the ornamental motifs of the 17th and 18th centuries. Their efforts marked the beginnings of the Garland style, which evolved up to and through the First World War.

The advent of platinum, which replaced silver, allowed for an open lacework and embroidery pattern as a polished background for diamonds and pearls. More important, however, were the production and fame of the Fabergé workshops in Russia which had successfully carried on the Versailles stylistic tradition. Fabergé's mastery of enameling also challenged Cartier to create similar *objets*.

Opposite: *A PRIDE OF PANTHERS*
The brooch with the sapphire and diamond panther straddling a 152-carat cabochon sapphire was purchased by the Duke of Windsor in 1949. Above it are various companions in the panther series, the earliest being the onyx and diamond pendant watch that Pierre Cartier had commissioned in 1915, especially for his wife. The onyx and diamond panther reclining on the agate base was designed as a brooch by Cartier for the American boxer Gene Tunney and made by the Lavabre workshop in 1928.
The sapphire and diamond recumbent panther ring was made in Paris for Nina Dyer in 1962. The ear clips, brooch and bangle bracelet illustrating onyx and diamond panthers with emerald eyes were all made in the Paris workshop between 1963 and 1970.

IN THE GARLAND STYLE

Top, a diamond and platinum dog collar sewn on a black velvet ribbon (Paris 1906). Centre, a
bow-top diamond and platinum brooch with a floral design inspired by the 19th-century crown
jewel look (Paris 1908). The diamond and platinum lapel watch brooch on black grosgrain ribbon
was made as a special order by Cartier New York in 1926, but the design reflects the customer's
18th-century taste. Cartier Paris in 1906 designed and made the platinum and gold brooch formed
by two intertwined sapphire and diamond Gothic motifs. The pearl, diamond and platinum corsage
basket produced by Cartier New York in 1918 is reminiscent of the 18th century.

THE FABERGE INFLUENCE

The gold and silver desk tray with mauve, blue, green and white enamel decoration, made for Cartier Paris by the Bako Workshop in 1908, consists of a clock framed by two inkwells and a pen resting on a holder. The gold, enamel and ivory standing desk clock in the shape of a Louis XIV-style barometer was made by Bredillard & Prevost for Cartier Paris in 1904 and sold that same year to J.P. Morgan. The gold, enamel and diamond parasol handle was made in 1907, and the two watches c. 1911 and 1913.

INDIA

Top, a cabochon emerald, coral and diamond pendant brooch, and below it, a carved emerald
bead, pearl and diamond necklace with an engraved Moghul emerald pendant, both made by
Cartier New York (1925). In the carved coral chimera bracelet with carved emerald beads,
sapphires and diamonds, directly inspired by the Indian tawiz arm bracelet, Cartier included the
blue and green enamel decoration prevalent in Jaipur pieces. The coral heads were carved by the
lapidary Dalvy and then given to the Lavabre workshop who completed the piece in 1928. The
fourth piece is a linear pendant brooch with a drop emerald suspended from onyx, coral and
diamond motifs, made by the Renault workshop in 1922.

INDIA

Top, *a ruby bead and diamond 18 kt. gold bib necklace with two Indian motifs (enamel on reverse) with a palm tree ornament suspending two bunches of ruby beads (Paris 1949). The "tree of life" platinum brooch with two birds is made of carved emeralds, rubies, cabochon sapphires, and diamonds (Paris 1927). The "Kashmir palm" jabot pin, with carved jade, rubies and diamonds, is a classical Moghul design reinterpreted by Cartier Paris and made by the Renault workshop in 1925.*

The bracelet with the diamond branch running down the centre was made by the Picq workshop (1925) and sold the following year to Cole Porter.

197

CHINA

The jade belt is composed of Chinese medallions carved in the 19th century. The carved rubies were set by Cartier London when the piece was completed in 1930 and then bought by the opera diva Ganna Walska. A 14 kt. gold vanity case with a carved jade and diamond centre engraved with Chinese cloud motifs (New York); opposite it, a 19th-century jade plaque carved in China and framed in a diamond and cabochon sapphire brooch, which was designed and made by Cartier New York in the Art Deco style (1950).

The lady's platinum and gold pendant lapel watch brooch (Paris 1929) has a 19th-century jade Buddhist seal carved as a lion suspended from ruby bead and diamond motifs.

CHINA/JAPAN

Left, a jeweled and wood-paneled vanity case made by the Lavabre workshop (1924), with Chinese mythological figures inlaid with mother-of-pearl, malachite, lapis-lazuli, turquoise, coral, and diamond motifs. On the cover, a Taoist shepherd, seen conversing with a warrior, who is able to transform rocks into sheep. Inside there are two powder compartments, a comb and a lipstick holder. The two decorative panels (reverse not shown) were made in the Far East during the 19th century and bought by Louis Cartier in Paris.

The mystery clock, with a large faceted topaz face decorated with mother-of-pearl numerals, green jade plaques and coral, was made by the Couet workshop in 1927. The octagon is a classic Art Deco stone cut, yet identical geometric shapes are seen in Chinese architecture and design of the 18th century.

The jeweled vanity case, from the Lavabre workshop (1928), is decorated with a floral vase and fallen flower; it combines Chinese stylization with the Japanese sentiment of the nursery rhyme: "Though the colour be fragrant, the flower will fall; who in the world lives forever?"

Right, front and back of a jade, coral, onyx and diamond mantel clock by Couet (1926); the Cartier chimera plays against the 18th-century Chinese carved white jade screen in the form of a diamond hand and a gold and enameled motif at the back.

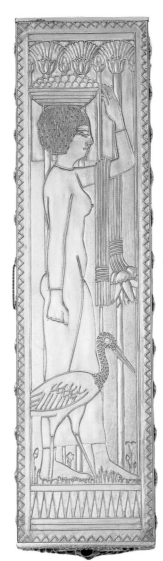
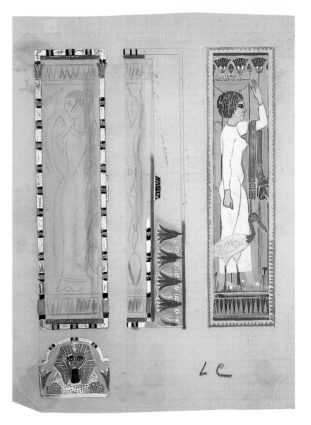

Above, *a jeweled enamel, gold and platinum vanity case shaped as an Egyptian sarcophagus designed by Jacqueau (design initialed by Louis Cartier) and made by the Lavabre workshop in 1925. It was bought that year by Mrs George Blumenthal, wife of the New York investment banker. Louis Cartier had bought from a Paris antique dealer what he thought to be a piece of ivory. The concave cover is actually bone, carved possibly in the 18th century, and depicts a* Persian princess with a tulip. The lid is framed by carved emerald lotus columns, emerald and onyx rondelles and pavé diamond tubes.

On the reverse, reminiscent of 19th-century archaeological style jewelry, is a gold cloisonné panel showing a female Egyptian almsbearer standing against a lotus flower background, with an ibis at her side. The two sides of the piece are decorated with blue, green, white champlevé lotus flowers and applied gold floral motifs.

The genius of the case lies in the two ends, each of which is set with a jeweled sphinx with an onyx and diamond body, emerald paws, and a pharaonic face carved out of one piece of emerald. Reflecting the mania for Tutankhamun and the 1922 excavations, Cartier recalled his funerary mask with sapphires and the diamond cobra, symbol of his rule over Lower Egypt.

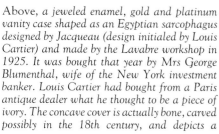

An ancient Egyptian blue faience scarab set in an 18 kt. gold and platinum brooch of citrine topaz, diamond, emerald, ruby and onyx wings. When originally designed and made by Cartier London in 1925, the brooch could be converted to a buckle and mounted on a plaited silk belt.

A platinum brooch with ancient Egyptian blue faience profile of a hawk decorated with coral, onyx, and diamond stylized lotus flowers (Lavabre 1925).

Ancient Egyptian faience head emerging from an onyx, emerald, ruby and diamond lotus flower brooch (Paris c. 1925).

In 1904 and again in 1905, Pierre Cartier was despatched to Russia, not only to meet new clients, but also to commission pieces from Russian workshops that the French could not yet produce. Animals and flowers carved out of semi-precious hardstones and enamel wares in exotic colours were ordered by Cartier from the famous Moscow atelier of Yahr. It was ironic that a French jeweler had to go as far afield as Russia to bring back a 200-year-old style that was first created at Versailles. But the Russian aristocracy, at least up to 1917, were the greatest consumers of jewels in the European market. What better resting-place for the spirit of the defunct French monarchy?

During his two exploratory trips to Russia, Pierre Cartier successfully opened up a foreign market for Cartier jewelry, just as he would later do in America. The social contacts he established (as each of the Cartier brothers was expert in doing the world over) would serve him well throughout his professional life. Grand Duchess Vladimir, her son Boris, Grand Duchess Xenia, daughter of the Tsar, and Prince Felix Youssoupov all assisted Cartier in opening a St Petersburg branch in 1909. Although the venture was considered commercially successful, it was short-lived and closed down in 1914, through a combination of anticipated wartime restrictions and Alfred Cartier's intention to concentrate all the firm's overseas efforts on the new store in New York.

The important contribution of Russian design and workmanship to 20th-century jewelry was not limited to Fabergé and the renewal of the Versailles style. Another strong influence was exerted by the Ballets Russes. The explosive launching of Diaghilev's ballet company in Paris in 1909 shook the traditions of Western European art and fashion. The cultural wall that had isolated the Orient was breached. From the stage emanated movements, sounds, and colours which proclaimed an exotic taste unfamiliar to Western palettes. The contribution of Léon Bakst in particular was the use of vibrant, clashing greens, yellows, oranges, and blues to highlight textured costumes and sets. Together with dance and music, this visual shock served to contrast the exotic image of the Eastern woman with her bland and old-fashioned Western counterpart.

For Cartier this dramatic kaleidoscope of Eastern exoticism could not have been more propitious. The fresh energy brought to the House by the three brothers had resulted in new personnel and an expansion of overseas ventures. In 1909 Louis hired a twenty-four-year-old designer, Charles Jacqueau, who was a graduate of the Ecole des Arts Décoratifs. At first, Jacqueau's personal creativity did not match his technical mastery of 18th-century forms. He was inspired by the Ballets Russes to visit the Louvre frequently to study the arts of India, Egypt, China and Japan. It was in this early period that he developed what would later be known as Art Deco jewelry. Only four years after he came to Cartier, Jacqueau designed a collection for the Paris shop that was exhibited and catalogued as "a choice of Persian, Indian, and Tibetan jewels adapted to the latest fashions". Jacqueau's studies in the Louvre allowed him to concentrate on the details of Persian miniatures, Moghul enamels, stylized Egyptian birds and flowers, the simplicity of Far Eastern inlay. For nearly twenty-five years he converted Oriental images into Western Art Deco jewels, clocks and *objets* that Cartier so successfully produced. From 1911 to 1935 he directed eleven designers in Paris towards this end.

Although both Pierre and Jacques Cartier had brought French designers with them to New York and London, it was under Jacqueau's influence in Paris that elegance and refinement set the international tone for Cartier jewelry, wherever it was made. From the beginning, he worked closely with Louis Cartier, who also enjoyed, when his administrative duties permitted, visualizing a piece and then having the designer do renderings. Their closest collaboration occurred after 1922 and the discovery of Tutankhamun's tomb. During the 19th century the House of Cartier had been duly influenced by the Egyptian revivals revered by European fashion; but the discovery of the tomb's treasures served to underscore the message of the Ballets Russes. Not only were the colours and designs exceptionally strong, but the workmanship of the artifacts surpassed modern creations. Louis Cartier was inspired to find original pieces to incorporate in modern jewels; collecting rare books, fine furniture, and drawings

*The extraordinarily talented
Jeanne Toussaint (1887–1978),
who made an invaluable
contribution to Cartier during
the years of its greatest successes.*

sharpened his taste and assisted him in finding suitable antiquities.

If Louis Cartier relied on Jacqueau for design excellence, he depended entirely on Jeanne Toussaint to share his responsibilities as the head of the firm. Joining Cartier in 1910 at the age of twenty-three, Toussaint rounded out the creative and merchandising team that Louis was organizing. During the half-century that she worked for the House, Tousssaint ranged over all its activities. Her approach to jewelry was modern, perfectly attuned to the changing attitudes of society towards women. Emerging from the Victorian closet, the 20th-century woman was shedding the restrictions of anonymity. Apart from the achievement of political equality with men, her most visible gains appeared in fashion and society. Following the First World War, smoking in public became acceptable for women; make-up and cosmetics, once considered the emblems of moral depravity, became decorative necessities. The sleekness and relative simplicity of clothes emphasized the body and provided a fitting backdrop to the new jewelry.

Accordingly, Cartier designated Toussaint to acknowledge this new image and to oversee the production of jeweled articles for women. During the 19th century Cartier had emphasized men's accessories – such as cigarette cases, cigar cutters, hair and moustache brushes, desk sets; now the time had come for women's articles to share equal billing. With this objective, Jeanne Toussaint organized and directed Department S to produce in precious metals and materials a quantity of accessories for men, women, and the home. In retrospect, this successful effort was the precursor of the Must creations which were to originate fifty years later on a mass-production scale.

Department S produced objects which were functional and yet stylish: handbags of gold and silver covered in alligator or crocodile skins or textured brocades from the Far East; men's cigarette cases made flat for the pocket and decorated in a geometric style; picture frames in precious metals and hardstone materials; night lamps; desk pieces such as magnifying glasses and letter openers – all enlisted the creative energies of the House to reach a broader public.

In the case of high jewelry, Toussaint's taste was for Indian design and Moghul jewels. Along with Jacques Cartier and Jacqueau, she devised that Art Deco classic – what future generations would call the "fruit salad" look. Jeweled European renditions of the Tree of Life and Indian gardens were set with a profusion of carved rubies, sapphires, emeralds, and diamonds. The combination of colours in Jaipur enamels, opulent gold mountings holding large stones, and the Eastern shapes of tassels and turban ornaments all served to divert Cartier jewelry from the conventional diamond look which had held sway at the end of the 19th century. This acknowledgement of the Indian style was not an isolated phenomenon, but merely the continuation of a tradition that had started in the 16th century when European jewelers scoured India for designs and stones. The three-dimensional enamel jeweled pendants depicting human and animal forms produced in Europe during the Renaissance were directly inspired by their Indian counterparts. For three hundred years the Indian continent was for European jewelers the primary source of diamonds, pearls, and coloured stones.

During the 20th century Cartier was able to develop a reciprocal tradition with India. Because of England's imperial status, London had taken on the role of cultural and political centre for the maharajahs on their European visits. Naturally Jacques Cartier and the London store became their contacts for the House. Jacques had taken his first trip to the Persian Gulf and India in 1911. In the following years, he was designated by his brothers to purchase pearls and precious stones for company designs and production. Jacques hired a full-time purchasing agent in New Delhi who would report directly to him and send back to London Moghul pieces as well as raw materials. Just as Pierre developed an affinity for the brahmans of American society, so Jacques cultivated and enjoyed their counterparts in the Indian continent. The maharajahs still held an astounding wealth of native jewels, but in the process of being Westernized, they were inclined to update their holdings. Jeweled turbans, armlets, ankle bracelets, nose rings, necklaces – all were in need of a contemporary look, and Cartier design and workmanship were the most impressive available to them. It was ironic that Cartier should be asked to transform the very pieces which served as an inspiration for their Art Deco creations. Patiala, Baroda, Mysore, Hyderabad, Kapurthala were among the potentates who entrusted their Moghul jewels to Cartier for remounting. Jacques Cartier's success in India, coupled with the creative efforts of Jacqueau and Toussaint, allowed the House to set a pace in the design and production of Art Deco jewelry which outclassed all other European and American jewelers.

Along with the artifacts of ancient Egypt and the carved stones of India, Cartier borrowed from the art work of China and Japan in its Art Deco creations. Far Eastern motifs and symbols from architecture and gardens were also converted to this 20th-century idiom, appearing on vanity cases, clocks, perfume bottles and the like.

Large carved jade and agate figures, screen panels, lacquered mother-of-pearl plaques were purchased by Cartier in the Orient as well as from antique dealers in Paris and London. In the United States, Pierre would buy similar treasures from New England families whose forebears had traded in China during the 19th century. Cartier did not depend entirely on the old pieces, but also encouraged and patronized small, independent Paris workshops which specialized in the Oriental traditions of inlay and lacquer. France's involvement with Indo-China had brought to Paris an Oriental work force capable of handling lacquer – not so proficiently as the ancient Chinese, but skilled enough to make an important contribution to the Art Deco style.

Jeanne Toussaint found the coordination of design and manufacturing an exhilarating task, for until 1940 Paris was the world centre for fine jewelry production. European and American retailers would come twice a year to see the latest fashions and to purchase stock. The manufacturers formed a very competitive and yet interdependent circle. Whatever their relative strengths, they needed each other, as retailers would use them for their specialities and then pass a particular piece on to another atelier for more work and completion. Although there were specialists in enameling, lapidary, clock-work, box-making, and jewelry manufacture, it was a rare atelier that could undertake all or even several of these activities.

Since its beginnings Cartier had established its own in-house facilities to repair customers' jewels and to create new jewelry. Simultaneously, commissions for special pieces were farmed out to independent workshops. With the dynamic growth and ambitions of the House at the beginning of the 20th century, Cartier was well aware that outside manufacturing had to be greatly increased, but this had to be achieved within the framework of exclusive contracts in order to protect Cartier styles and designs.

For example, in exchange for a loan of 50,000 francs, Henri Lavabre agreed in 1906 that his shop of twenty men would work exclusively for Cartier. Although this formal arrangement was terminated in 1921, Lavabre continued his relationship with the House until the mid-1930s when the effects of the Depression forced him to close. His workers produced beautiful vanity cases and jewels that survive as Cartier classics.

Picq, in the Rue de Quatre Septembre, was another workshop to which Cartier gave its designs for execution. Picq's speciality was platinum jewelry, and though he was used by other retailers and dealers, he designated a team of workmen within his shop to devote themselves exclusively to Cartier designs. It was an arrangement that would last about forty years. Renault, Dubois, Allard et Meyer, Droguet, the Rue Bachaumont shop set up outside of the Rue de la Paix facility – these were among the manufacturers that supplied Cartier in the years between 1918 and 1940 when the House dominated the world of jewelry.

In the creation of clocks, however, the Couet workshop was considered unique. Founded and directed by Maurice Couet, who descended from a family of clockmakers, the establishment produced a small number of boxes and flower vases in the Fabergé style; their main production involved table clocks. Maurice had been responsible for reviving the "mystery clock" and transforming its 19th-century design into the highly stylized and jeweled creations of the 1920s. The technique of manufacturing these clocks was as simple as it was baffling, but it required the expert's touch. In time, the Couet mystery clock became a symbol of Cartier excellence just as the Imperial Egg stood for the best of Fabergé.

The outbreak of the Second World War shut off all creativity in European high jewelry. It marked the end of the Art Deco style, which had undergone transformations during the Depression but nonetheless survived. Coincidentally, the generation which had pioneered the new jewelry at Cartier and thrust the firm to the forefront of international jewelry was disappearing. In 1942 both Louis and Jacques Cartier died, leaving Jeanne Toussaint and Pierre Cartier to lead the House during the war years. Stylistically, the detail of design and Orientalism that Charles Jacqueau had so beautifully expounded gave way to a more abstract and metallic look: a younger generation of designers was at work. The passing of Louis Cartier deprived Jacqueau of his mentor and chief supporter. Toussaint, ever aware of the fickleness of fashion, had promoted Peter Lemarchand as designer of the new jewelry. Twenty-one years younger than Jacqueau, Lemarchand had joined Cartier in Paris in 1927. He was transferred to London in 1935, travelled to India in 1939, and then returned to Paris to work with Toussaint. Lemarchand's drawing technique and spirit were freer and more open than Jacqueau's. He was attracted to nature, not the constraints of stylization. It seems appropriate, therefore, that he and Toussaint should have picked up an earlier Cartier motif – the panther – and finally given it enough body and style to create an entire line of jewels.

The panther's noble bearing and sensuality prompted Louis Cartier in 1914 to use it as the House symbol. He hired the illustrator George Barbier to design aigrettes and feather jewelry, but few of them were ever made. What did bear fruit was Barbier's design for the firm's advertising logo: a black panther with a jeweled collar reclining by a standing lady, bedecked in an endless strand of pearls. In 1915 Pierre Cartier had ordered for his young American wife the first of the panther jewels, a diamond châtelaine watch spotted with black onyx dots. Throughout the 1920s and '30s, an assortment of panther pieces were made in jewels, boxes and *objets* – always within the style and discipline of Jacqueau's Art Deco imagery.

By the late 1940s, however, Lemarchard was designing a new generation of panthers, more natural, more physical than their predecessors. The first important Cartier client to order post-war panther pieces was the Duke of Windsor, who enjoyed participating in the various stages of design and manufacture. This last incarnation of panther jewelry is also the final entry in the great design styles that Cartier created. It was inevitably a sentimental project for Toussaint, because "panthère" was the nickname Louis Cartier had always used for her, indicating possibly a special intimacy and emotional link.

Toussaint continued to work with designers and clients until a few years before her death in 1978. She was indeed the last survivor of her creative generation. In 1945, Jean-Jacques Cartier had assumed his late father's role in London. Pierre Cartier returned to Paris in 1948, exchanging the New York store for Rue de la Paix with Louis's son, Claude. Shortly afterward, when Pierre retired to Switzerland, his daughter Marion Claudel became director of the Paris store. The least artistic of the three brothers, Pierre left behind in New York the legacy of a great retail merchant who had mixed comfortably with high society and adopted the dynamism and business flair of industrial America. Unlike Louis and Jacques, he usually undertook projects that had to do with marketing strategy, rather than jewelry design or production: he depended on Paris and London for that element. Pierre Cartier lived to see his nephew Claude begin the dismantling of the family empire with the sale of the New York store in 1962. The Paris and London branches were sold separately, after Pierre died in 1965. In 1972, Robert Hocq, Joseph Kanoui, and Alain Perrin organized the eventual purchase and reunion of Paris, London and New York. And Pierre Cartier's merchandising vision became a reality in 1973 with the creation of *Les Must de Cartier*, a mass production line of articles to be marketed in Must boutiques and concessions throughout the world.

As long as human societies feel the need to distinguish rank and wealth, as long as man must express his devotion and adorn his beloved, jewels will be created. There will always be great designers, jewelers and merchants, but the *consistency* of quality and the variety of the Cartier production in the first half of the 20th century remains a unique achievement.

VAN CLEEF & ARPELS

Julien and Louis Arpels, who with their brother Charles were the founders of the firm.

Opposite, the bejeweled Prince of Nepal, photographed here in the early 1930s, was one of Van Cleef & Arpels' important clients from the East.

The House of Van Cleef & Arpels, universally recognized as one of the leading and most stylish jewelry dealers of the 20th century, had its origins in 1906. On 16 June of that year, three enterprising young men – Alfred Van Cleef, and the brothers Charles and Julien Arpels – opened a small shop in the Place Vendôme, at that time the prime centre of fashion and luxury in Paris.

Alfred was the son of Charles Van Cleef, a young lapidary craftsman who had left his native Amsterdam to work in Paris. Born in 1873, Alfred served as an apprentice in the workshops of Messrs David et Grosgeat, for whom he later became a salesman. In 1898 he married his cousin Estelle Arpels, the daughter of Léon Arpels, a dealer in precious stones. Coming from a comparable background, her brothers Charles and Julien shared Alfred's vision of creating distinctive jewelry, and so the partnership was born.

Before launching themselves properly in the Paris luxury market, they developed their skills and expertise in small office premises at 34 Rue Drouot. Their move to 22 Place Vendôme (an address which Van Cleef & Arpels still occupies today) was calculated to attract the attention of a wealthy and stylish clientele. Their gamble paid off, and they were rewarded by an immediate success, which led them to increase their staff. From the beginning, Estelle contributed to the family enterprise by keeping the accounts, and in 1912 a third Arpels brother, Louis, joined the partnership.

The partners' various talents fortunately balanced each other. Charles's charm and salesmanship and Julien's judgment of stones were an excellent complement to Alfred's understanding of stone cutting and skill as an administrator and master strategist. Louis's affable personality enabled him to establish a special rapport with many important clients as well as personal friendships with such celebrities as Marlene Dietrich and Maurice Chevalier.

The firm's jewelry archives for the years preceding 1920 have unfortunately not survived, but it is well known that certain themes have always been characteristic of the House's product: fluid lines, graceful curves, colour, and a sense of movement which might be suggested by the lines of the design or produced mechanically by mobile elements in the jewelry.

Throughout the 1920s Van Cleef & Arpels' designs reflected contemporary fashions. The discovery of Tutankhamun's tomb in 1922 provided the inspiration for a whole range of jewels, the most extraordinary of which was a series of flat bracelets decorated with ancient Egyptian symbols such as the ibis and sphinx, the lotus and scarab, and the god Horus. The Oriental influence was pervasive; in 1924, for instance, vanity cases were decorated with Persian arabesques or even a Chinese landscape. Once the vogue for Art Deco was launched by the 1925 exhibition of Arts Décoratifs et Industriales Modernes in Paris, geometric patterns made their appearance in Van Cleef & Arpels' designs. It was at that exhibition, too, that the firm's reputation for excellence of design and technical innovation was enhanced by the award of a Grand Prix for a magnificent bracelet of roses in rubies and diamonds with emerald leaves.

Popular items during this period included the *sautoir*, a long necklace sometimes worn with a pendant; bold bracelets which complemented the bare-armed fashions of the day; and pendant ear clips which were shown off to advantage by the new shorter hairstyles. "Convertible" jewelry, designed to be worn in different ways (for

instance, a necklace which could be converted into a bracelet by undoing some small fasteners, or a large clip which could be separated and worn as two small clips), was a notable success.

Van Cleef & Arpels' collections have traditionally concentrated on the major gem stones – diamonds, rubies, emeralds and sapphires – and the firm is renowned for creating unique pieces of jewelry. Some items, however, such as bracelets with "invisibly set" rubies or sapphires, became such classics that they are still being produced.

In the 1930s Van Cleef & Arpels' patrons wanted a look of luxurious extravagance in their jewelry. The coloratura soprano Lily Pons, for instance, was given a clip by her husband for her debut in Donizetti's opera *La Fille du Régiment* which bore a likeness of the part she was singing, the "vivandière" Marie, fashioned from gold, rubies, sapphires and rose-cut diamonds.

Van Cleef & Arpels experimented with items other than conventional jewelry. In the 1920s they began to produce clocks. A hand mirror made in 1930 was unusual in combining black and red lacquer with agate and gold, with cabochon ruby accents. In 1931 the firm created a striking night light, made with gold, green and black enamel. When the lamp was turned on, the light streamed through sections of rock-crystal. One of the most unusual items the firm ever produced was a cage, intended to house a live frog, which was made from agate, jade, coral, lapis-lazuli, onyx and gold.

An item which came to be particularly associated with the firm was the *nécessaire*, or vanity case, which had been used by fashionable European women since shortly after the First World War. The relatively spacious surface of the cases allowed the designers and craftsmen of Van Cleef & Arpels to use their skills without the limitations imposed by conventional jewelry.

The *nécessaire* lent itself to a wide range and combinations of materials: precious and semi-precious stones, enamel, mother-of-pearl, textured gold. Some boxes were covered in highly polished gold which acted as background to a design set off by the imaginative use of stones; this was the technique used to create a charming view of Avenue Foch in Paris on the surface of one case, while on another flamingos formed from buff-topped, calibrated rubies and emeralds stand in a pool of emeralds against a gold background.

The design themes chosen for the boxes were as varied as the materials, ranging from the starkly simple to the intricate. Some were inspired by motifs from China, Japan and Persia, while others were based on fabric or wallpaper patterns or design elements drawn from the past.

In the early 1930s the small box was endowed with an even greater degree of sophistication. Louis Arpels observed Florence J. Gould, the wife of an American tycoon, using a long metal "Lucky Strike" box as a handbag. Inspired by her ingenuity, Louis invented the *minaudière*, a sleek gold box with hidden latches which could be opened to reveal compartments especially designed to hold face powder, lipstick, rouge, a miniature comb, and all the small items essential to a lady of fashion. Some even contained a tiny hidden watch. Their appeal was such that they quickly replaced the chic woman's evening bag. The term *minaudière* was coined by Alfred Van Cleef from the word *minauder* ("to simper"), with which he teased his wife.

Like the *nécessaire*, the *minaudière* allowed the designer and craftsman great scope because of its shape. In addition to the usual precious and semi-precious materials, lacquer was also used as a substitute for enamel, which is too fragile to cover a large surface. *Minaudières* often had an elaborately ornamented clasp, decorated with pearls or precious stones; sometimes the clasp was detachable so that it could be used as a clip.

Opposite, the ornament at the top (1924), designed to be worn on the upper sleeve, was inspired by motifs from India. The intricate design is composed of calibrated rubies, sapphires and emeralds on a round diamond background.
The bracelet from the "Egyptian" series is a masterpiece of workmanship (1924). Buff-topped, calibrated emeralds, rubies and sapphires are set amidst diamonds in a platinum setting.
The platinum Art Deco clip of 1931 has an outer ring covered with round diamonds. The centre motif is movable and has baguette and round diamonds.
The unusual diamond brooch of 1928 is set in platinum and has five pear-shaped drop emeralds suspended from intricately designed ropes of diamonds.

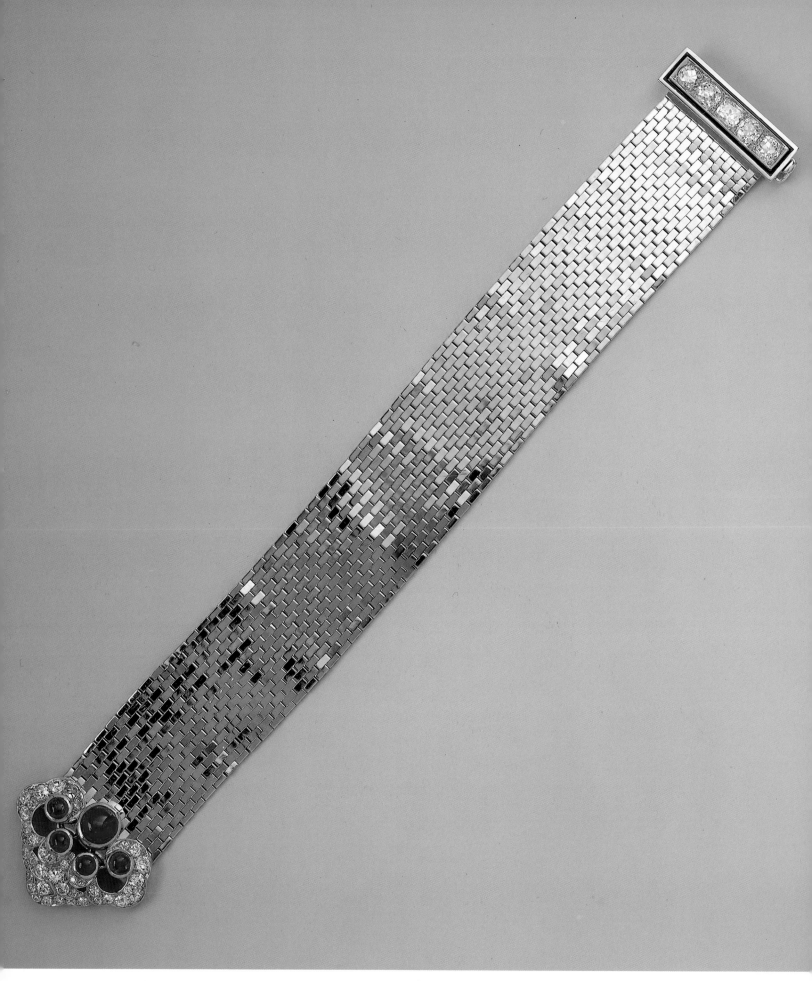

This supple bracelet (mid-1930s), one of a series of many "Ludo" bracelets, has thin gold rectangular panels in a brickwork pattern. The clasp is decorated with cabochon rubies and round diamonds.

Opposite, a Van Cleef & Arpels "Zipper" necklace (1950s) made of supple gold with round diamonds. When the back section is removed, the front can be zipped to make a bracelet with a gold tassel.

The famous Van Cleef & Arpels line of "minaudières" were fitted boxes with compartments for everything a woman might need on an evening out. This example of 1930 is in black lacquer on 18 kt. gold.

Below, this Art Deco compact of 1927, with a design of diamonds, has a cabochon sapphire on a surface of pink and violet enamel on gold.

Below left, the back of a 1930 mirror decorated with black and red lacquer, agate, cabochon rubies and gold.

Opposite, three unusual Van Cleef & Arpels vanity cases. Top, a gold case with a blue and black enamel top decorated with an Art Deco design in diamonds (1925). The sides have a floral motif in enamel with diamonds. Centre, an example of 1930 in plique-à-jour, a technique which required many layers of transparent enamel. Bottom, an Art Deco case of 1925 made of gold and blue enamel imitating lapis-lazuli; the centre band on each side is decorated with a different peacock.

Opposite, top, *a graceful clip that combines yellow diamonds with round and baguette diamonds in a setting of platinum and gold (1938).*

Centre, *this clip of two birds in a hat was produced in red, white and blue to celebrate the end of the Second World War (1946). The two nesting swallows are made of diamonds with ruby eyes, and the flowers are rubies, sapphires and diamonds. The hat is of gold, treated to look like weaving, with a hatband of calibrated rubies.*

Below, *one of Van Cleef & Arpels' many popular dancer clips (1940s). The ballerina has a rose-cut diamond head and her gold skirt has been cut to resemble pleats. Her tutu is decorated with faceted sapphires and rubies.*

Above, top, *a "swallow" clip, one of many Van Cleef & Arpels made with bird motifs, is composed of black onyx and baguette diamonds with a pear-shaped diamond head, set in platinum.*

The three flower clips (two in rubies and one in sapphires) make use of the "invisible setting" technique made famous by Van Cleef & Arpels. The stones are carefully cut to fit the contour of each petal with no visible prongs. Round diamonds are used in the centre of each clip and the stems are baguette diamonds. The leaves on the ruby clip on the lower left have round diamonds and the sapphire clip has leaves of round diamonds (1950s).

In the centre clip of intertwining leaves, one is made of round diamonds and the other of invisibly set sapphires. The veins and stem are of baguette diamonds set in platinum.

A gold serpent chain with a "passepartout" clip in yellow and blue faceted Ceylon sapphires and faceted rubies (1939). The clip could be worn alone or with the serpent chain as a necklace, belt or bracelet.

Normally each *minaudière* was unique. On one occasion, however, thirty identical ones, richly decorated with precious stones, were produced for an Emir who wished to avoid provoking jealousy among his thirty wives!

Innovation, whether technical or conceptual, was by no means limited to women's accessories. In 1935 Alfred Van Cleef and Julien Arpels developed into a work of art the technique of "invisible setting". The technique is to set each stone directly against the next in a beautiful monochromatic mosaic without any visible prongs or signs of setting. Rubies and sapphires, perfectly matched in colour and depth, are precisely cut and grooved by a highly skilled lapidary to fit exactly into their assigned places. Each stone is then slid onto concealed tracks and into its specific location in an intricate lattice-work of gold. The fit must be perfect, and the technique is therefore time-consuming. Sometimes as many as 800 stones are required to make a single clip, and many stones may be broken in the process and discarded. This revolutionary technique provides such flexibility that a bracelet can be moved like a ribbon of satin.

During the mid-1930s and the 1940s the second generation of the firm began to emerge. Julien's three sons, Claude, Jacques and Pierre, learned the business by working with their father and uncles. Jacques was blessed with great energy and a keen business sense which fitted him ideally to take on eventually the position of Director of Van Cleef & Arpels in Paris; and going into the 1990s he still provides guidance for the firm in Europe. Pierre's personality suited him for new projects, including development of the Van Cleef & Arpels boutique and the introduction of Van Cleef & Arpels in Japan. Claude accompanied his uncles Julien and Louis on a visit to the United States and ended up managing the firm there until his retirement in 1986. He was succeeded by a member of the third generation, Jacques's son Philippe, who had learned the business in the 1970s by working alongside his father in Paris.

During the 1930s geometric motifs began to be replaced by softer designs, and it was in collections of this period that the "padlock" watch and the graceful "swallow" clips both appeared. Indeed, clips of all kinds continued to be shown every year; detachable clips, corsage clips, clasps for necklaces or bracelets that could be worn on their own as clips. Several became "classics": the flame clips in platinum which were introduced in 1934 were revived again in the 1950s, while the four-leaf clover clips continued to be made into the 1960s.

The "Ludo" bracelets, affectionately called after Louis Arpels who was nicknamed "Ludovic", first appeared in 1934. The bracelets were supple ribbons formed either from flat panels of highly polished gold in the shape of hexagons, set side by side in a beehive pattern, or from rectangular panels arranged in a brickwork pattern. Often precious stones were "star" set in the centre of each panel and additional stones adorned the clasp. The versatile decorative theme was also used for rings, clips and ear clips.

Invisible setting was extended to new items: clips, cufflinks, ear clips, bracelets and boxes. The technique proved especially successful in highly contoured, sculpted items such as sumptuous flower and leaf clips and the "boule" ring. The double holly leaf clip, a remarkable example of invisible setting, was favoured by the Duchess of Windsor and made popular by her.

Floral themes were popular in the 1930s, and indeed into the 1960s, especially the "Hawaii" motif, sprays of multicoloured flowers on clips, ear clips, bracelets and necklaces.

Van Cleef & Arpels received a particularly prestigious commission in 1938, when the firm was requested to create jewels to be worn at the wedding of Reza Pahlavi, Shah of Iran, and Princess Fawzia, the daughter of King Fouad of Egypt. Van Cleef & Arpels jewels adorned not only the bride (who remained a loyal client of the firm), but also Queen Nazli and the entourage of the Egyptian royal family.

It was also in 1938 that the first of the "passepartout" clips appeared. Decorated with cushion-cut Ceylon sapphires in pale tones of yellow, pink and blue, they could be worn alone or attached to a gold snake chain which could also serve as a belt or be coiled round the arm. These were successfully revived in the 1940s and 1950s.

Van Cleef & Arpels had seen their international business grow so rapidly that

States of the policy of being represented at the resorts favoured by those who could afford luxury jewelry. Beverly Hills was another obvious objective, and a salon was opened there on Rodeo Drive in 1969.

The clientele of Van Cleef & Arpels has always been illustrious, and while many have preferred to remain anonymous, others have made no secret of their patronage. Over the years its glamorous customers have included Maria Callas, Elizabeth Taylor, Gloria Swanson, Marlene Dietrich, Christina Onassis, Madeleine Carroll, Barbara Hutton, the Vanderbilts, Mellons, Kennedys, the Duke of Westminster, the Aga Khan, King Farouk and the Maharajah of Baroda.

The Duchess of Windsor was often photographed wearing a Van Cleef & Arpels clip of a spray of wild flowers in diamonds and sapphires. She was a widely emulated leader of fashion, and the success of the flower style in the United States has been attributed to her influence. In a similar way, Marlene Dietrich made famous the *manchette*, or cuff bracelet, decorated by sapphires with baguette, round- and square-cut diamonds.

During the 1940s and '50s several popular new themes were introduced, such as the "Snowflake" motif (1945), the "Marine" motif depicting waves and shells, and meteors of gold and platinum. The first of the successful ballerina clips was created in 1945, and during the latter half of the decade birds of all kinds, from finches to parakeets and birds of paradise, were in favour.

The scarcity of precious stones during the Second World War led Van Cleef & Arpels to explore the use of textured gold. As the result of technical innovations, gold could be fluted, twisted and perforated to resemble basketweave, lace or fabric. The "pochette" clip cleverly imitated the pocket handkerchief.

The same delight in imitating everyday items inspired the "col Claudine", a "collar" made of highly polished gold panels, with a detachable clip of white and jonquil diamonds; and also a cuff bracelet, complete with buttonhole and diamond button.

It was during the 1950s that the firm recognized the need for lighter jewelry for daytime wear, which might also have a greater appeal to the young. In 1954 the

they reached the conclusion they were missing excellent opportunities by restricting their activities to the Place Vendôme. They decided to follow their colourful clientele to the fashionable resorts and casinos of Europe. Their first venture was the opening in 1921 of a salon in Cannes, next door to the leading couturier of the period, Paul Poiret. Before long they opened further establishments in Deauville, Vichy and Nice, and over the years they have continued this policy of judicious expansion all over the world from Monte Carlo to Hong Kong.

In 1939 Julien and Louis Arpels travelled to the United States on the *Queen Mary* in search of new challenges and markets. An exhibition of the firm's jewelry in the French Pavilion of the New York World's Fair during that summer was so successful that they rented a two-room office in Rockefeller Center.

Americans were so enthusiastic about the style and sophistication of the French jewelers' *haute joaillerie* that Van Cleef & Arpels had little difficulty in developing a loyal clientele. In 1942, having outgrown the Rockefeller Center premises, the firm opened a salon on Fifth Avenue between 57th and 58th Streets, adjoining the exclusive shop of Bergdorf Goodman. Julien and Louis began to divide their time between Europe and the United States, while Jacques and Pierre oversaw the firm's expansion in Europe.

In 1940 a Van Cleef & Arpels salon was established on fashionable Worth Avenue in Palm Beach, an extension to the United

Opposite, *among Van Cleef & Arpels'
clients of note: King Constantine of Greece
with his then fiancée, Princess Anne-Marie
of Denmark, wearing a "Swan" clip made of
gold and diamonds (c. 1963); the Duchess of
Windsor at the Bal des Petits Lits Blancs at
Cannes (1938), wearing a necklace and
earrings of faceted rubies and diamonds and
a large clip depicting a double holly leaf; and
Queen Nazli of Egypt at her daughter's
wedding in 1939, wearing the jewels created
by Van Cleef & Arpels for the occasion.*

first Van Cleef & Arpels boutique was
opened as a special outlet for this casual –
and more reasonably priced – jewelry,
which was often produced in limited numbers and comprised semi-precious as well
as precious stones. As with the traditional
haute joaillerie, certain of these pieces, for
instance, the "Mischievous Cat" clip of
1954 and the "Baby Lion" of 1964, became
classics which the firm continued to
produce.

At the same time the House had no
shortage of important commissions for its
haute joaillerie. In 1957 Prince Rainier of
Monaco ordered a magnificent diamond
and pearl parure, consisting of a necklace,
bracelet and ear clips, as a wedding gift for
Princess Grace. In addition, the National
and Municipal Council gave her a bracelet
with five rows of diamonds, which was also
from Van Cleef & Arpels. Princess Grace
wore a tiara of pear-shaped, marquise and
round diamonds created by the firm at the
wedding of her daughter Princess Caroline
in 1978.

Since the 1960s, Van Cleef & Arpels'
traditional pursuit of the opportunities
offered by the globe-trotting life-style of
their clientele has led them to organize
exhibitions all over the world which are
often timed to coincide with special events
or the seasonal migrations of high society.
It was after just such a series of exhibitions
in Japan that Van Cleef & Arpels established a presence there by opening 14
outlets under a franchise agreement with
Seibu department stores.

*Prominent clients in the entertainment world:
Richard Burton and Elizabeth Taylor wearing a tiara and earrings of pear-shaped and
navette diamonds and brilliants; Joan
Fontaine wearing a flexible diamond necklace with matching earrings (c. 1948); Sophia Loren sporting a long chain made of
gold, diamonds and cabochon rubies; the
necklace and earrings of pearls and diamonds worn by Grace Kelly in 1955 were
given to her by Prince Rainier to celebrate
their engagement; Maria Callas is trying on
an exceptional diamond parure.*

In 1965, after competing with more than sixty other jewelers, the firm was commissioned by the Shah and Empress of Iran to create new jewels from the existing Crown Jewels. As the stones could not be taken from Iran, Pierre Arpels had plaster impressions made of them, so that exact replicas could be fashioned and used to create the new settings. These were taken back to Iran when the actual work was carried out.

In 1967 Barbara Hutton commissioned a tiara with six pear-shaped diamonds, the largest of which weighed 54.82 carats. On one occasion when he visited her during an indisposition, Pierre Arpels was surprised to find her wearing it in bed!

Claude and Jacques made numerous trips to India during the 1960s and '70s, and this proved a fertile source for their designs. For instance, precious and semiprecious stones were combined in multicoloured jewelry based on the collarettes worn by the maharajahs over their tunics. The brothers also took advantage of these Indian visits to indulge their family's passion for magnificent stones, and it was while in Bombay in 1965 that they acquired the 114-carat "Neela Ranee" ("Blue Princess") sapphire.

Other notable acquisitions by Claude and Jacques Arpels included the "Princie" diamond at a London auction in 1960 and the "Mazarin" diamond in 1964. The "Princie" diamond is a splendid pink stone weighing 34.64 carats, re-named in honour of the Maharajah of Baroda who was known as "Princie" to his friends. The "Mazarin" diamond is an emerald-cut stone of 30.58 carats which still shows traces of the cushion cutting carried out by Parisian lapidaries in the 17th century for Cardinal Mazarin.

Although the Arpels preferred to buy extraordinary stones, they have often also purchased jewelry with an interesting history. The firm bought a *sautoir* and tiara from Queen Mary of Serbia, daughter of Ferdinand I of Roumania and wife of Alexander I of Serbia. She had acquired the tiara from the Romanoffs and had had the matching *sautoir* made.

As far back as 1925, Van Cleef & Arpels bought the famous "Liberty" necklace. According to legend, when Philadelphia was captured in September 1777, a beautiful Countess of Polish extraction became so distraught with anxiety about the fate of Tadeusz Kosciuszko, the freedom-loving Pole who had joined the American cause, that she called on Benjamin Franklin for comfort. Upon being assured by him that her beloved friend was not in danger, she took off her emerald necklace and earrings and donated them to the cause of Liberty.

In 1953 Van Cleef & Arpels purchased a tiara which had been given by Napoleon to the Empress Marie-Louise in 1811 to mark the birth of their son, the King of Rome. At a client's request, the firm sold the emeralds individually, while the diamond-studded mount was bought by Mrs Merriweather Post, who had it set with turquoise. In 1966 she donated it to the Smithsonian Institution.

Another acquisition with Napoleonic connections was a diamond tiara with a motif of butterflies and flowers which had been placed by Napoleon on Josephine's head on the day of his coronation. It is believed that Josephine bequeathed the tiara to her daughter Hortense, who in turn gave it to her son, the future Napoleon III. When Empress Eugénie fled from Paris, she entrusted her jewels to her friend Madame de Metternich, who arranged for them to be sent to London. The tiara was listed among some jewels sold by Eugénie in May 1872.

During the 1970s and '80s Van Cleef & Arpels concentrated on consolidating their status and success in the luxury market. In 1972 their first *Boutique des Heures* was launched in the Paris salon with a collection of exclusive watches, and in 1979 (and again in 1987) the firm diversified its activities by creating its own perfume. But of course jewelry remained the firm's major concern. "Ribbons" and "Bows" proved particular favourites among the motifs in the collections of the 1970s and '80s, while the firm's continuing use of the natural world as a source of inspiration is seen in the "Everest" necklace (1981), a series of scalloped motifs with diamonds and coloured stones. A variant of "Everest" with a characteristic invisible setting was also produced.

Today the firm is still in the hands of the Arpels family, who are anticipating the handing on of their skills and experience to yet another generation.

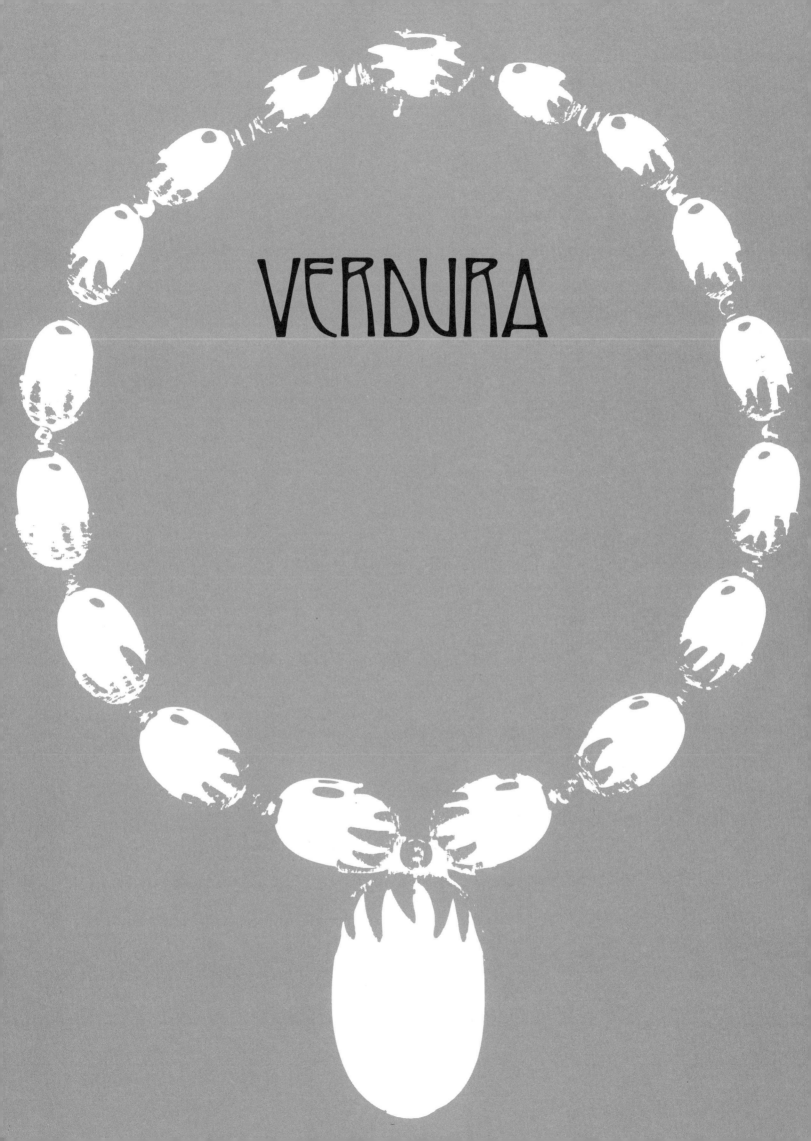

B ut what of myself? Well, I was a sturdy little boy well planted on my short legs, seemingly in perpetual motion, running ("May I skip?"), jumping on furniture, climbing up trees or trying to stand on my head, then suddenly stopping in my tracks to lose myself in some faraway daydream.

FULCO DI VERDURA *The Happy Summer Days*

Verdura's childhood propensity for intense activity combined with the whimsy of a daydream lasted a lifetime. An elegant aristocrat, wickedly witty and vastly talented, he used his energy and skill to produce some of the most innovative and imaginative jewelry of the 20th century. Although he was not particularly well known outside his circle of celebrated friends, his work reached a wide audience. Throughout the 1940s and 1950s, month after month, his exquisite designs adorned the beautiful women who graced the covers and interiors of *Harper's Bazaar*, *Vogue*, *Town & Country*, and other fashionable magazines. His creations captured the mood of an era, inspiring other designers who copied them freely. Ultimately, they have withstood the test of time; they are as fresh and appealing today as when they were first made.

Born in 1898 and christened Fulco Santostefano della Cerda, the Duke of Verdura, he was the only son of a delightfully eccentric Sicilian family. He and his sister Maria Felice were fiercely loved and indulged by their relatives. Their world included the Villa Niscemi just outside the city of Palermo, the Palazzo Verdura within it, and Bagheria, a country estate. There were lush, almost tropical gardens with meandering paths and wide avenues, landscaped with plants to delight any child – cherry trees, oranges, lemons, tangerines, peaches, quince, figs, and more. There was a little lake with a miniature island. There were trips to the beach through the orange groves in a valley called La Conca d'Oro (The Golden Shell). There were family libraries filled with old volumes that fired a young imagination. And there were the animals: dogs, cats, horses, ponies, a reddish dwarf mule, a ferocious ram, a mongoose, several pet squirrels who were known to bite, white mice, a short-lived chameleon, a couple of baboons, swans, and mandarin ducks.

During these years, Verdura was accumulating a rich mental portfolio of themes and motifs that he would later explore in his jewelry designs. After his father died, in 1919, he left Palermo with his inheritance and spent the next several years pursuing high society and its pleasures in Cannes, Venice, and Paris. It was a glorious time to be young and independent, with an income and without a care, and Verdura enjoyed it to the full. In 1926, while in Venice, he attended one of the legendary fêtes hosted by Linda and Cole Porter in the Palazzo Rezzonico. Thus began a friendship that would last for just over forty years. The Porters recognized Verdura's talent and encouraged him to pursue a career that would allow it to flourish.

Verdura took their advice and went to Paris in 1926, to work as a textile designer for Coco Chanel. Before six months had passed, Chanel too had seen Verdura's flair and asked him to redesign her wonderful, but outmoded jewelry. Most of the collection had been given to her by her extravagant lovers, the Duke of Westminster and the Russian Grand Duke Dmitri. Over the next six years or so, as Chanel's head jewelry designer, Verdura created pieces to complement Chanel's collection, including those that became Chanel's signatures – two wide, enameled cuff bracelets encrusted with a jeweled Maltese cross, and a pair of pearl earrings surrounded by gold braid.

Verdura often accompanied Chanel to the glittering costume theme balls that lit up the Paris nights. In fact, he spent the last of his inheritance on an enormous party

Fulco di Verdura and Coco Chanel admiring one of the famous Maltese Cross cuffs he designed for her in 1926.

of his own in the old palazzo in Palermo. Because it had once belonged to Lady Hamilton, the days of the First Empire were set as the theme, and Verdura naturally dressed as Napoleon. Lady Mendl came as Mrs Siddons and Elsa Maxwell, the society party-hostess, was "a cross between a drummer and an admiral", as Verdura later recalled.

At a similar fête, the second Empire Ball, Verdura and Baron Nicolas de Gunzburg, an old friend whose style and panache matched his own, made a momentous decision. They would go to America, Verdura to design jewelry and the Baron to establish himself in the world of fashion. They arrived in 1934 and, armed with a list of introductions from friends in Europe, they toured the States making new friends in New York, Hollywood, and Palm Beach.

While Nicky de Gunzburg pursued his own career, becoming a fashion editor at *Harper's Bazaar* and *Vogue*, and editor-in-chief at *Town & Country*, Verdura began designing for jeweler Paul Flato in New York. When Flato opened a store in Los Angeles in 1937, he chose Verdura to run it. There Verdura found both friends and clients among the film colony: Gary Cooper, James Stewart, Marlene Dietrich, Jack Benny, Rita Hayworth, Olivia de Havilland, Katharine Hepburn, and many others. Verdura spent almost five years working as head designer for Flato.

Set adrift again in 1939, Verdura returned to New York and, with the encouragement and financial support of Cole Porter, started his own business at 712 Fifth Avenue, in premises once occupied by Cartier. His showrooms opened for business on 1 September 1939, on the eve of the Second World War. Despite the turbulent situation in Europe, Verdura's was an immediate success.

It was as though the events in his life had led up to this moment; he had had an enchanted childhood and had hobnobbed with famous and fashionable people in Europe and America, intimates who were only too happy to buy his delightful creations or to promote them. With his friends Diana Vreeland and Baron de Gunzburg guiding the influential magazines, Verdura and his work were soon familiar to those in the know. The Duchess of Windsor was drawn to Verdura and identified herself with his flamboyant style. As the fashion photographer Horst recently recalled, "He transformed her. She bought from other jewelers, but he alone understood how to make her a duchess." Laurence Olivier, the ever-faithful Porters, Clare Booth Luce, Marjorie Merriweather Post, and myriad others from the social and show-business circles on both sides of the Atlantic arrived on Verdura's doorstep to visit with their elegant, charming friend and leave with his latest designs.

Verdura's famous "woven ribbon" motif is shown to advantage in this diamond and platinum brooch set with round and baguette-cut stones which give dimension and direct attention to the large round-cut centre diamond. Verdura felt that this design had weight and importance, but he allowed sufficient fabric to show between the ribbons to give the piece a light, airy quality so important in a large jewel. The design was made in the 1940s for the film star Pola Negri.

Below, *this yellow gold leaf brooch, made in 1943, is set with masses of facet-cut sapphires and zircons in the warmest colours ranging from golden yellow to rich brown. Throughout his career, Verdura created brooches in the shape of oak and maple leaves in various autumn colours.*

Above, *in the late 1930s, when Verdura was working for Paul Flato, he designed this pomegranate brooch in yellow gold with a skin of facet-cut peridots and seeds of cabochon rubies. The stem is set with yellow diamonds.*

Below, *a set of cufflinks and shirt studs, of black baroque pearls set with tiny diamonds and mounted in yellow gold, made for Baron Nicolas de Gunzburg, one of Verdura's inner circle of talented friends. This dress-set is now in the private collection of Paul Briger.*

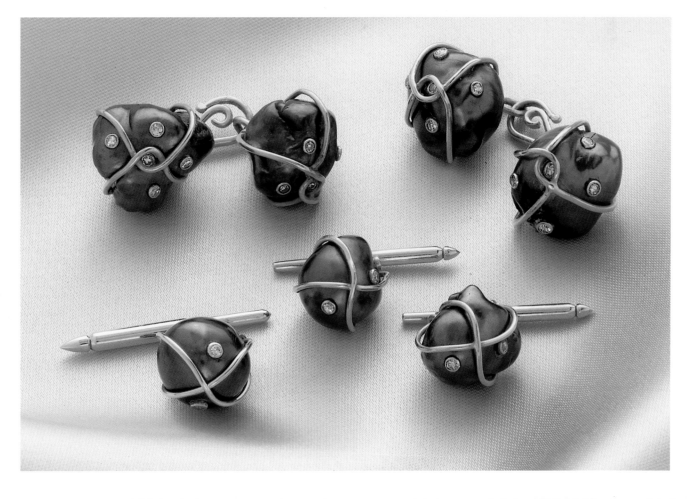

Left, *Verdura was original in using large
coloured stones together to create a
stained-glass effect, as in the two brooches
shown here (left and centre), designed for
Chanel around 1930 and providing the
look of medieval jewelry from a completely contemporary design technique.
Similarly, the Maltese cross motif appears frequently in Verdura's repertoire.
In the brooch designed for Clare Booth
Luce in 1943, large emerald-cut diamonds are mounted in layers with brilliant-cut and baguette-cut stones, giving
depth and dimension. The diamonds are
displayed on a background of yellow gold
rays to create the look of an order of
chivalry or a foreign decoration – items
which Mrs Luce would receive in abun-
dance in later years.*

Left below, *a pair of cuff bracelets in
baked enamel, set with gold, coloured
stones, pearls and diamonds. First designed for Chanel in black and white, they
signaled the revival of baked enamel, a
process by which many thin layers of
enamel are applied over a gold base. The
result is a rich, intense colour, with the
gold shimmering through, and with a
softness and sheen not possible with ordinary enamel.*

Right, *almost as soon as he opened his
New York salon in 1939, Verdura began
to use actual seashells in his fine jewelry.
The Duchess of Windsor was one of the
first to accept these innovative designs,
and by the 1950s the fashion had swept
the USA. The example shown here (along
with its original sketch) is made of a
Lion's Paw shell mounted in yellow gold
and set with diamonds and cabochon
Ceylon sapphires.*

Far right, top, *Verdura brought the
insect motif, which goes back as far as the
17th century, into the 1960s with this
stylized bee brooch with a coral body, four
enormous pear-shaped diamond wings
and an onyx head.*

Far right, centre, *a twin Blackamoor
brooch in yellow gold, extravagantly set
with diamonds, pendant pearls and various coloured stones, made during the
1960s. It reflects Verdura's fascination
with the exotic influences of the Orient
and the Middle East.*

Far right, bottom, *a splendid platinum
and diamond-set wing brooch, which
suspends a large pear-shaped pearl pendant from a diamond-set cap (c. 1946).
The "wing series" was one of Verdura's
most successful designs. It was inspired by
Egyptian mythology and the heraldic
attributes of St Michael.*

This amusing opal, diamond and platinum brooch in the form of an inquisitive mouse wearing a ruby and emerald necklace (early 1970s) was among the most charming animalier jewels made by Verdura.

In this ruby "wrapped heart" brooch, Verdura contrasts the smooth, almost liquid quality of the blood-red cabochon stones with the sharp white bite of the diamond-set platinum ribbon applied in a random crisscross that became one of his trademarks.

The warm pink tourmaline heart pendants on this pair of pavé diamond bow earrings provide a sentimental and completely feminine feeling to the design. In choosing a gem, Verdura's criterion was colour rather than price.

A shell brooch of yellow gold and platinum set with diamonds, which seems to open to reveal a treasure of pearls of various colours and sizes.

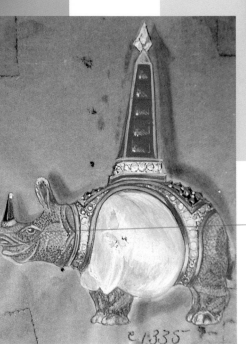

A comedy-and-tragedy mask brooch, intricately composed of yellow gold, openwork platinum, cabochon emerald, cabochon sapphire and cultured pearls, was made in the early 1940s for Clare Booth Luce to celebrate her successful play, The Women.

One of Verdura's vast production of enchanting design drawings – showing a yellow gold rhinoceros brooch (1956), its body formed by an enormous baroque pearl with emeralds, rubies and diamonds added for contrast and brilliance. The design recalls Bernini's mid-17th-century composition for the Piazza of S. Maria sopra Minerva in Rome.

Opposite, a necklace, representative of Verdura's special sensitivity to colour and unusual combinations of materials, in which the iridescence of the black baroque pearls is carried forward in a stronger tone in the magnificent Siberian amethyst pendant. The two elements are joined by a platinum and pavé diamond wreath, while the pendant is topped by a pavé diamond cap in points of irregular length. The earrings are pavé diamond loops, each with a large oval-cut diamond centre stone.

Above, an example of one of Verdura's earliest and most copied innovations: the rope motif. In this yellow gold and diamond necklace, he makes the diamonds seem almost incidental to the intricate goldwork. The earrings were designed to complement Verdura's famous wreath motif with a pavé diamond centre and beautiful pendant pearls.

Left, two pairs of mabe pearl earrings, in which Verdura used gold twisted wire and pavé diamonds to add importance and interest to the large surface area of the pearl. The pair on the left were made for the Duchess of Windsor.

230

In this sapphire and diamond necklace, evocative of the 1950s, Verdura used a variety of carefully positioned stones in shades of blue ranging from almost purple to pale gray-blue, with an occasional cabochon of rich cornflower blue thrown in for good measure. Round-cut diamonds are sprinkled among the sapphires like stars, and the sharply defined crossed bands of calibré-cut sapphires of very dark blue provide contrast. The earrings match the design of the necklace and are accented by centre starburst motifs of pavé diamonds.

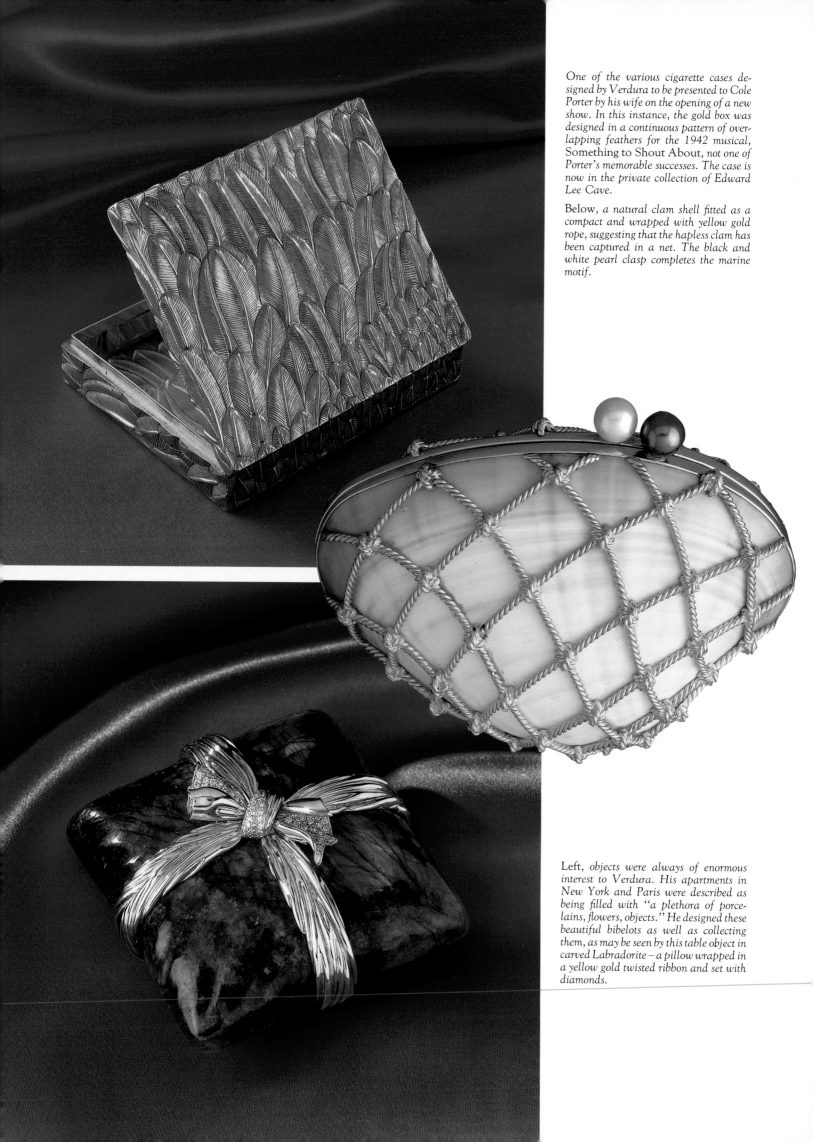

One of the various cigarette cases designed by Verdura to be presented to Cole Porter by his wife on the opening of a new show. In this instance, the gold box was designed in a continuous pattern of overlapping feathers for the 1942 musical, Something to Shout About, not one of Porter's memorable successes. The case is now in the private collection of Edward Lee Cave.

Below, a natural clam shell fitted as a compact and wrapped with yellow gold rope, suggesting that the hapless clam has been captured in a net. The black and white pearl clasp completes the marine motif.

Left, objects were always of enormous interest to Verdura. His apartments in New York and Paris were described as being filled with "a plethora of porcelains, flowers, objects." He designed these beautiful bibelots as well as collecting them, as may be seen by this table object in carved Labradorite – a pillow wrapped in a yellow gold twisted ribbon and set with diamonds.

He accepted many special commissions from his clients over the years, designing pieces for everything from Christmas celebrations and anniversaries to opening nights at the theatre. Even before Verdura had his own showroom, Linda Porter made it a first-night ritual to give her husband a cigarette case designed by Fulco, each case in some way reflecting the specific musical. "I designed more than twenty," Verdura recalled in an interview. "It was a puzzle, a challenge, trying to fit them into the theme. *Du Barry Was a Lady* was especially difficult. On one side I had the fleur-de-lis of France and the royal crown, and on the other I had a lady's hat with the ribbons flying and all the fleurs-de-lis sort of bebopping along in two different golds." For another Cole Porter show, *Red, Hot and Blue*, in 1936, the case had stripes of rubies, diamonds and sapphires; and a gold case woven like fine straw celebrated the opening of *Panama Hattie* in 1940.

When another client and friend, John Hay Whitney, was appointed Ambassador to the Court of Saint James in the 1950s, his wife Betsy, who would be presented at court, turned to Verdura for her tiara. He produced a highly imaginative design, based on an American Indian headdress, with golden feathers rising from a narrow circlet and glittering with diamonds. It was not only appropriate but elegant and witty as well.

Clients would often give Verdura their old pieces to be cleverly reworked into new designs that bore the stamp of his humour and imagination. In discussing his work, he once addressed the problems of such commissions: "If I do a thing for stock, then I do my own design and choose my stones, but very often I have to make a design, a sketch, for a stone or several stones that belong to somebody, and then it's much more difficult. You can't bend them to your power; you must have respect for the stone."

Unlike many other jewelers, who simply turned a design over to their craftsmen, Verdura worked closely with his, so that each piece is a direct reflection of his personality. His earliest association was with the firm of Valliant and Deverne, until in 1952 he met André Chervin. This talented young Frenchman translated Verdura's designs into the beautiful enamel pieces that became one of the firm's trademarks and revived interest in fine enamel jewelry.

Fulco had no fear of competition and was generous and open with other designers. When Jean Schlumberger arrived in New York, Verdura not only gave him a place to stay but shared his portfolio of drawings. Comparisons are often noted between their work; Schlumberger's early designs are certainly derivative of Verdura pieces. Kenneth Jay Lane, David Webb, Angela Cummings, Paloma Picasso and others also acknowledge their debt to Verdura.

Verdura drew from a wide range of sources for his designs, from personal memories of his ancestral home and its frescoes in Palermo, to the Renaissance jewels he discovered in the Munich Schatzkammer which he visited with Chanel. He had an instinctive feeling for nature and all its rich variety, and delighted in designs of ripe pomegranates bursting with ruby seeds, of birds in flight or pecking at jeweled berries, of ears of corn, and golden pineapples. He created a menagerie of jeweled animals and an Eden of jeweled flowers. There were funny little poodles in velvet jackets, cats playing with pearl balls, sea horses, dolphins, and mythical sea creatures – a mermaid admiring herself in a mirror and a pearl-breasted merman brandishing two sapphire torches.

Verdura's work struck a balance between tradition and innovation. While he might be inspired by the Renaissance, by medieval heraldry, by motifs borrowed from Egypt and ancient Rome, he would realize his designs in new or newly discovered materials. He broke the rules to suit his designs. During the war years, as Diana Vreeland recalled, "He was the first to use colored stones and gold when platinum and diamonds were being produced by the other houses. It certainly took the other jewelers a long time to catch up with him." He decried huge stones, particularly the icy diamonds prized by other jewelers, which he dubbed "mineralogy, not jewelry". He wrinkled his nose at large solitaire diamonds set in rings, calling them "swimming pools".

He was also the first to incorporate actual shells and pebbles into his work. Some of these he found on the beach at Fire Island where he spent several summers, and others he bought at the American

Top, *Verdura's unusual imagination was given full rein in his use of antique carved ivory-and-bone chessmen, collected during his world travels. These exotic and often crudely carved figures were then set with colourful gems, dressed in gold turbans and given real or fantasy animals as pets on gold or pearl leashes. The two figures shown here appear against a background of the original design drawings.*

Below, *the bow motif appears time and again in Verdura's work. He loved its soft asymmetric quality and was fascinated by the ability of his goldsmith to give hard, unforgiving metal a look of supple flexibility. This bow brooch of 1939 is set against the original design drawing.*

Museum of Natural History in New York. It was reported in a *New Yorker* article (24 May 1941) that it amused him to "buy a shell for five dollars, use half of it, and sell it for twenty-five hundred". By the time he had finished with a lowly pebble, it might be covered with colourful jewels and set in gold.

Verdura produced unusual and exuberant responses to prevailing trends. He revived the gold knotwork of Leonardo da Vinci and the basketwork of Giulio Romano, the 16th-century designer for the Gonzagas of Mantua, and produced rich ropes of necklaces – wreaths of diamond leaves with emerald berries, garlands of pink topaz flowers tied with ribbons, and stars twinkling amid dark blue sapphires, strings of pearls or coral beads twisted into torsades and secured with a ribbon motif or a double crescent. Such pieces were a perfect complement to the fashion for bare-shouldered, full-skirted evening gowns. When women began to sweep their hair away from the face, a style preferred by the Duchess of Windsor, Verdura softened the look with large Mabe pearl earrings with twisted gold borders, or surrounded by golden laurel wreaths, highlighted with diamonds, and occasionally covered in a trellis of gold basketwork.

Unless they were personal friends, those who found their way to his quiet second-floor establishment were invariably told that the Duke was out, although Verdura always instructed his employees to say that he was dead. Rather than meet with clients, he preferred to spend hour after hour in his private office making wonderful gouache sketches for designs. Far more prolific than most people realized, he filled several large volumes with these exquisitely detailed miniatures, many of which are yet to be executed. His extraordinary energy enabled him to work long hours and still find time each day for lunch at the Caravelle and dinner at other restaurants, followed by visits to nightclubs or parties with his friends.

The war years were painful for Verdura, who could only witness from afar his beloved Europe being torn to pieces. The old Palazzo Verdura, which had survived for so many centuries, was destroyed in a bombardment, but the Villa Niscemi survived. In New York, Verdura himself was treated as an enemy alien by the authorities,

who actually seized his office radio, thus depriving him of the pleasure of listening to classical music while he sketched.

Even so, his business thrived and he found time to collaborate in 1941 with Salvador Dalí on a collection of painted jewels – paintings by Dalí, jewels by Verdura. Dalí's notebooks hinted at their surreal relationship, and *Vogue* published excerpts (15 July 1941), calling them "Dalí's Aphorisms" – "1. Fulco and I have tried to discover whether it was the Jewel that was born for Painting or Painting for the Jewel; we are sure, however, that they were born for each other; it's a love marriage. . . . 5. The ideal Object to me is an Object that is useful for absolutely nothing; that could not be used for writing or removing superfluous hair or for telephoning; an Object which could not be placed on the mantelpiece or a Louis XIV commode; an Object which one is forced simply to wear – a Jewel. 6. Uselessness is the first condition of luxury."

A portrait of Verdura in his Paris apartment taken by Horst in 1930, at a time when the jeweler, at the height of the European success, was about to set his sights on New York and Hollywood.

235

VERDURA

When peace was declared, Verdura designed a V-for-victory brooch and in 1947 he opened a small shop in Paris, on the Rue de Boissy, mostly to provide himself with an excuse to travel regularly to Europe. He still called New York home, and lived for years in a brownstone apartment on Park Avenue above The Rosary flower shop. He surrounded himself with books, piling them everywhere, and collected porcelains and wonderful *objets*. However small, the apartment had a European elegance and richness that reflected the warm, lively personality of its owner. Here he entertained his intimates from society and the arts – the Cole Porters, Hélène de Rothschild, Diana Vreeland, Babs Simpson, and others. He loved cooking, company, and opera, and he served up sprightly conversation and opera recordings with his carefully planned dinners. Elsa Maxwell once compiled a guest list for what she called "the most perfect dinner party for twelve", and Verdura was high on the list.

By 1972, however, he was beginning to feel somewhat world-weary. He decided to retire to London and sold his business to his long-time associate Joseph Alfano. In the few years that remained, he worked on a series of much admired miniature paintings – landscapes, still-lifes, and interiors. He finished his book of memoirs, writing only about his childhood, and he kept up with his many friends. In the summer of 1978, he died and his ashes were taken to Palermo, to the family chapel in the Church of the Holy Spirit.

After Verdura's retirement, the firm continued to produce his designs, upholding his high standards. Today, there are still many vibrant designs in his sketchbooks to be fulfilled, made in limited quantities for clients who have remained faithful to the Verdura tradition. His work has been discovered by a new generation as part of a return to elegance in the 1980s. But whatever the era, Verdura's work possesses a timeless beauty that enhances without overwhelming, often making the viewer smile and draw closer to discover the surprise that Verdura worked into his small-scale masterpieces.

W hen I'm in Rome I always visit Bulgari, because it is the most important museum of contemporary art.

ANDY WARHOL

The Rome-based jewelers Bulgari are virtually the only House to have made a world-wide reputation in the production of high jewelry since the Second World War. Most of the names which have remained famous in this recent period were originally established either towards the end of the 19th century or in the years between the two global wars. Bulgari had, in fact, made its appearance in the Via Condotti as early as 1905, but it was not really until the 1960s that the imprint made by its distinctive combination of style, quality and craftsmanship won over the international jewelry world.

Throughout history, jewelry and the wearing of jewelry have had different meanings for different cultures. Among primitive people, a piece of metal, wood or stone personal adornment seems to have been a totem of superhuman powers, a charm with magical properties. In various phases of our own civilization, jewelry has been looked on as a status symbol, an element of fashion, a craft, and – in rare instances – a form of art. It is precisely as an art that Bulgari interprets jewelry, following an Italian tradition that originated in the 15th century.

During the Italian Renaissance, the craftsmen involved in the making of jewelry developed a new approach to design. Since the humanist philosophy reversed medieval cosmological teaching and placed the individual firmly at the centre of the universe, anything which helped to express this novel view was considered to be highly desirable. Jewelry, being directly related to the essence and circumstances of individuals, and being besides one of the oldest forms of decorative art, finally entered into the mainstream of social life. Its prevalence and connotations are documented in the work of all the great Renaissance painters.

The essence of jewelry design during the Renaissance was colour, and the predominance and original use of colour in its creations was later also to be a hallmark of the House of Bulgari.

The first of the family in Italy was Sotirio Bulgari, a silversmith who came there in 1881 from his native Greece. A specialist in the engraving of precious objects in silver, he settled first in Naples, where he opened a small shop in the Piazza dei Martiri. Beginning from nothing, he seems quickly to have flourished in that city. But he was robbed of his earnings and decided to start over again in Rome. In 1884 he opened his first shop there, in the Via Sistina. It was not until some twenty years later that he moved the business to the Via Condotti, but not yet at the address where Andy Warhol liked to make his visits.

Sotirio had begun in the meantime to deal in stones and jewels, and brought up two sons, Giorgio and Costantino, whom he taught all he knew of the art of engraving. It was these two who gradually took over the running of their father's business, and turned from engraving to the production of modern jewelry.

During the 1930s the Bulgari brothers called on the services of an important architect of the period to design a new store at 10 Via Condotti, the same address where the main business is still conducted today. By the time of Sotirio's death in 1932, Bulgari's was a thriving concern and had grown enormously in stature, but was not yet universally regarded as one of the world's leading fine jewelers.

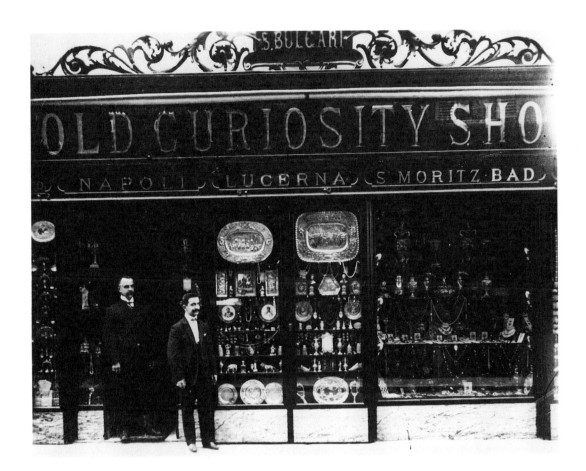

Sotirio Bulgari, Greek-born founder of the jewelry firm, in the doorway of his shop in the Via Condotti, Rome, shortly after it was opened.

The same shop after it was rebuilt and modernized in the 1930s.

The up-to-date, remodelled and enlarged Roman headquarters of Bulgari, still in the Via Condotti, and now the centre of a world-wide enterprise.

The sons had begun their introduction into the business from the early part of the century. In fact, Giorgio Bulgari made the first of many visits to Paris in 1900 and imbibed there the intoxicating splendours of the Ballets Russes which were to have such a significant influence on jewelry design. As was the case with a number of jewelry dynasties, the two brothers were different but complementary. Giorgio became the creative genius of the House, with an expert knowledge of stones and jewelry-making techniques; Costantino specialized in antique silver and art objects, building up a collection of snuff boxes, jade and Italian and English silver. Costantino made it his life work to publish *Argentieri, Gemmari e Orafi in Italia*, the only existing directory of hallmarks of Italian silver of all periods.

Since the 18th century, the jewelry business had been concentrated in France, and Paris was the mecca to which all the world's potentates and millionaires came to buy their extravagant baubles. In the early 20th century, jewelry designers were addicted to the so-called "French style" which, basically speaking, implied the use of round diamonds set in prongs, surrounded by emeralds, rubies or sapphires. With these elements the Paris jewelers were able to make the magnificent parures, diadems, tiaras and crowns for which they had become world-famous.

Another strand in the design of jewelry at that time was the Oriental influence, based not only on the costumes and decors of the Ballets Russes, but also on archaeological discoveries and contacts with the Middle East and India. Motifs were freely borrowed from ancient Egyptian, Assyrian and Chinese prototypes.

The most revolutionary change that took place in the 20th century was the application of Art Deco motifs to jewelry; from about 1925, the clean, bold shapes of Art Deco jewels and costly *objets* were spread throughout the world by the Houses of Cartier, Van Cleef & Arpels, and Boucheron.

In its turn, Bulgari introduced a new aesthetic into the art of jewelry. In place of the "French style" diamond with its surround of other precious stones, Bulgari proposed a coloured stone, not set in prongs but in a hand-crafted gold bezel, in a frame of tapered baguette diamonds. The centre, instead of being held around the neck by more diamonds in prongs, was encased in a heavy gold chain. The first thing which became apparent in this new arrangement of precious materials was the use of forms. Bulgari brought to jewelry a new compactness and purity of form.

Opposite, necklace and matching pendant earrings, dating from the late 1950s. Cabochon-cut sapphires, rubies and emeralds are set amid brilliant-cut diamonds.

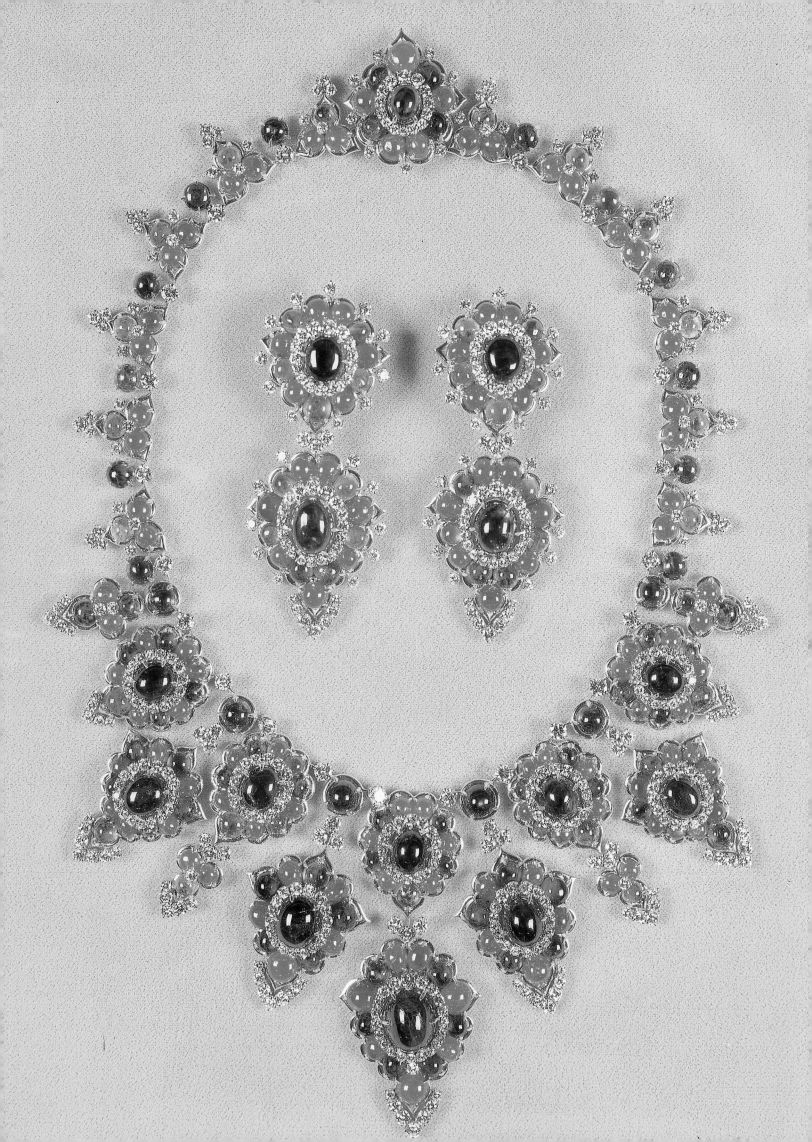

Opposite, *a yellow gold and diamond necklace composed of a row of twenty-one round diamond balls. These are linked by baguette diamond motifs, from which are suspended seven emerald drops which increase in size towards the centre of the necklace. (Late 1970s)*

Top, *a collar of yellow gold and cultured pearls. The cabochon emerald in the centre of the ruby and emerald motif weighs 12.53 carats.*

Centre left, *one of a pair of yellow gold earrings, set with brilliant-cut diamonds, rubies, emeralds and an oval cabochon emerald weighing 10.7 carats. Next to it, one of a pair of yellow gold ear clips, decorated with rubies, sapphires, diamonds and an oval cabochon emerald weighing 7.5 carats.*

Below, *detail of a yellow gold necklace, made up of heart-shaped emeralds set amid brilliant and baguette-cut diamonds.*

Two brightly coloured rings of yellow gold, set with rubies, emeralds, diamonds and amethysts.

Two rings in which the central oval emeralds are enhanced by ruby and emerald "pippoli" (small stones embellishing the central gem) in the manner characteristic of Bulgari jewelry.

Two rings of yellow gold. The one on the left is set with brilliant and baguette-cut diamonds, baguette-cut rubies and a large oval cabochon emerald. Next to it, an oval-cut sapphire is embellished by baguette diamonds and rubies.

A necklace of yellow gold, set with round and baguette diamonds, baguette rubies, triangular
cabochon amethysts and five large cabochon emeralds.
Below it, a diamond "carpet" necklace set with forty fancy oval-cut sapphires amid sinuous ruby
and amethyst motifs.

Opposite: above, *a necklace of cultured pearls and square-cut diamonds has as its central motif*
an 81.94-carat oval-cut sapphire with a pear-shaped diamond at each corner, set amid bands of
baguette sapphires and diamonds.
Below it, a yellow gold necklace and matching clip bracelet set with brilliant-cut diamonds and
cultured pearls.

Above, *necklace composed of graduated round and drop pearls, encircled by brilliant-cut diamonds.*

In itself, this was not strictly a step forward, but instead a sophisticated return to historical patterns. In Etruscan art Bulgari found a point of departure – a new attitude towards jewelry founded on a re-thinking of Etruscan values.

Similarly, Bulgari researched the workmanship of ancient Rome, and reinterpreted this in a contemporary key. For example, the House introduced for the first time the use of antique coins and handmade gold chains in fine jewelry.

Bulgari's aim in its designs has always been to maintain close ties with Italian history and art. Thus it has harked back to the Renaissance in its use of cameo and intaglio, and above all colour. Modern jewelry had been characterized for a long time by an unvarying colour triad created out of emeralds, rubies and sapphires. Bulgari introduced into the design vocabulary such new shades as violets, pinks and yellows. In numerous jewels, one finds such colour combinations as yellow gold together with white, red, or other materials – for example, white and burnished steel. The use of "pippoli" – small coloured stones which embellish the central stone – is also frequent. From the techniques per-fected in the Renaissance, Bulgari revived the cabochon cut for precious stones, marking a reversal in the dominant tradition of the early 20th century.

Bulgari's continuing and growing success has been sustained by its good fortune in having a family business tradition. The fruitful combination of Giorgio and Costantino was succeeded by Giorgio's three sons, Paolo, Gianni and Nicola, who took over the management in 1967. In their hands, the Rome shop, already the pre-mière establishment in Italy, took on a truly international character. It had been one of Giorgio's dreams to export the Bulgari production to the whole world, and his sons realized this ambition when they opened the first Bulgari shop abroad – New York in 1970. Soon afterwards, their expansion became irresistible: Geneva in 1974, Monte Carlo in 1977, Paris itself in 1979, Milan in 1986, Tokyo in 1987, and Hong Kong, Osaka, Singapore and London in 1988. In 1989, there were two additional launchings in Munich and in a second location in New York on the southwest corner of Fifth Avenue and 57th Street. The year 1990 was earmarked for St Moritz.

Above, left, *Sotirio, Leonilde and Giorgio Bulgari in the summer of 1932 at the Lido of Venice.*

Above, *in a photograph of 1989: Paolo Bulgari (chairman), Francesco Trapani, and Nicola Bulgari.*

Opposite: top, *a flexible ribbed clip bracelet of yellow gold, set with a silver drachma minted on the island of Rhodes in the 3rd century* BC.
Centre, *a "gas pipe" clip bracelet in three colours, set with a rare Roman silver coin of the Emperor Augustus (43* BC–14 AD*).*
Below, *watch with a white and yellow gold "gas pipe" bracelet (c. 1965).*

BULGARI

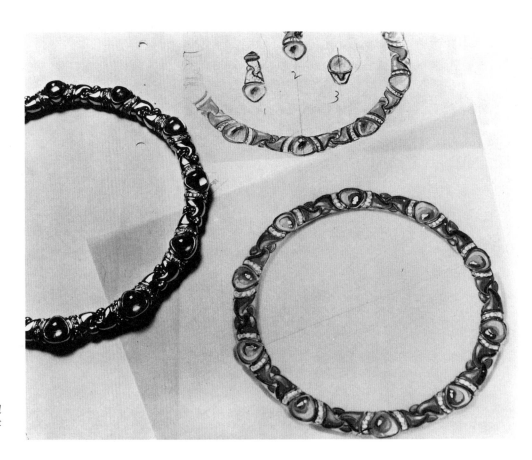

Right and opposite, *examples of typical Bulgari necklaces being made from the careful and detailed design drawings that set down the creative ideas.*

Gianni Bulgari has ceased to take an active part in the firm's activities; on the other hand, in 1981 a nephew, Francesco Trapani, representing the fourth generation, joined his uncles and brought with him organizational skills which have facilitated Bulgari's tremendous international growth.

The Bulgari brothers now in charge are as different in their characters as the brothers in the preceding generation were. Nicola, who spends a good deal of time in the United States, is ebullient and outgoing. A born salesman, he is gifted at creating the right atmosphere in which to display and sell fine jewelry. After a period of training in diamond-cutting in Amsterdam, he learned the trade at the side of his father and uncle in Rome. He loves America because he was a young boy growing up in Rome at the time the city was liberated by American troops in 1945. In fact, the House of Bulgari received a citation from Generals Alexander and Clark for their help to Allied troops parachuted into Italy during the war.

Paolo prefers to keep a low profile, out of the reach of publicity; but his quiet façade belies the depth of his creative talents. He is widely acknowledged as one of the world's foremost jewelers, in terms of both technical skill and inspiration. In his capacity as the artistic director of Bulgari, he works in close collaboration with a team of seasoned designers, craftsmen and artists. One of his greatest talents is his ability to translate his understanding of his family's traditions into recognizably Bulgari jewels while continually moving forward with new and exciting forms and ideas.

The ideas may emerge from a simple combination of various stones or from a particular flash of intuition. Most often they are based on the prior study of certain motifs, certain themes of specific historical epochs, which are analyzed into their essential elements and reinterpreted in terms of contemporary jewelry or silverware. The creative idea takes shape as a watercolour or tempera drawing, which shows the depth and life the jewel will acquire, thus anticipating the emotion it will arouse once it is actually made. From this first drawing, the idea is explored and developed creatively to determine the materials and colours best suited to it, to see how it will be worn and how it fits in with the Bulgari tradition and style.

One of the characteristic elements of Bulgari jewelry is the influence of ancient Greek objects and models. The symmetry and proportions of Bulgari products are based more upon art and architecture than on nature – a factor which distinguishes the Bulgari jewel from that of the French masters.

Bulgari has made many breakthroughs in creating what is now recognized as "the Bulgari style". It was the first, for example, in the 1950s, to substitute the use of yellow gold for platinum or white gold in the setting of precious stones, and it was a pioneer in the use of cabochon semi-precious stones in fine jewelry to obtain particular chromatic effects.

Bulgari's importance as one of the most influential of contemporary jewelry Houses derives mainly from two factors: the passion of the Bulgari brothers for beauty and quality, and the firm's innovations in the field of design. It looks on jewels, as well as its other products (such as watches, pens, lighters, and a whole range of silverware), as the culmination of beautiful forms and colours created and adapted specifically for the world of today.

NOTES

BIBLIOGRAPHIES

ACKNOWLEDGMENTS

FONTENAY

Acknowledgments

To Marie-Nöel de Gary, Hannah Helms, Françoise Maison, Marie-Madeleine Massé, Sylvie Nissen, Katherine Purcell, Judy Rudoc.

Daniel Alcouffe, Fritz Falk, Michael Koch, Geoffrey Munn, Michel Tonneleau.

Bibliography

WORKS BY EUGÈNE FONTENAY

Fontenay, *Exposition Universelle de 1867: Classe 36 Pièces de Joaillerie exécutées et gravées à l'eau-forte, à Messieurs les Jurés*, Paris 1867

"Le Rôle du Bijou Moderne dans le Costume", *Revue des Arts Décoratifs*, Vol. 2, 1881–82, pp. 341–45

"Le Bijou à travers les Ages", *Revue des Arts Décoratifs*, Vol. 5, 1884–85, pp. 569–577 and Vol. 6, 1885–86, pp. 23–27

"Confession d'un Orfèvre", *Revue des Arts Décoratifs*, Vol. 6, 1885–86, pp. 262–65

Les Bijoux Anciens et Modernes, Paris 1887

WORKS BY EUGÈNE FONTENAY WITH OTHERS

JANNETAZ, ED., FONTENAY, EU., VANDERHEYM, EM., and COUTANCE, A., *Diamants et Pierres Précieuses: Bijoux, Joyaux, Orfèvreries*, Paris 1881

The best study devoted to Eugène Fontenay remains that of Henri Vever in his work *La Bijouterie Française au XIXème Siècle*, Paris 1906–08, Vol. II, pp. 157–80. (The illustrations begin on p. 147, and continue in Vol. III, pp. 342, 355–56, 365, 368, 375, 393 and 449.)

HANCOCK

Acknowledgments

The present-day directors of Messrs Hancocks have been unfailingly helpful and encouraging during the writing of this brief account of the firm's history. In particular David Callaghan arranged for special photography of their collection, and allowed me unrestricted access to their archive material.

I would also like to thank Judy Rudoc of the British Museum for her continued help in solving the puzzles that emerge at every turn in the study of 19th-century jewelry.

C. G.

Notes to the text

p. 48 The quotation from *The Illustrated London News* is again taken from the edition of 9 May 1857, p. 441.

Lady Granville wearing the stomacher at the Graziano Palace: see *Treasures from Chatsworth*, The Royal Academy, 1980, no. 176, catalogued by Diana Scarisbrick.

The description of the temporary ballroom is to be found in *The Illustrated London News*, 18 October 1856, p. 392.

For the account of the inauguration of the State Supper Room, see *The Illustrated London News*, 18 July 1857, p. 51.

p. 58 The account of Hancock approaching the Duke with the idea of remounting the gems from the Devonshire collection appears in the *Morning Chronicle*, 30 April 1857 (also cited above on p. 48).

The report of the 1871 Exhibition is taken from *The Queen*, 30 September 1871, p. 208.

p. 59 For the suggestion that the brooch with the libation scene was made by George Goodwin, see "Assyrian-Style Jewellery", *The Antique Collector*, April 1989, p. 48. Goodwin registered his "Assyrian" designs in October 1873 and June and July 1874.

p. 59–60 The tiara is illustrated in the *Art Journal* for 1873, p. 152.

p. 60 The Empress Eugénie's brooch is illustrated in the *Lady's Pictorial*, 8 July 1893, and *The Queen*, 15 July 1893.

FALIZE

Acknowledgments

I am grateful to HRH Prince Paul of Hohenzollern-Roumania for his help concerning the Roumanian commissions of Falize's work and I am indebted to Ljiljana Mišković-Prelević of the Historical Museum of Serbia in Belgrade for her kind attention regarding the regalia for King Peter I of Serbia.

I would like to express my very special gratitude to Monsieur Robert Falize who provided previously unpublished biographical details of his father Jean and grandfather Lucien.

K. P.

Bibliography

BURTY, PHILIPPE, *Les Emaux Cloisonnés Anciens et Modernes*, 1868
—— "Les Industries de luxe à l'Exposition de l'Union Centrale", *Gazette des Beaux-Arts*, 1869, 2e période, pp. 529–49
FALIZE, LUCIEN, "Claude Popelin et la Renaissance des Emaux Peints", *Gazette des Beaux-Arts*, 1893, 3e période, IX
—— "Exposition Universelle de 1889. Les Industries d'Art. III. Orfèvrerie d'art, Bijoux, Joyaux", *Gazette des Beaux-Arts*, 1889, 3e période.
—— "Jeweller's Work", *Artistic Japan*, Part V
—— "L'Art Japonais: A propos de l'Exposition organisée par M. Gonse", *Revue des Arts Décoratifs*, 1882–83, III, pp. 239–338
—— "L'Art Japonais par M. Louis Gonse", *Revue des Arts Décoratifs*, 1883–4, IV
FONTENAY, EUGÈNE, *Les Bijoux Anciens et Modernes*. 1887
MIŠKOVIĆ-PRELEVIĆ, LJILJANA, "Valtrovic's designs for the coronation objects of Peter I Karadordevic", *Annual of the Museum of Applied Arts*, Belgrade, Vol. 24–25, 1980–81
VEVER, HENRI, *La Bijouterie Française au XIXe Siècle*, 1908
WARING, J.B., *Masterpieces of Industrial Art and Sculpture at the International Exhibition of 1862*

FABERGÉ

Note on the photographs

The photographs in this chapter are from the archives of Wartski, London, who are also the owners of the Fabergé record books from which the watercolour designs reproduced here have been chosen. The jewels illustrated are all signed by one of Fabergé's workmasters in St Petersburg or the Moscow branch unless otherwise stated.

TILLANDER

Bibliography

In addition to the archives of A. Tillander in Helsinki, the following were consulted:
A. Tillander Jewelers, *Annual Reports, 1901–17*, St Petersburg
TILLANDER, ALEXANDER THEODOR, *Family Chronicle*, unpublished, 1935
—— *Diaries, 1898–1934*, unpublished, St Petersburg and Helsinki

VEVER

Bibliography

ANON., *Ville de Metz, Exposition Universelle de 1861 sous le Patronage de S.M. l'Impératrice. Agriculture, Industrie, Horticulture, Beaux-Arts, Concours d'Orphéons* (Metz 1861)
BÉNÉDITE, LÉONCE, "Le Bijou à l'Exposition Universelle", in *Art Décoration*, v. 8 (1900), pp. 65–82
GEFFROY, GUSTAVE, *Les Industries Artistiques Françaises et Etrangères à l'Exposition Universelle de 1900* (Paris 1901), p. 40
MARX, ROGER, "La Décoration et l'Art Industriel à l'Exposition de 1889", conference at the Congrès de la Société Centrale des Architectes Français held on 17 June 1890 (Paris 1890), p. 43
—— "Les Arts à l'Exposition Universelle de 1900. La Décoration et les Industries d'Art", *Gazette des Beaux-Arts*, January 1901 (v. 25), pp. 53–83
MONOD, E., *L'Exposition Universelle de 1889* (Paris 1889), v. III ("Les Industries de luxe"), p. 539

VEVER, HENRI, *La Bijouterie Française au XIXème Siècle*, 3 vols (Paris 1906–08), v. 3, pp. 652–89

FOUQUET

Notes to the text

p. 158 Alphonse was apprenticed first to Henri Meusnier in the Rue Saint-Martin. His various employers after that included Sustendal, Robin Père, Dobbée Frères and Savard.

From 1854 onwards all Alphonse Fouquet's sketches and designs in albums or on loose sheets were preserved. They were deposited with the Musée des Arts Décoratifs in Paris and form an exceptional archive which, joined to the production of Alphonse's successors, his son Georges and his grandson Jean, gives us access to the complete production (about 3,500 designs) of one firm.

p. 160 The four pieces owned by the Musée were the gift of Alphonse Fouquet (1908, Inv. 14851. A, C, D, F) along with three other pieces: a châtelaine, showing a chimera and a serpent fighting (Inv. 14851 E), a belt buckle showing two lions face to face, with the monogram of Marie-Henriette of Austria, Queen of Belgium (Inv. 14851 G), and a hand-mirror (Inv. 14851 B).

Oscar Massin's remark appears in A. Fouquet, *Histoire de ma Vie Industrielle* (Paris 1899), p. 59.

The model of the necklace shown in 1889 is in the Musée des Arts Décoratifs.

p. 169 The quotation from Vever's book is in vol. 3 (Paris 1908).

The orchid brooch of 1898 is at the University of East Anglia, Norwich (*cf.* M. N. de Gary, *Les Fouquets, Bijoutiers et Joailliers à Paris 1860–1960*, Paris 1983, repr. p. 72).

Eugène Grasset was to design jewels for Henri Vever in 1900.

Bernhardt's snake bracelet came up for sale at Christie's, Geneva, on 12 November 1987. More recently another bracelet, unknown until then, was sold on 11 May 1989, again at Christie's.

p. 170 The Mucha bodice clip is in the collection of Johanna Walker (*cf.* de Gary, *op. cit.*, pp. 66, 67).

The central ornament of a necklace is in the collection of S. and L. Lewis (*cf.* de Gary, *op. cit.*, p. 68).

For an example of fragments remounted in different settings, see the pendant of 1905 reproduced in de Gary, *op. cit.*, p. 157.

The elements of the Rue Royale location were distributed as follows: the façade and the interior furnishings were given by Georges Fouquet to the Musées de la Ville de Paris at the time of the demolition; other elements were more recently given by the Fouquet family to the Musée des Arts Décoratifs. The floor, the ceiling and other missing elements were reconstructed in the Hôtel Le Peletier de Saint Fargeau after Mucha's designs.

Houillon: a text of his in manuscript, housed in the Bibliothèque de la Chambre Syndicale de la Joaillerie, describes the technique used by Tourette.

Fouquet's remarks on Tourette are from a letter he wrote to the Conservateur of the Musée des Arts Décoratifs in 1950.

p. 171 In connection with Georges' position in the Milan exhibition, *cf.* G. Fouquet, *Bijouterie, Joaillerie, Médailles à l'Exposition Internationale de Milan en 1906* (Paris 1913).

The book organized by Georges Fouquet after the 1925 Exposition was published in Paris in 1934.

p. 172 With reference to the originality of design and new sources of inspiration to form the basis of the 1925 Exposition, the admissions committee under G. Fouquet was specifically instructed to respect this condition.

The 1929 quotation of Georges Fouquet appeared in *Le Figaro* (supplément artistique), 13 June 1929, pp. 607–14.

Jean Fouquet's book appeared in the series called *Art International d'Aujourd'hui*, No. 16, published in Paris by Charles Moreau.

In connection with the pieces shown in 1937, there are designs and a brooch in the Musée des Arts Décoratifs (*cf.* de Gary, *op. cit.*, pp. 122–25).

TIFFANY

Bibliography

ANON., "The Art of the Modern Goldsmith", *Town and Country*, 29 October 1904, pp. 16–17

—— "The Jewelry Department", *The Jewelers' Weekly*, Vol. 8, No. 6, 6 June 1889.

—— "Louis C. Tiffany and His Work in Artistic Jewellery", *The International Studio*, Vol. 30, No. 117, November 1906, pp. xxxii–xlii

—— "Recent Work in Objets d'Art and Artistic Jewellery by Paulding Farnham", *The International Studio*, Vol. 29, No. 116, October 1906, pp. xciii–xcix

—— "Tiffany & Co. at the Saint Louis Exposition", *The Craftsman*, Vol. VII, No. 2, November 1904, pp. 169–83

BECKER, VIVIENNE, *Art Nouveau Jewelry*, New York 1985

—— "Schlumberger: A Look at His Life and Career", *Jewel*, Premiere Issue, Winter 1988, pp. 28–37

CARPENTER, CHARLES H., JR, with GRACE, MARY, *Tiffany Silver*, New York 1978

—— and ZAPATA, JANET, *The Silver of Tiffany & Co. 1850–1987*, Museum of Fine Arts, Boston 1987

DEKAY, CHARLES, *The Art Work of Louis Comfort Tiffany*, New York 1914

EDWARDS, HARRIET, "The Goldsmith's Art at Paris: An American Triumph", *The Home Journal*, Vol. 55, No. 29, 20 September 1900, pp. 6–7.

GARSIDE, ANNE (ed.), *Jewelry: Ancient to Modern*, Baltimore 1979

GERE, CHARLOTTE, *American & European Jewelry 1830–1914*, New York 1975

HARLOW, KATHERINA, "A Pioneer Master of Art Nouveau", *Apollo*, Vol. 116, No. 245, July 1982, pp. 46–50

HEYDT, GEORGE FREDERICK, *Charles L. Tiffany and the House of Tiffany & Co.*, New York 1893

—— "A Glimpse of the Tiffany Exhibit at the Columbian Exposition", reproduced in *Godey's Magazine*, August 1893

HOVING, THOMAS, "Cellini, Fabergé and Me", *Connoisseur*, April 1982, pp. 82–91

KUNZ, GEORGE FREDERICK, and STEVENSON, CHARLES HUGH, *The Book of the Pearl*, New York 1908

—— *Gems and Precious Stones of North America*, New York 1890

LORING, JOHN, *Tiffany's 150 Years*, New York 1987

MARX, LINDA, "Tiffany Designers . . . Perpetuating the Schlumberger Tradition", *Palm Beach Life*, January 1983, pp. 73–78

McKEAN, HUGH F., *The "Lost" Treasures of Louis Comfort Tiffany*, New York 1980

NOVAS, HIMILCE, "A Jewel in His Crown", *Connoisseur*, October 1983, pp. 134–140

PRODDOW, PENNY, and HEALY, DEBRA, *American Jewelry: Glamour and Tradition*, New York 1987

—— and SCHNEIRLA, PETER, *Tiffany: 150 Years of Gems and Jewelry*, New York 1987

PURTELL, JOSEPH, *The Tiffany Touch*, New York 1971

SATALOFF, JOSEPH, *Art Nouveau Jewelry*, Bryn Mawr 1984

SEEBOHM, CAROLINE, "Natural Affinities", *Connoisseur*, Vol. 215, No. 885, October 1985, pp. 120–27

SPEENBURGH, GERTRUDE, *The Arts of the Tiffanys*, Chicago 1956

TAIT, HUGH (ed.), *The Art of the Jeweller, a Catalogue of the Hull Grundy Gift to the British Museum* (2 vols), London 1984

ZAPATA, JANET, "Authenticating Tiffany Jewelry", *Heritage* insert in *Jewelers' Circular Keystone*, August 1988, pp. 226–230

CARTIER

Acknowledgments

I wish only to thank the late Hans Nadelhoffer whose vision and accomplishment have given us the monumental *Cartier: Jewelers Extraordinary*.

Photographers: David Behl, Bruce Field and Tjerk Wicky.

R. E.

VERDURA

Acknowledgments

Several people were helpful to me in the preparation of this chapter. I would like to thank especially my wife Judith, as well as Eve Auchincloss, Martina D'Alton, Prince Jean-Louis de Faucigny-Lucinge, Neil Letson, Tom Parr, Elizabeth Price, and Diana Scarisbrick.

E. L.

INDEX

(Page numbers in italics refer to illustrations)